Child Neglect

Planning and Intervention

Jan Horwath

palgrave
macmillan

First published 2013 by
PALGRAVE MACMILLAN

Palgrave Macmillan in the UK is an imprint of Macmillan Publishers Limited, registered in England, company number 785998, of Houndmills, Basingstoke, Hampshire RG21 6XS.

Palgrave Macmillan in the US is a division of St Martin's Press LLC, 175 Fifth Avenue, New York, NY 10010.

Palgrave Macmillan is the global academic imprint of the above companies and has companies and representatives throughout the world.

Palgrave® and Macmillan® are registered trademarks in the United States, the United Kingdom, Europe and other countries

ISBN: 978–0–230–20666–3

This book is printed on paper suitable for recycling and made from fully managed and sustained forest sources. Logging, pulping and manufacturing processes are expected to conform to the environmental regulations of the country of origin.

A catalogue record for this book is available from the British Library.

A catalog record for this book is available from the Library of Congress.

In memory of my father Jan Lasota, 1915–2012, and for my grandsons Oscar Jan and Toby Owen.

Contents

Illustrations

Figures

Boxes

Tables

Case studies

Acknowledgements

So many people have supported and helped me to write this book and I would like to thank them all. I owe a particular debt of gratitude to Ann Godfrey and Tony Kennedy for providing me with a peaceful and beautiful location in which to concentrate on writing. Zarah Newman and her colleagues made a significant contribution by commissioning the Anytown study and I am grateful to the practitioners who participated in the research. A special thanks to the parents and children who were prepared to let me read their case files, to Carol Marsh for sharing some of her experiences and to Helen Richardson-Foster and Sukey Tarr for assisting with data collection and analysis. Thanks also to Julie Taylor for her valuable comments on an early draft of the book and to William Baginsky, Maureen Howard and Denise Chandler for their assistance with the final draft. My husband Baz has, as ever, supported me in my writing endeavours. Whether that meant transporting hard copies of articles and books back and forth across the UK or calming me down when I feared I had wiped out chapters from my computer, he has done it all with a smile.

The author and publishers would like to thank Jessica Kingsley Publishers for permission to reproduce the following material:

Figure 5.1, source: Bentovim *et al.* (2009) *Safeguarding Children Living with Trauma and Family Violence: Evidence-based Assessment, Analysis and Planning Interventions* (London: Jessica Kingsley Publishers); figure 5.2, source: Bentovim *et al.* (2009) *Safeguarding Children Living with Trauma and Family Violence: Evidence-based Assessment, Analysis and Planning Interventions* (London: Jessica Kingsley Publishers); figure 5.3, source: Daniel *et al.* (2010) *Child Development for Child Care and Protection Workers*, 2nd edition (London: Jessica Kingsley Publishers).

Introduction

> What causes neglect? Why does it happen? These are natural questions in the mind of the child welfare worker. Our work can be steered more intelligently and will have a more lasting impact if it can be directed to rooting out sources of difficulty, rather than rubbing balm on its symptoms. (Polansky *et al.*, 1972, p. 5)

Polansky *et al.* posed these questions and made this comment over 40 years ago. Is it as relevant today? We are certainly more aware of the significant and detrimental impact that neglect has, for example, on the development of the brain of the child and adolescent. Moreover, our knowledge and understanding of factors that can contribute to parents neglecting their children is becoming more sophisticated. Nevertheless, we still remain in a situation where practitioners are 'rubbing balm on the symptoms' rather than addressing the root causes of neglect. For example, recent studies of serious case reviews following the death or serious injury of a child from neglect in England found that the focus of workers' attention was on resolving the presenting problem through short-term interventions with little attention paid to the underlying issues, past family history and patterns of behaviour (Brandon, Belderson *et al.* 2008; Brandon, Bailey *et al.* 2009). In a recent survey completed in the UK by the NSPCC (2011), 9 per cent of young adults and one in ten young people between the ages of 11 and 17 years reported that they had been severely neglected by parents or guardians during childhood. In an Action for Children study (2010) involving 3,000 eight- to twelve-year-olds, 63 per cent had seen suspected signs of neglect in other children. These included the child looking dirty and unwashed, wearing clothes that did not fit or were soiled, not getting meals at home and having no friends. This pattern appears to be repeated across the developed world. Indeed, the statistics gathered in different countries bear out the fact that neglect is a common experience (Dubowitz, Newton *et al.*, 2005; Gardner, 2008; Mardani, 2010). If one considers the number of children subject to neglect in the developed world it would appear we continue to fail to address the root causes of neglect.

In my previous book, *Child Neglect: Identification and Assessment* (Horwath, 2007), I not only attempted to answer the two questions Polansky *et al.* posed but also considered how the answers should inform the way in which professionals identify and assess child neglect. Since I wrote that book I have had numerous discussions with practitioners who have indicated that national assessment frameworks and tools, such as

1

the Graded Care Profile (Srivastava, Fountain *et al.*, 2003), have enabled them to go beyond the presenting problem when assessing child neglect. However, they then encounter a new challenge: struggling to find effective interventions that will lead to better outcomes for children living in neglectful families. This quote from a conference chair who participated in the Anytown neglect study, which is summarized in Box 0.1 and described in more detail in the Appendix, explains what often occurs:

> I was doing a conference yesterday and this is the fourth period of registration…the concerns are exactly the same, every initial conference that has been held…There's been several written agreements put in place but they've been breached and there's no real understanding or answers.

The quote highlights for me how practitioners can often be left floundering, not knowing how to intervene to address the root causes of neglect in a way that will improve the daily lived experience of children in the family. Part of the problem is that resources are limited and professionals feel constrained by their often prescriptive roles and responsibilities (Daniel, Taylor *et al.*, 2011; Munro, 2011b; Davies and Ward, 2012). However, the issue goes beyond this, with practitioners often unsure about what works for families with different, often complex needs.

My intention, therefore, in writing this book is to draw on research and practice developments to assist practitioners and managers make the move from patching up and dispatching the child and their family, until another symptom of neglect brings the family to the attention of practitioners, to addressing the root causes of neglect. This book is not a revised version of my previous book on neglect; rather, it complements the first book by exploring how practitioners can build on a meaningful assessment to plan and intervene effectively to improve the lives of neglected children. In the last ten years interventions that are effective in addressing child neglect have received increasing attention from researchers (Davies and Ward, 2012). Thus, in writing this book I have been able to draw on a plethora of research studies, from randomized control trials to small-scale qualitative studies, to consider what we know about the effectiveness of various interventions. These interventions range from population-based approaches to prevent neglect through to protecting children from harm in cases of chronic neglect.

Despite the increased attention paid to ways in which the needs of the vulnerable and neglected child can be met, there is remarkably little written about planning in general and more specifically in relation to child neglect. This would appear to be a significant oversight because planning is the crucial link between identifying and meeting the needs of the neglected child. I have sought to go some way to adding to the limited body of knowledge on this topic by drawing on the findings of a small-scale study on planning in cases of chronic neglect recently completed in the UK. The details of the study are summarized in Box 0.1. I will be referring to the findings from this study – known as the Anytown study – throughout the book. For the reader who requires more information about the study, this is provided in Appendix 1.

Box 0.1: *The Anytown neglect study: brief summary of research design*

The Anytown neglect study

What follows is a brief summary of the study aim, sample size and research methods. For more detailed information regarding the research design and study findings, see the Appendix.

The overall aim of the study was to further understanding of multidisciplinary planning and intervention in cases of chronic neglect. (For the purposes of the study, chronic neglect was defined as either the child being registered[1] under the category of neglect and remaining on the register for over two years, or the child having their name placed on the register because of neglect, subsequently being de-registered and then being re-registered on at least one further occasion in a two-year period).

The study was commissioned by a local safeguarding children board (LSCB)[2] in Wales and was completed in a mixed urban and rural community with high unemployment.

Four different research methods were used:

1. *An analysis* of case conference minutes, chronologies, reports, child protection plans, core group minutes and reports contained in the case files of 21 children (12 boys and 9 girls). A purposive sampling method was used to ensure that the sample reflected the definition of chronic neglect used for this study but also included: adolescents; children who are members of the same sibling group; disabled children.
2. *Semi-structured telephone interviews* with six chairs of initial child protection conferences and 12 social workers who act as lead professionals for child protection plans. The purpose of these interviews was to explore the themes from the case review.
3. *Multidisciplinary focus groups.* Four groups were facilitated for a total of 34 participants. The aim was to further explore the emerging themes from the previous two stages of the study with professionals who are members of core groups and work with the family and other professionals to implement the child protection plan.
4. *The survey.* Whilst the data collected and analysed thus far provided some insight into planning in cases of chronic neglect in that LSCB area, it was difficult to ascertain whether the key practice issues

identified by the respondents were unique to that area. With this in mind, a survey was completed by 162 frontline practitioners to establish whether practitioners with similar cases in other parts of the UK encountered comparable issues. Fourteen statements and questions were developed to identify the extent to which professionals working in a diverse range of practice settings felt that some of the key findings that emerged consistently from the data analysis of the first three stages of the study reflected their practice experience.

Key findings are considered throughout the book and summarized in the Appendix.

1. In Wales, as in Northern Ireland and Scotland, if there are concerns that a child is suffering and likely to continue to suffer significant harm and therefore is in need of a child protection plan, then a decision is made at the initial child protection conference to place the name of the child on the child protection register. In England, instead of being registered, the name of the child is recorded as being the subject of a multidisciplinary child protection plan.
2. LSCBs consist of service directors and senior managers who have a statutory duty to coordinate and ensure the effectiveness of what is done by each person or body represented on the LSCB for the purposes of safeguarding and promoting the welfare of children.

Key concepts: being 'crazy about the kid'

In order to develop normally, a child requires progressively more complex joint activity with one or more adults who have an irrational emotional relationship with the child. Somebody's got to be crazy about that kid. That's number one. First, last, and always. (Bronfenbrenner, quoted in National Scientific Council on the Developing Child, 2004, p. 1)

In this quote, Bronfenbrenner captures exactly what children need if they are to achieve their full potential. I have, therefore, endeavoured to explore, within the book, how this can be achieved and drawn on four concepts that I believe should inform practice. First, in order for parents to provide the 'complex joint activity' and emotional relationship necessary to meet the needs of the child, the parents not only require the necessary ability and motivation, they also need a parenting environment that is supportive and facilitates quality child rearing. Therefore, the theoretical approach I have taken in writing this book draws on an ecological perspective (Bronfenbrenner, 1979) and a multilevel systems approach. Conceptualizing neglect in this way means recognizing and understanding the influence of the child's relationship with their carer, the world of the immediate and the extended family, the community in which that child and family lives and the influence of the wider society on the family through, for example, legislation, culture and religion. It means that child development is inextricably linked to the interrelated contexts within which children grow up, which either support or inhibit each child's progress.

Second, the first step to becoming 'crazy about the kid' is having an understanding of the individual child and how they experience their world. In 1988 Dame Butler-Sloss reminded practitioners that 'the child is a person and not an object of concern' (Butler-Sloss, 1988, p.245). This perspective challenges what was the view at the time, namely that children are biologically and socially immature and that powerful groups of adults construct representations of the child and impose this construction on groups of children – in the case Butler-Sloss was referring to, sexually abused children. In the last 20 years there has been a move towards a more socially constructed view of childhood that recognizes children as social actors and agents who live and experience family and community life in very different ways (James and James, 2000). Thus, in order to make sense of neglect so that practitioners can intervene effectively in these children's lives, it is important to understand the daily lived experience of the neglected child, and to recognize that neglect affects each neglected child differently. However, one of the tensions when working with neglect is determining the extent to which the voice and views of the child should determine actions. As Gittens (1998) notes, whilst maltreatment is experienced by and affects children differently it is also a problem that is categorized and defined by adults and remains an act of harm inflicted by those who have some power and control over children: namely their parents. Moreover, as Littlechild (2000) comments, the very phrase 'child protection' reflects a view that the child cannot safeguard itself and therefore needs support from the state and its agents. In this book I have sought to address this tension by placing considerable emphasis on the importance of practitioners ensuring that they fully appreciate what a good and bad day is like in the life of each and every neglected child they are working with. This picture should be constructed by not only taking into account the child's experiences and views but also what can be learnt about their lived experience from other professionals and family members. I also believe, as noted by Littlechild (2000), it is important to validate and ensure representation of the child's views whilst also taking account of the duty of the state to protect children from harm.

Third, if interventions are to be effective, it is not only the caregivers that should be 'crazy about the kid'; practitioners and the organizations they work for also need to be demonstrating they put the needs of the child first. All too often workers appear to go through the motions of following guidance and procedures aimed at meeting the needs of the children without demonstrating a commitment to the individual child (Munro, 2010). This was evident in some of the comments from participants in the Anytown study, who talked about 'doing an assessment', 'holding a core group on the X clan', 'meeting the threshold', 'your classic chronic neglect case', 'when there are a group of siblings we do a cut and paste job for each form'. These quotes indicate a lack of focus on the individual child. What is crucial is that professionals recognize that each child, even those in the same family, will have a different experience of neglect. Being 'crazy about the kid' and ensuring their particular needs are met also means that workers need to establish meaningful relationships with children and families. As noted by Lambert and Barley (2001), the quality of the relationship between worker and service user has more influence when addressing concerns than the use of a specific intervention or technique. Without a meaningful relationship with family members the practitioner will not be able to access information about past experiences and the current concerns and anxieties that influence child rearing (Barlow and Schrader McMillan, 2010; Platt, 2012). If workers are to be 'crazy about the kid' they need to work in organizations where managers demonstrate, through the implementation of operational systems, that they are crazy about frontline workers and create an environment that promotes practice associated with positive outcomes for children. This requires systems that ensure the needs of the child are given priority over the needs of the organization and that staff feel valued, supported and have manageable workloads (Hemmelgarn *et al.*, 2006).

Finally, if practitioners are to intervene effectively in the lives of neglectful families, in a manner that improves the quality of parenting and the child's daily lived experience, they need to have an understanding of the way in which individuals respond to change. All too often families believe change is imposed on them: they are told what needs to change and how to achieve this by professionals (Morrison, 2010). As Senge *et al.* (1994) note, people do not resist change, they resist being changed. Therefore, if practitioners wish to improve the quality of the daily lived experience of the neglected child, they need to pay attention to the process of change, as, for example, outlined by Prochaska and DiClementi (1982), and support parents through recognizing the need to change, deciding how to make the necessary changes and sustaining any changes that are made. Throughout the book I consider how processes for planning and intervening in the lives of neglected families promote or inhibit engagement with the change process.

Having provided an overview of the key concepts that have informed this book I now consider the contents of the book in more detail.

Overview of the book and chapter contents

The overall aim of this book is to provide a readily accessible publication grounded in research and best practice in order to assist practitioners and managers, irrespective of discipline and jurisdiction, to plan to meet the needs of neglected children and, in light of these plans, work effectively with neglectful families. This will be achieved by exploring the research and practice developments that should inform planning and interventions in cases of child neglect. As part of this process, the tensions and dilemmas encountered by professionals working with neglectful families will be identified and possible ways in which practitioners can work together to promote better outcomes for neglected children considered.

What follows is a summary of the content of each part of the book and the individual chapters.

The book is divided into three parts. In the first part I attempt to set the scene by exploring the concept of neglect and the impact that neglect has on children. In Chapter 1 I consider how operational definitions of neglect are of limited use and can be particularly unhelpful when attempting to identify ways of intervening in cases of neglect. I argue that neglect is socially constructed and perceptions of neglect will change with time and place. This means that nation states at a particular time may emphasize different elements of neglect, minimizing other aspects of neglect which may be as damaging for the child. As a consequence the legislative framework, as well as cultural, religious and community norms, will inform the way in which professionals view the family. This, combined with personal and professional values and beliefs, means that practitioners are likely to view neglect through different lenses and hold different views as to what is 'good enough parenting', at what point professionals should intervene in family life and the ways in which they should work with families. This in turn will dictate which families receive services. Whilst neglect is associated with a parental failure to meet the needs of the child, I consider how professional, organizational and societal neglect may also contribute to a failure to intervene effectively to meet the needs of the child.

In Chapter 2 I focus on the multifaceted nature of neglect and explore the factors that contribute to neglectful parenting, including the parent's ability to understand the needs of the child as well as the socio-emotional reasons why they may not be 'crazy about the kid'. The part played by family and environmental factors in shaping parental behaviours is also considered. In the final chapter of this section, I explore the bleak and miserable daily lived experience of the neglected child and young person and discuss the different ways in which neglect affects the child's health and wellbeing. I argue that if interventions are to be effective it is essential that professionals recognize the cumulative effect of neglect and ensure they focus on how each child within a family is affected by their neglectful environment.

The second part of the book is about planning interventions. In this section I focus on cases of chronic neglect where the child is suffering or likely to suffer significant harm. In Chapter 4 I consider assessment, the foundation from which plans and interventions are constructed. As I have written extensively about the assessment process in cases of neglect elsewhere – see, for example, Horwath (2007) – I focus on one particular aspect: assessing parental capacity to change. I argue that this is a neglected aspect of the assessment process and, as a consequence, parents do not engage meaningfully in plans designed to change their behaviours and improve outcomes for children. I explore the challenges that practitioners encounter engaging with parents and eliciting and sharing information in a way that motivates parents to take their first steps on the pathway to change. Drawing on the Prochaska and DiClementi model of change (1982), I consider ways in which practitioners can complete more effective assessments, using this model. In Chapter 5 I move on to consider how the initial child protection conference can be used as a vehicle to assist parents identify a pathway for change that leads to better outcomes for the child. I argue that information should be shared and analysed and decisions made about interventions in such a way that the child's lived experience remains centre stage. I emphasize the importance of ensuring that by the end of the conference both family members and members of the conference understand the causes for concern as they relate to the child's lived experience, the rationale behind the proposed interventions and ways in which progress will be measured. In the final chapter of this section I discuss plans to safeguard the neglected child from harm. I consider the tensions that practitioners encounter in obtaining meaningful parental engagement with the plan whilst at the same time balancing the care and control functions in their interactions with the family. I propose a framework that enables practitioners to both assess the extent to which parents are actively engaged in bringing about change that improves outcomes for the child, and identify why parents may be superficially compliant with, or disengage from, the plan. I use the same framework to argue that practitioners may mirror parents' behaviour and not engage meaningfully in implementing the plan, and consider why this is the case and what practitioners require from their organizations to ensure this does not occur. Traditionally, when assessing effective interventions, practitioners have focused on whether family members have completed the tasks negotiated between themselves and practitioners (Munro, 2011a). Success, no thanks to a recent overemphasis on performance indicators, is frequently measured in terms of compliance and short-term, tangible improvements to the lives of children. Little consideration is given to the long-term impact of these interventions in promoting better outcomes for children. I therefore consider ways in which professionals can measure the effectiveness of interventions, not only in terms of safeguarding and promoting the current welfare of the child but also in terms of the long-term wellbeing of the child. Whilst the focus in this part of the book is on child protection processes, the information regarding assessment and planning and establishing a pathway for change is just as relevant to practitioners who are working with families where there are emerging concerns about neglect and where the children are considered vulnerable.

The final section of the book focuses on the diverse range of interventions available to neglectful families. I begin by arguing in Chapter 7 that it is not only 'neglect' that is a vague term and open to interpretation; so is 'intervention'. This word can be used to describe very different actions: for example, a social worker receiving a referral from a teacher may consider this to be the beginning of a process of identification and assessment that may lead to intervening in the family through service provision, whilst the teacher may consider that the very act of referring is an appropriate intervention on her part to meet the needs of the child. The factors that influence what services are available and how thresholds are established for accessing services are explored. This is achieved by considering how personal, professional and organizational factors inform the way services are allocated. The next three chapters centre on interventions aimed at parents, primarily in cases where young children are vulnerable to, or actually experiencing, neglect. This section of the book draws on research findings and practice developments regarding effective interventions for neglected children and their families, and considers the range of interventions from population-based services to prevent neglect, services designed to provide early help, through to interventions that are aimed at meeting the needs of the complex families where chronic neglect is a concern. In Chapter 8 I focus on population-based services and consider why parents vulnerable to neglecting their babies and children in the early years find it hard to access these services. In the following chapter the emphasis shifts to early help and, whilst recognizing that early help does not equate to early years, bearing in mind the importance of providing children with a positive start in life I consider the services that are available for families with pre-school-age children to address emerging concerns about neglect. I discuss three different types of service: home visiting services, such as the *Family Nurse Partnership*; centre-support services, such as *Triple P* parenting programmes and two-generation services designed to improve interactions between the parent and child. I consider which services are most relevant where the concerns are about a lack of parental knowledge and skills, and those interventions which lend themselves more to meet the needs of children and families where there are concerns about the parent–child relationship. Chapter 10 centres on working with complex cases: chronic neglect. The importance of a team around the family approach, combined with meaningful relationships between workers and the family, is emphasized. Recognizing that the behaviours that are being addressed as part of the intervention in these cases are often entrenched, consideration is given to the need for support of sufficient duration to ensure changes to behaviours are sustained even during times of stress and family crises. In Chapter 11 there is recognition that rates of neglect are higher amongst carers who have mental health issues, who misuse drugs and alcohol, are victims of domestic violence or have a learning disability, than amongst other groups of carers. In this chapter the specific issues encountered and the specialist interventions available for both carers and their children are considered. Chapter 12 moves away from a focus on parents to neglected primary school aged children and adolescents. I discuss ways in which their needs can be met within the community. Different levels of need, from building resilience, addressing early signs of vulnerability through to damage limitation are considered. Neglect, particularly in adolescence, often comes to the attention of professionals through antisocial behaviour, such as offending or the young person running away, and attention is given to addressing both the presenting problem and the underlying neglect. In Chapter 13, acknowledging that the needs of neglected children cannot always be met in the community, I consider what we know about best practice with regard to placing neglected children in out-of-home placements. I explore factors that practitioners should take into account when planning to remove children, placement stability and potential reunification, as well as the needs of those neglected children when they become care leavers.

Target readership

This book has been written specifically for a multidisciplinary audience. It provides a helpful and important resource, that draws on theory and research, for practitioners and managers who are in contact with or working with children and families where there are potential or actual concerns about child neglect. The material in this book will be of relevance to students completing social work, health, social care and education qualifying and post-qualifying training. The book will not only help students in terms of their academic studies but will provide valuable guidance to assist students completing practice placements. Trainers and educators will also find the book useful for accessing the underpinning knowledge required for preparing courses on planning and intervening in cases of child neglect. The chapters provide valuable material that can also be used to prepare handouts. As the book has been written for a multidisciplinary audience, the content will prove invaluable to interagency as well as in-house trainers. This book also provides managers with a very clear overview of high quality practice. Therefore, the book can be used to enable managers to identify the resources, operational context, supervision and support practitioners require to work effectively with child neglect.

Whist the research informing this book was completed in the UK and I make some reference to UK legislation, I also draw on international research and I have attempted to write the book in such a way that the content is relevant to both practitioners planning and intervening in cases of neglect in all jurisdictions and the managers supervising their practice.

In conclusion, in a recent study by the Children's Rights Director for England (Morgan, 2011), children were asked how adults can keep them safe. The most common responses given by the young people, aged between five and twelve years of age, was having a family looking out for them, parents giving boundaries and advice, and people who care for them: that is, being 'crazy about the kid'. The intention in writing this book is to provide practitioners with theoretical perspectives, research findings and practice developments that enable them to plan interventions and work with families to create this type of safe environment for children both vulnerable to neglect and those actually experiencing neglect.

Part 1

Making Sense of Neglect

Chapter 1

The Neglected Child: Are We on the Same Wavelength?

Neglect is essentially parental failure to meet the needs of the child (Greenbaum *et al.*, 2008). The simplicity of this definition, however, belies the complexity associated with identifying neglect and determining when services should be provided to the child and their family. Mennen *et al.* (2010a), in an American study, found that the one-word term 'neglect' described a diverse and heterogeneous range of behaviours experienced by the young people. This is a consequence of neglect being socially constructed and dependent on perceptions of what constitutes good enough parenting at a particular time within a particular society. This social construction goes some way to explaining why operational definitions of child neglect vary across nation states, as shown in Table 1.1. Whilst all the definitions included in the table refer to parental failure to meet the needs of the child, there are variations in the focus on different needs. All the operational definitions mention the child's basic physical needs and providing adequate supervision. Yet, whilst both the Scottish and Northern Irish definitions include 'lack of stimulation', 'failure to educate in line with that required by law' is also considered neglect in some American states. However, this specific focus is absent from the UK definitions. These variations occur because a number of factors – such as social and cultural influences, research, legislative frameworks and state thresholds for intervention into family life – influence the way in which neglect is constructed in each state (Daniel *et al.*, 2011; Gilbert *et al.*, 2011). In Australia, for example, operational definitions vary from state to state and consideration is given to 'cultural tradition'. The way in which neglect is constructed and defined will inform both the children that are labelled 'neglected' at a particular time and the interventions required by the community, professionals and the state to meet their needs (Dickens, 2007; Mardani, 2010).

The problem with prescriptive operational definitions is that professionals can become so exercised by marrying concerns about neglect with the operational definition that the focus on the individual child and their needs is lost. For example, the 1991 definition of neglect in English national guidance included 'non-organic failure to thrive' (Home Office *et al.*, 1991). This has been removed from subsequent versions of the guidance because research in the field indicated that whilst neglect may be associated with

Table 1.1: Variations in operational definitions of neglect

Country	Operational definition of neglect
England	The persistent failure to meet the child's basic physical and/or psychological needs, likely to result in the serious impairment of the child's health and development. Neglect may occur during pregnancy as a result of maternal substance abuse. Once a child is born, neglect may involve a parent or carer failing to: • provide adequate food, clothing and shelter (including exclusion from home or abandonment) • protect a child from physical and emotional harm or danger • ensure adequate supervision (including the use of inadequate caregivers) • or ensure access to appropriate medical care or treatment. It may also include neglect of, or unresponsiveness to, a child's basic emotional needs (HM Government, 2010).
Scotland	Neglect is the persistent failure to meet a child's basic physical and/or psychological needs, likely to result in the serious impairment of the child's health or development. It may involve a parent or carer failing to provide adequate food, shelter and clothing, to protect a child from physical harm or danger, or to ensure access to appropriate medical care or treatment. It may also include neglect of, or failure to respond to, a child's basic emotional needs. Neglect may also result in the child being diagnosed as suffering from 'non-organic failure to thrive', where they have significantly failed to reach normal weight and growth or development milestones and where physical and genetic reasons have been medically eliminated. In its extreme form, children can be at serious risk from the effects of malnutrition, lack of nurturing and stimulation. This can lead to serious long-term effects such as greater susceptibility to serious childhood illnesses and reduction in potential stature. With young children in particular, the consequences may be life threatening within a relatively short period of time (Scottish Government, 2010).
Wales	Neglect is the persistent failure to meet a child's basic physical and/or psychological needs, likely to result in the serious impairment of the child's health or development. It may involve a parent or caregiver failing to provide adequate food, shelter and clothing, failing to protect a child from physical harm or danger, or the failure to ensure access to appropriate medical care or treatment. It may also include neglect of, or unresponsiveness to, a child's basic emotional needs. In addition, neglect may occur during pregnancy as a result of maternal substance misuse (Children In Wales, 2008).

Continued

Table 1.1:   Continued

Country	Operational definition of neglect
Northern Ireland	Neglect is the persistent failure to meet a child's physical, emotional and/or psychological needs, likely to result in significant harm. It may involve a parent or caregiver failing to provide adequate food, shelter and clothing, failing to protect a child from physical harm or danger, failure to ensure access to appropriate medical care or treatment, lack of stimulation or lack of supervision. It may also include non-organic failure to thrive (faltering growth) (DHSSPS, 2005).
USA	Neglect is frequently defined as the failure of the parent or other person responsible for the child to provide basic care such as food, clothing, shelter, medical care and supervision to the extent that the health, safety and wellbeing of the child are affected. In approximately 24 states failure to educate the child in line with that required by law is included and seven states specifically mention medical neglect, describing it as failure to provide special medical treatment or mental health care to the child, whilst four additional states describe medical neglect as withholding of medical treatment or nutrition from disabled infants with life-threatening conditions (US Department of Health and Human Services, 2011). In some states, consideration is given to parents being financially able to or having financial support to meet the needs of the child. In other states, consideration is given to neglect associated with foetal alcohol syndrome and exposure to prenatal substance abuse (Munro and Manful, 2012).
Australia	Operational definitions of neglect vary from state to state. However, the federal government-run Australian Institute for Health and Welfare defines neglect as: any serious omissions or commissions by a person having the care of a child which, within the bounds of cultural tradition, constitute a failure to provide conditions which are essential for the healthy, physical and emotional development of a child (Australian Institute of Health and Welfare, 2011).
Norway	Norway takes a different approach and does not have an operational definition of neglect. Rather, 18 categories are used to identify concerns. A number of these categories indicate issues associated with neglect, such as a child's psychological and behavioural problems, parents' inability to care for children and domestic conditions (Munro and Manful, 2012).

failure to thrive this was not necessarily the case (Wright, 1995; Batchelor, 1999, 2008). Yet the combination of neglect and failure to thrive, as outlined in the Scottish definition, can be devastating (Mackner and Starr, 1997; Ben-Galim *et al.*, 2010). This might explain why, as shown in Table 1.1, non-organic failure to thrive as a possible form of neglect is included in both the Scottish and Northern Irish definitions. Does this mean that a practitioner in England would work with a child suffering non-organic failure to thrive differently from a colleague in another part of the UK? What if the family move? In England the parents may not be labelled as neglectful whilst in other parts of the UK they could be, resulting in engagement with statutory services. Daniel *et al.* (2011, p. 18) argue that trying to pin down neglect in this way, when there are so many factors influencing its construction, is not helpful. Rather, practitioners, service commissioners and providers should accept that neglect is a 'fluid concept' and that definitions are useful as the 'key not the padlock' to identifying and meeting the needs of children.

Defining actual or potential neglect: the challenges

As neglect is a 'fluid' concept it means that practitioners and managers encounter a number of challenges when defining actual or potential neglect with a view to accessing services for children. These challenges are explored below.

Establishing good enough parenting

Identifying the point at which the quality of care can be described as neglectful begs a question: what is reasonable caregiving? Dubowitz (2007) concludes that national definitions, such as the ones in Table 1.1, can only offer general guidance. Therefore, if the definitions provided by states do not in their own right help practitioners, and indeed the community, identify neglect then alternatives need to be considered. A more helpful way to identify neglect, he argues, is to consider the basic minimum that children and young people need from their parent or caregiver if they are to develop satisfactorily. This notion is found in the *Framework for the Assessment of Children in Need and Their Families* (DH *et al.*, 2000; Jones, 2010), where minimum parental competences are brought together as the dimensions of parenting capacity. The Assessment Framework, as it is referred to, is also used in Wales, in Australian, Canadian and American states, the Council for Europe and the World Health Organization (Daly, 2007). The Framework includes six parenting activities and behaviours that are necessary if carers are to meet the needs of their child (the Framework is considered in more detail in Chapter 3). These dimensions are recognized as important to the health and wellbeing of children irrespective of age, gender, ethnicity, disability, culture or faith (DH, 2000). Different types of neglect can therefore be described in relation to a failure to meet these various minimum competences, as shown in Table 1.2.

The focus, however, cannot be merely on parental competencies. Dickens (2007) reminds us that seemingly identical behaviours by carers can affect individual children differently. Thus, in order to make sense of neglect it is necessary to consider not only the parenting behaviours but also the *impact* of those behaviours on the particular child and the way in which

Table 1.2:   Types of neglect linked to parenting capacity

Dimension of parenting capacity	Type of neglect
Basic care	Failure to provide appropriate diet, warmth, shelter, clothing, and address personal hygiene and care of child in an age-appropriate manner. Lack of medical care, including meeting complex health needs; audio, optical and dental care; and failing to address mental health needs.
Ensuring safety	Failure to ensure child is supervised appropriately and protected from harm and danger, both within the home and the community.
Emotional warmth	Failure to meet the child's emotional needs, including developing their sense of a positive self. Recognizing their identity: racial, cultural, religious, identity as young carer, child of a parent with parenting issues, stepchild, and so on.
Stimulation	Failure to provide a stimulating environment with opportunities for learning and intellectual development for both pre- and school-age children, including language and communication, play, social opportunities, and attendance at school.
Guidance and boundaries	Failure to demonstrate and model appropriate displays of emotion and interaction with others. Failure to provide guidance to enable the child to develop and internalize moral values, a conscience and appropriate social behaviours.
Stability	Failure to provide a sufficiently stable home life, ensuring the child develops a secure attachment to the caregiver.

their needs are being met, as discussed in Chapter 3. The needs should be related to the age of the child or young person and set within the context of the developmental tasks facing children at specific ages (Rees *et al.*, 2010), with neglect linked to 'measurable developmental damage' (Gardner, 2008, p.7). Moreover, as the needs of the child change during development what may be neglectful at one stage may not be at another. For example, leaving a two-year-old unsupervised in the house for half an hour when the child has no sense of danger is neglectful, yet leaving a 14-year-old for the same period of time, provided they have the necessary skills to keep themselves safe, would not be.

Making judgements about the quality of parenting

Differences in the way in which good enough parenting is interpreted by communities and societies can lead to judgements being made about the quality of parenting, which do not always seem to be just and raise questions as to whether different standards of parenting apply depending on the parent, their socio-economic group and their culture. The press coverage of two cases in 2008 in England demonstrates this point. Both cases raised questions about good enough parenting with regard to the supervision of children. The first case concerned a three-year-old girl, Madeleine McCann, who was abducted one evening from a holiday apartment in Portugal whilst her parents were eating a meal in a nearby restaurant with friends. The parents and their friends (who also left their children unsupervised) indicated that they made checks on the children every half hour. The response by the UK press to the child's disappearance was one of overwhelming support and sympathy for the parents, with only a minority of articles blaming the parents for leaving Madeleine and her two younger siblings unsupervised. In addition, the McCanns reported that only 1 per cent of their mail was hate mail (Williams, 2008). In this case the parents were doctors – white, middle-class, articulate professionals. Their attempts to find Madeleine were considered laudable and the popular press gave the case significant, supportive news coverage, despite a short period when the Portuguese police considered the McCanns official suspects involved in Madeleine's disappearance. In one popular paper, the *Daily Mail*, Mrs McCann was described as 'tearful', 'a broken figure' and 'fragile' (Boffey and Wilkes, 2008).

The second case was reported very differently in the UK press. The case concerned Scarlett Keeling, a 15-year-old who was left with a 25-year-old local, male guide in Goa whilst her mother and the rest of the family went travelling for a few days. Scarlett was raped and murdered. In this case, whilst the mother was articulate and also described as middle class, the same paper, the *Daily Mail*, which showed sympathy for the McCanns, described the mother of Scarlett as an 'aging hippy' who led an alternative lifestyle, and the paper heavily criticized her for leaving her daughter. The article concluded that 'articulate middle-class people should know better' – a comment the paper did not make of the McCanns (Pearson, 2008). One could argue that in both cases the parents were neglectful as they had failed to provide adequate supervision for their children. However, one could also argue that Scarlett's mother had actually made attempts, in good faith, to provide reasonable supervision, even though in hindsight this was not the case; therefore, she was less culpable than the parents of Madeleine, who left very young children and only made half-hourly checks.

The impression made by parents has also been found to have an effect on assessments of accidents that could be associated with neglect. Accidents can be defined as incidents where parents or carers take reasonable care to meet the needs of the child but there are unexpected circumstances leading to unintentional consequences. A question that professionals often have to answer, however, is when does (what appears to be) a series of accidents become evidence of neglectful caring? A study of a hospital child protection team in Israel sought to answer this question and found that judgement making in this regard was inconsistent. They conclude that the impression the parents made on the professionals at the hospital had far more influence on decisions as to whether this was a pure accident or an indicator of possible neglect or abuse than did the child's characteristics or the parents' socio-economic background (Davidson-Arad *et al.*, 2010).

The Israeli study demonstrates that professional judgements about the quality of parenting will be influenced by professionals' individual perceptions. This is supported by other studies that have been completed in relation to professional perceptions of neglectful parenting. A number of studies completed in the USA and the UK have highlighted that professionals hold different views regarding appropriate standards of care to those held by the general public (Portwood, 1998; Truman, 2004; Daniel *et al.*, 2010). Moreover, there are differences in standards of reasonable care between professionals from different disciplines, with social work personnel appearing to tolerate lower standards of care than other professionals (Rose and Meezan, 1997; Rose and Selwyn, 2000). There is also evidence that professionals belonging to the same profession do not necessarily agree on standards (Horwath, 2005). Professional interpretations of neglect will be influenced by not only the experiences of the individual and their professional values but also the communities and networks to which the professional belongs in both a personal and working capacity (Korbin and Spilsbury, 1999; Ferrari, 2002; Owen and Statham, 2009). A stark example of this was highlighted in a serious case review completed in England on the 'W' children, who were severely neglected. The report writer criticized the school for accepting particular parental behaviours, such as sending the children to school in winter with no underwear, as the community norm without considering the impact on the individual children (Sheffield Area Child Protection Committee, 2005). This raises questions as to whether, irrespective of guidance and definitions, the judgement of individual workers has a considerable part to play in determining which children are labelled as neglected and require services.

Cumulative harm and emerging concerns

In cases of neglect the cause of harm is rarely linked to one specific incident; rather, it is the day-to-day adverse effects of poor parenting on the health and wellbeing of the child that are so damaging. This is recognized in all the UK operational definitions, which focus on the 'persistent failure' of the parents to meet the needs of the child. But what is meant by 'persistent'? Dickens (2007) notes that this term raises questions as to how to gauge the number of incidents, over what period of time and under what circumstances. Sadly, as will be discussed in Chapter 4, it is often a specific incident, such as the child being left alone and being harmed, that leads professionals to uncover the damaging and miserable lives led by these neglected children. This focus on specific incidents is particularly likely to occur in countries with forensically driven child protection systems, such as the UK, USA and Australia, where the emphasis is on obtaining medical evidence that a child has been maltreated (Parton, 2006).

Focusing on persistent behaviours can also result in some neglected children being ignored. One-off or episodic incidents, rather than chronic or persistent failure to provide good enough parenting, may seriously impair a child's health and development. For example, as will be discussed in more detail in Chapter 11, a parent or carer may be able to provide good enough parenting whilst their mental health issues are being controlled with medication. At times when this is not the case, however, the quality of parenting may deteriorate and the children suffer. But, as this suffering may be for short periods, the long-term impact of erratic parenting may not be identified by professionals in contact with the child and family.

If practitioners focus on the persistent failure on the part of the parent to meet the needs of the child, there is a danger that attention is diverted from identifying emerging concerns regarding potential neglect. As will be discussed in Chapters 8 and 9, the use of universal and targeted services has a considerable part to play in preventing neglect and addressing parental behaviours, which, if unchecked, could lead to harm to the child. By focusing on the minimum competencies a parent requires to meet the needs of the child, it is much easier to identify ways in which the parent can be helped, through service provision, to prevent cumulative harm occurring.

Neglect: an ever-changing phenomenon

Operational definitions of neglect do not remain static: they evolve and change, influenced by research and current concerns within a particular society. The problems associated with this have already been demonstrated in relation to non-organic failure to thrive. There is, however, another issue – and that is the selective use of research to influence what is included in operational definitions. A recent addition to some operational definitions of neglect is the acknowledgement that neglect can occur during pregnancy as a consequence of maternal substance misuse and, in some USA states, foetal alcohol syndrome. As discussed in Chapter 10, there is no doubt that drug and alcohol use by a mother-to-be can have serious implications for her unborn baby. However, it is not drugs and alcohol but also disease and poor diet that can affect the unborn child (Schaffer, 2004). Overeating during pregnancy can lead to excessive weight gain, which has been associated with obesity in childhood (Rooney and Schauberger, 2002); a pregnant mother failing to address her own medical conditions, such as diabetes, can lead to malformations in the baby (Feig and Palda, 2002); and using other 'drugs', such as cigarettes, can lead to premature or low birth-weight babies (Schaffer, 2004). In addition, living in a situation of domestic violence during pregnancy increases the risk of miscarriage or harm to the unborn child through assault (Humphreys and Stanley, 2006). With this in mind, it might be more useful, rather than specifying particular issues in relation to neglect during pregnancy, for practitioners and policy makers to refer to prenatal neglect, which is a more encompassing term and describes the parent's failure to engage with the antenatal care necessary for the development of the foetus and neonate (Polonko, 2006).

The influence of legislative frameworks

One of the challenges for practitioners, when attempting to identify and work with neglect, is recognizing the influence of legislation. In the paragraph above, consideration was given to the nature of prenatal neglect. Whether practitioners can act in these cases will depend on the legal frameworks that guide practice. Using Australia as an example, in New South Wales, Queensland and Tasmania statutory child protection services are able to accept notifications of concerns of neglect in relation to unborn children, whilst in other jurisdictions, such as South Australia, these agencies have no legislative mandate to receive notifications until immediately prior to the birth of the child (Australian Institute of Health and Welfare, 2011).

Culpability

Legislation will also determine whether neglect is considered a criminal offence or not. Whilst the behaviour may be unreasonable, the carer may be either without a motive to cause harm or unaware of the potential danger, and therefore cannot always be considered to be deserving of blame. For example, a parent may drink alcohol and lie on a sofa with their baby. The parent may fall asleep and lie over the baby who consequently suffocates. The parent had no intention to harm the child and was not aware of the dangers of co-sleeping. This view would support the often cited judgement made by Lord Hailsham re W in England in 1973 (AC682, 1971) where he stated that unreasonable behaviour was not to be equated with culpability. The judgement implies that the focus of culpability should therefore be on intention or recklessness as to the consequences of particular behaviour. This is made explicit in England in the Children and Young Person Act 1933, c12 Cruelty to Persons under Sixteen in Section 1, which indicates that a crime has been committed if any person *wilfully* neglects a child or young person.

However, there is a danger that viewing neglect as harm caused unintentionally may mean it is seen as less serious and more remediable than other forms of maltreatment (Gardner, 2008). Thus, in more recent legislation, the scope, in relation to culpability, has broadened in England with the Domestic Violence, Crime and Victims Act 2004 to focus not so much on wilful behaviours but rather on 'reasonable' ones. Whilst the focus is on significant risk of serious harm, in this case to a child, consideration has to be given as to whether the perpetrator 'was or ought to have been aware of risk' of serious harm through their actions; or that another person in the household 'failed to take steps as he could reasonably have been expected to take to protect the child from the risk'. The same emphasis on 'reasonable' behaviour is made in other countries and federal states. For example, in New South Wales, Australia, neglect is considered a criminal offence where: 'a person ... without reasonable excuse neglects to provide adequate and proper food, nursing, clothing, medical aid or lodging for the child or young person' (NSW Children and Young Persons (Care and Protection) Act 1998 s228 cited by Lawrence and Irvine, 2004). Thus, the question to answer in relation to the example given above of the parent who was co-sleeping with the baby is: would it be reasonable to expect the parent to be aware of the dangers of co-sleeping?

Another challenge for professionals, when considering the reasonableness of parents' behaviours, centres on the degree to which parents have a right to decide what is in the best interests of their child. For example, it is well established that placing an infant on their back to sleep reduces the likelihood of Sudden Infant Death Syndrome (SIDS) (Foundation for the Study of Infant Deaths, 2007). However, Epstein and Jolly (2008) found that some new mothers justified placing the baby on its stomach as the baby seemed to like it better, despite the parents knowing that placing the child to sleep on their back reduced the risk of SIDS. Is this neglect?

Neglect beyond the family

All the operational definitions used in the UK and Australia centre on the failure of the parent or caregiver to meet the needs of the child. Whilst this is clearly important, it distances others from their responsibilities towards children. For instance, to what extent can carers be held responsible for failing to meet the needs of the child if the resources are not available, or they are living in poverty and poor housing conditions? In some states in the USA there is recognition that parents can only be considered neglectful if they fail to meet the needs of the child whilst financially able to do so. Spencer and Baldwin (2005) argue that whilst child neglect takes place mainly within families, as societies provide the economic, social and cultural context for child rearing they are associated both directly and indirectly with neglect.

There are at least three types of neglect committed by individuals or groups outside the immediate family that can have a significant impact on children. First, professional neglect. This can take various forms – from a failure by a doctor, for example, to wash their hands between child patients through to professionals engaging tokenistically with the child and family. Overviews of serious case reviews involving the death of, or serious injuries to, neglected children provide examples of neglect by professionals which include failing to see the child, not communicating concerns to relevant agencies or avoiding carers because of fears of violence and aggression (Brandon *et al.*, 2008; Brandon *et al.*, 2009). Music (2009) identifies another way in which professionals can neglect children, which is by failing to provide them with the necessary input because the professional finds it difficult relating to the child or does not 'warm' to them. It is all too easy to see how this can occur. A teacher once described to me a neglected child in her class. The child smelt, had a constantly running nose and was forever whining and demanding her attention. One way he did this was to pull at her skirt and wrap it round his face, in the process wiping his nose all over her skirt. Despite her best efforts, he would not use a handkerchief or sit with the other children. She found she lost patience with the child far more easily than with other children in the class and breathed a sigh of relief on the many days he did not attend school.

Types of professional neglect and their impact on planning and intervening in cases of child neglect are discussed in detail in Chapter 5.

Professionals, however, cannot always be blamed for failing to meet the needs of the child and family. Heavy workloads, limited time available to spend with families, inadequate training and supervision can all affect their engagement with the child and their family. Polonko (2006) has described how organizations that are short staffed or have an unstable workforce are not well placed to work with neglect. And both Hemmelgarn *et al.* (2006) and Glisson and Green (2011) have identified how organizations where morale is low, staff feel stressed and overburdened, the needs of the organization take precedence over the needs of families and there are constantly changing structures and systems are ones that are associated with poor outcomes for children. Therefore, the second form of neglect outside the family is organizational neglect. If practitioners are to work effectively to meet the needs of children, those managing organizations should operate to a minimum level of competence to ensure the needs of staff are met and they in turn work effectively with families to keep children safe. The following have been found to be associated with improved outcomes for children:

- recognising the impact of the work on staff and consequently providing staff with opportunities to discuss concerns and support to manage the stresses of the work
- promoting an environment where errors can be expressed, mistakes acknowledged and solutions found
- ensuring workers are clear about roles and have manageable workloads
- making workers feel valued and positive about the job and organization. (Hemmelgarn *et al.*, 2006; Glisson and Green, 2011)

The third type of neglect can be described as societal neglect. Spencer and Baldwin (2005) argue that society can neglect children in different ways by failing to provide sufficient basic resources to families – such as shelter and nourishment, ensuring access to adequate health care and education services, by failing to respect the rights of children and denying citizens' rights to religious and cultural freedom. As noted above, some American states recognize that parents cannot meet the needs of children if they do not have the financial resources to do so. The approach taken by the state towards public services can also be significant. Indirect societal neglect can occur, according to Spencer and Baldwin, if economic policies and societal attitudes adversely affect child rearing. So, for example, the economic priority given to providing family support services and generous state benefits will influence what is available to support vulnerable families. Indirect societal neglect is evident in the application of a public management approach to child welfare services, which has shaped practice in a number of countries in recent years. The emphasis on quantitative performance indicators and targets has resulted in organizational targets – rather than the needs of the child and their family – driving service delivery (Broadhurst *et al.*, 2009; Munro 2011b). In contrast, a reduction in central government oversight – in favour of localism, such as that advocated by the Coalition government in England – is likely to result in significant variation across the nation depending on what priorities local councils place on the provision of services to vulnerable families. (State policy and its implications for planning and intervention in cases of neglect will be discussed further in Chapter 2.)

Finally, each and every member of a society can also be held to account for failing to recognize and act if they have concerns about neglect. In describing the circumstances surrounding the death from neglect of three-year-old Tiffany Wright, Levy and Scott Clark (2010, p. 30) put this well:

> Her case…challenges the British notion of community: family and friends, neighbours, pub regulars, staff, all watched as a sickening child faded from view, and not one of them called for help.

Conclusion

'Child neglect' is a vague term and is difficult to define for a number of reasons. First, neglect is socially constructed. Therefore, what is perceived to be neglect will change with time and place. Second, neglect is usually described in relation to a failure to meet the basic minimum standards that young people and children require from a parent or carer. This raises questions as to what can reasonably be expected of carers, and indeed what contribution professionals, the state and society should make to support child rearing. Third, the complex and multifaceted nature of neglect means that it is difficult achieving consensus as to what constitutes neglect. Moreover, different professionals and indeed members of the public may hold dissimilar views and standards regarding good enough parenting. These standards are also likely to be influenced by the legislative framework, and cultural, religious and community norms. Fourth, whilst neglect tends to be associated with persistent failure on the part of the carer to meet the needs of the child, resulting in cumulative harm to the child, this is a very narrow focus and minimizes the potential impact of episodic neglect and one-off incidents on the child. Furthermore, it diverts attention away from identifying and addressing emerging concerns about neglectful parenting behaviours.

Taking these challenges into account, operational definitions of neglect, if interpreted literally, are of limited use. In order to identify neglect in a meaningful way, rather than being driven by definitions, a focus on minimum parenting competencies can be useful. This approach enables practitioners to consider in a more holistic manner ways in which the parent is or is not meeting all the developmental needs of their child, rather than those specific needs that are listed in operational definitions.

Chapter 2

Neglectful Parenting: Ability, Motivation and Opportunities

Case study 2.1: Gemma, Dylan and Ethan

Gemma is 22 years old and lives on her own with her two children: Dylan, who is six years old and Ethan, who is just eight weeks old. She depends on state benefits and lives in a run-down part of the city in a damp, dirty and poorly equipped flat. She is on medication for depression and drinks heavily. Gemma has a troubled relationship with Jamie, the father of Ethan, who does not live in the flat but visits occasionally; she is not sure who fathered Dylan. She has one female friend, who visits irregularly. They quarrel frequently and Gemma does not see her friend for months following these arguments. Other than that she does not have any friends, has few social skills and lacks the confidence to join a parent–toddler group. She does, however, see her mother, who lives on the other side of the city, but their relationship is volatile. Gemma did not do well at school: she was bullied and called 'stupid' and, as a result, her attendance was erratic and she did not obtain any qualifications.

Gemma's birth family was well known to social workers and other professionals and Gemma, because of concerns regarding neglect and physical abuse, spent short periods in foster care with her two younger siblings. This was always a result of a request by her mother that she could not cope with her children. Gemma's father has been in prison since Gemma was ten. He is still serving a sentence for armed robbery and she has no contact with him. Gemma lived at home for two years after the birth of Dylan. Both the midwife and the health visitor were concerned about her ability to care for him but, with the support of her mother, Gemma appeared to meet his needs. She was offered a place on a local parenting programme for young mothers but did not take it up. When Dylan was four, Gemma quarrelled with her mother, left home and moved in with Jamie, her then boyfriend and father of Ethan. This was into a privately rented flat where she still lives.

The police received a number of phone calls over the following year from neighbours who were concerned that Jamie was violent and verbally abusive towards Gemma, but Gemma always denied this was the case.

The police did refer the family for family support because of the state of the flat and concerns that Dylan appeared to be dirty and looked thin. A family centre worker was allocated to work with Gemma. She visited the home but Gemma would not engage in any centre-based activities. Gemma's care for Dylan improved and the case was closed.

A further referral was made to social services by the health visitor following a visit when Ethan was six weeks old. The health visitor reported that Jamie had left whilst Gemma was pregnant, although he occasionally visits unexpectedly and, according to Gemma, 'upsets us'. Gemma appeared to be depressed and admitted to drinking heavily. The flat was dirty, there were piles of dirty clothes and rubbish bags everywhere and both children were filthy. Dylan had head lice and, according to Gemma, was 'out of control', and he was constantly shouted at by Gemma. Ethan had a severe nappy rash and Gemma was concerned that he was not gaining weight as he should. She said he never seemed hungry and would shut his mouth when she tried to give him his bottle. Moreover, Gemma appeared to find it difficult to engage with Ethan.

The school has also identified concerns about the quality of parenting. They reported that Dylan's attendance at school has always been erratic, that he is attention seeking and easily wound up by the other children, who tease him because of his appearance and the fact that he smells. He often falls asleep in the classroom and complains about being hungry. He should attend the breakfast club but usually arrives too late to join in. Gemma is usually late collecting Dylan from school and his class teacher is worried that she has sometimes collected him when she has been drunk.

This case example is one that must be familiar to many practitioners, as Gemma's behaviour and the children's experiences, according to research studies in a range of countries, are common amongst neglectful families (Gaudin *et al.*, 1996; Dubowitz, 1999a; Schumacher *et al.*, 2001; Erickson and Egeland, 2002; Coohey, 2003; Wilson and Horner, 2005; Stevenson, 2007; Brandon *et al.*, 2008; Brandon *et al.*, 2009; Moran, 2010).

In order to intervene effectively to meet the needs of children like Ethan and Dylan, it is important that practitioners appreciate why parents struggle to meet the needs of their child. In other words, they must address the causes of the neglect rather than the symptoms alone (Gaudin, 1993). For instance, there may be a number of reasons why Gemma finds it difficult controlling Dylan's behaviour: she might not know how to provide him with suitable boundaries; she may be depressed and find she has not got the energy to set boundaries and adhere to them; or she may be finding Dylan difficult to relate to. It is only by looking beyond the parenting behaviour and considering why parents behave in the way they do that practitioners can ensure interventions are appropriate and are likely to improve the quality of parenting. In Gemma's case there would be little benefit in offering her a parenting programme designed to teach her parenting skills if the issue is not her ability to meet the needs of her children but, rather, the problem centres on her lack of motivation.

Planning and intervening in these types of cases also requires practitioners to look beyond the parent to understand how the development of the child is compromised by neglect. It is only by understanding how the needs of the child are, or are not, being met that it is possible to identify what services children require in their own right and what the parent needs to do to improve the quality of life for the child. For example, how is Ethan affected by Gemma's lack of emotional engagement with him? What are his needs and how can they best be met?

In this chapter I explore neglectful parenting with a particular focus on aspects of the parenting environment and parenting capacity that practitioners should take into account when assessing and making sense of the struggles that neglectful parents encounter in meeting the needs of their child, and the reasons why they may find parenting difficult.

Neglectful parenting: what do we know?

Good enough parents ensure their child is safe, adequately stimulated, receives love and affection, and is provided with age-appropriate guidance and boundaries within a stable environment (Pugh, De'Ath *et al.*, 1994; DH *et al.*, 2000). Parents who neglect their children, like Gemma, find this difficult. Research into neglectful mothering (sadly, there is very limited research on neglectful fathers) has highlighted that neglectful mothers have particular issues in relation to meeting the needs of their children. Before considering the research, however, a note of caution: the research can do little more than alert practitioners to the types of parenting behaviours that *appear* to be associated with neglect. To date, research in the field is limited, the studies are often small scale, many do not distinguish neglect from other forms of maltreatment and researchers do not use a common definition of neglect. Moreover, it is also important to recognize that many of the studies are completed in the USA and are therefore set within the American child welfare context and take account of American cultures and definitions of neglect.

Mothers and neglect

Moving on to the specifics, it should be noted that neglectful mothers find recognizing the age-appropriate needs of their children more difficult than their non-neglectful counterparts (Jones and McNeely, 1980). They tend to have more unrealistic and negative expectations of their offspring and consequently find it difficult setting behavioural boundaries and gaining the cooperation of the child in an age-appropriate manner. They also tend to become upset and angry with their children easily (Hansen *et al.*, 1989; Crittenden, 1996; Lacharité *et al.*, 1996). This can also affect their ability to offer appropriate guidance. Establishing appropriate guidance and boundaries is made even more challenging for these mothers as they find problem solving difficult, have poor negotiating skills, and do not recognize why a child might be misbehaving or have an appropriate response to that behaviour (Brayden *et al.*, 1992; Gaudin *et al.*, 1996; Coohey, 1998). These mothers tend to see things as black or white rather than recognizing shades of grey, which might explain why Hildyard and Wolfe (2007) found the neglectful mothers in their study were not good at identifying risk of harm to the child. They have particular difficulty understanding behaviour in terms of different contexts and situations and therefore cannot readily identify danger in different settings. Hildyard and Wolfe (2007) also found that neglectful mothers had difficulties processing social-emotional information and therefore struggled to identify children's emotions and actions accurately, which impedes their understanding of their children's feelings and behaviour and their ability to respond. Neglecting mothers have also been found to have a restricted emotional vocabulary and lack empathy with their children (Jones and McNeely, 1980). They appear to lack social skills and find it difficult to demonstrate both warmth and responsiveness in their relationships and a curiosity about others (Gaudin *et al.*, 1996; Coohey, 1998). Other studies indicate neglectful mothers also struggle to provide the child with appropriate stimulation, having particular difficulties with both verbal and social stimulation (Garbarino and Collins, 1999; Wilson and Horner, 2005). In addition, neglectful mothers are more likely to suffer depression; be tense, angry and have more mood swings; and experience more unresolved conflict than non-neglectful mothers (Pianta *et al.*, 1989; Gaudin *et al.*, 1996). Domestic abuse, mental health issues, child maltreatment, a history of substance misuse and poor parenting are also more prevalent in cases of maltreatment, including neglect (Polansky *et al.*, 1981; Daniel *et al.*, 2011; Davies and Ward, 2012).

Fathers and males in caring roles and neglect

Burgess and Daniel (2010), drawing on the key findings from studies of caregiving by fathers, found fewer behavioural problems amongst children whose fathers are heavily involved in their care. These children are also likely to have higher educational achievement and higher self-esteem and life satisfaction than children whose fathers are not so involved in their care. Unfortunately, little is known about male caregivers and child neglect. Lee *et al.* (2009) note that without this knowledge practitioners have problems

identifying the part played by men in both contributing to neglect and protecting children from harm. Brandon *et al.* (2009) have, however, analysed
the information obtained about fathers who caused death or serious injury
to a child from neglect in England and found they possessed similar histories of maltreatment in childhood to those of neglectful mothers.

Exploring various family structures in cases of neglect, Dufour *et al.*
(2008) found mothers and fathers were struggling with different personal
problems. Women faced problems such as poor mental health and social
isolation, whilst their male counterparts were more likely to be involved in
illegal activities; this is supported by the findings of Brandon *et al.* (2008).
According to Dubowitz *et al.* (2000), the father's involvement in family
life, including duration, feelings of effective parenting and participation in
household duties, can increase or reduce the risk of neglect. Four different
types of involvement of fathers in neglectful families have been described
by Lacharité *et al.* (1996):

- coercive involvement where the father is present yet abusive, violent,
  intrusive or hostile
- obstructive involvement where the quality and quantity of parental
  behaviour is low
- intermittent involvement which is positive but infrequent
- positive ongoing involvement.

In the latter, the father's contribution may be appropriate although the benefits can be diluted by the family's other numerous difficulties. In the case
example of Gemma and her two boys, the father of Dylan is not known
and Jamie, Ethan's father, has absented himself from the full-time care of
the child but appears on the scene infrequently, often upsetting Gemma
and the boys. This type of behaviour was noted in the analysis of cases in
the Anytown neglect study (see Box 0.1 and Appendix). Thus, two further
types of involvement can be added to the levels of involvement identified by
Lacharité *et al.* (1996):

- absent fathers with no involvement
- intermittent involvement which is negative.

It is not only the role of birth fathers that needs to be considered in relation to neglect, but that of other significant male caregivers. Recent serious
case reviews following death or serious injury to a child from neglect in
England (see, for example, Brandon *et al.*, 2008, 2009) have highlighted
that it is all too easy to ignore the role of men who are not fathers but
are living intermittently or permanently within the home. Although there
appears to be a strong correlation between lone mothers and neglect

(Connell-Carrick, 2003), many of these mothers have a partner, albeit on a temporary or transitory basis (Coohey, 1995). Thus, even in situations where it appears the mother is caring for children on her own there may well be another potential caregiver. These men may play a positive or negative role in relation to meeting the needs of the child. In the Anytown study, there were two examples of men, who were not the birth fathers of the children, providing quality caregiving, which enabled the mothers who had a history of neglecting their children to provide reasonable care: the problem was that these men only remained in the home for a short period, and when they left the standard of care deteriorated.

Understanding neglectful caregiving

It is all too tempting, when considering the challenges that neglectful mothers have in meeting the needs of their children, to conclude that all that these mothers need in terms of an intervention are services that provide them with the knowledge and skills to engage with the child in such a way that their needs are met. The Anytown study provided numerous examples of this response. For example, a mother who had difficulty stimulating her child was offered a place at a parent–toddler group so that she could learn how to play with her two-year-old. For some mothers this may be the solution to the problem, but unfortunately it will not work for all neglectful parents or may be just part of the solution, as was the case with the mother offered a place at a parent–toddler group who had problems bonding with her child. Effective parenting requires an ability to meet the needs of the child, the motivation to do so and the opportunity (Horwath, 2007). Therefore, if interventions are to be effective then practitioners need to take an ecological approach – not only going beyond the presenting concerns to identify the specific parental behaviours that are an issue, but establishing the parental beliefs, desires and needs that are shaping those behaviours and also considering how the parenting context is affecting their ability to meet the needs of their child.

Parenting ability and completing parenting tasks

The case study at the beginning of this chapter raises questions about Gemma's ability to provide basic care to her boys. Yet, if parents are to provide basic care, or indeed any other aspect of care, they must be able to understand what is required of them and translate this into actions. All too often, neglectful parents do not understand what appears to us to be the simplest of tasks. A case that immediately springs to mind is a couple who lived with their six children in the Republic of Ireland. The professionals were seriously concerned about the chronic neglect these children were experiencing, and an intensive package of support was provided by child welfare agencies. A significant concern was the mouth infections and gum disease the children were experiencing alongside tooth decay. The children received the necessary dental treatment and the parents were told they needed to introduce a regime of tooth brushing twice daily. Despite the parents assuring workers that they were ensuring the children brushed their teeth, the evidence was to the contrary. Eventually a family support worker asked the mother to show her how the children were brushing their teeth. The mother lined all the children up and took a rather worn toothbrush and a tube of toothpaste from the bathroom cabinet. Each child in turn stuck out their tongue and she proceeded to squeeze a drop of toothpaste onto their tongues. She then took the toothbrush and gave it to each child in turn asking them to suck on the brush, before removing it and putting it into the mouth of the next child. The mother turned triumphantly to the family support worker and said, 'See, I'm making sure they brush their teeth.' Both the parents came from families where neglect and physical abuse were rife. The mother had had all her teeth removed by the age of 17. Neither parent knew what brushing teeth effectively actually meant. In this case, with proper guidance, they were able to introduce a regime that had a significant, positive impact on the children's oral health. This case illustrates what has been found in a number of research studies, that parents who fail to meet the needs of their children may well have experienced abuse and neglect themselves and therefore had poor parenting role models (Polansky *et al.*, 1981), or because of their parenting experiences have less of an understanding of the complexity of caregiving tasks compared to those who have not been maltreated (Pianta *et al.*, 1989). Moreover, understanding the most basic parenting tasks may be challenging if the cognitive skills of the parent are impaired by prescribed or illicit drugs or alcohol (Cleaver *et al.*, 2011). It is often presumed that a parent with a learning difficulty will have problems acquiring and applying the knowledge and skills necessary to meet the needs of their child. Whilst this may be the case amongst some of these parents, it is not inevitable; the degree of intellectual disability and the support available will have a significant influence (Booth and Booth, 2004; National Child Protection Clearinghouse, 2009).

Parenting motivation: the parent–child relationship

Whilst parents may lack the knowledge and skills to meet the needs of their children, with appropriate guidance and support many parents can learn how to do this. What can be more challenging, when identifying meaningful interventions, is addressing parent–child relationship problems. Stith *et al.* (2009), using a meta-analysis of neglect studies, found five antecedents pertinent to neglect by carers: the quality of the parent–child relationship; the carer seeing the child as a problem; carers' stress levels; parental self-esteem; and parental responses of anger and hyper-reactivity. Many of these issues have their roots in how the parent themselves was parented, as carers' personal histories of being cared for influence their relationship with their own child. Wilson *et al.* (2008, p. 909), for example, found in a meta-analysis of observational studies of child neglect that:

> neglect is evident not just in a parent's failure to meet a child's basic needs (e.g. clothing and supervision) but also in a more subtle failure to display attentiveness and responsiveness. Lack of involvement may reflect a parent's own mental models about self and relationships and simultaneously communicate implicit messages about relationships to the neglected child.

Crittenden (1999), drawing on attachment theory, offers a theoretical explanation as to why this is the case. She argues that the way carers process information in terms of 'cognition' (appreciating what emotional actions cause specific outcomes) and 'affect' (feelings about danger and protection that motivate protective and affectionate behaviours) relates to neglect and is influenced by the parent's own experience of being parented. The style in which information is processed links to how carers perceive, interpret and respond to their child's signals and indeed to others within and beyond the family. In Crittenden's opinion, neglectful carers' responses differ from those of good enough parents, who are able to respond positively at both an emotional and a cognitive level. Drawing on this work, DePaul and Guibert (2008, p. 1064) conclude that neglectful carers lack empathy, or experience empathy that is then modified by cognitive processes, so they 'cannot develop the helping response needed to care for their children'. Concern for the child's welfare or recognizing the child is expressing a need does not trigger empathetic responses. Parents become 'empathy avoidant' as a means of circumventing the potential personal costs involved in satisfying the child's need.

Crittenden identifies three different types of neglectful caregiving styles: disorganized, emotional and depressed.

Disorganized neglect

Carers in this category have histories of emotional deprivation and of feeling worthless; their immediate feelings tend to dominate and suffocate cognition or thinking. Their behaviour is influenced by how they themselves are feeling at the time, resulting in volatile and unpredictable caregiving. So, for example, children may be 'little cherubs' one minute and 'little devils' the next. These carers tend to lurch from crisis to crisis. The parents can, if their feelings are right at the time, be genuinely committed to meeting the needs of their child. However, in reality, they are unable to sustain this commitment, and so little alters and children's needs remain unmet. The children brought up in this environment are experiencing unpredictable and inconsistent parenting.

Emotional neglect

For emotionally neglectful carers, emotional processing is dominated by cognition. The home may be materially comfortable and well organized, carers may be articulate with stimulation and basic care valued, yet there is an overwhelming absence of emotional warmth. Expectations of children can be unrealistic, resulting in children being criticized and belittled when they fail to live up to the carer's exacting standards. Emotionally neglectful carers have usually experienced insecure, avoidant attachments – that is, a low-warmth environment – themselves and keep their children at arm's length in order not to be overwhelmed by the emotional demands of the child. Feelings cannot be expressed in a healthy fashion, yet may be manifest through arguments, violence or intimidation (Howe, 2005). Growing up in an atmosphere of low warmth and high criticism is highly damaging to children, who may be lonely, open to bullying, unable to express emotions or form meaningful relationships. These families can be challenging for professionals to work with as they tend to use tactics, such as aggression or lack of meaningful communication, to keep practitioners at a distance.

Depressed neglect

This term is used to describe carers where both cognition and affect are absent from their emotional information processing systems. They appear to be unmotivated and often do not recognize that their child has needs, even if these are pointed out to them. These carers do not care for themselves or others; household conditions can be unhygienic and insanitary; basic physical care is lacking and general supervision is missing, resulting in a bleak home environment for the child. The overall atmosphere in the household is 'flat', as carers show no emotion and do not respond to children's signals for attention. Children are at risk of accidents due to the paucity of supervision and may suffer from nutritional or medical neglect. The children themselves become passive, expecting nothing from their carers and, in some situations, may become carers both for their parents, who have given up on life, and for other siblings. This type of neglect may be associated with drug and alcohol misuse.

Parenting opportunities

Parenting does not take place in a vacuum. Effective parenting requires adequate resources to meet the needs of the child, such as satisfactory housing, transport and employment (Field, 2010). Yet parents who, as described above, have very limited parenting skills are often attempting to meet the needs of their child in a context that even the most competent parents would find challenging. Rose and Barnes (2007), for example, found that neglected children who had been subject to serious case reviews following death or serious injury in England were living in inadequate housing with insufficient resources and little community support. The NSPCC (2008) also found a strong correlation between neglect and poverty in the UK, with parents struggling to provide adequate care and nourishment in very poor material environments. The link between poverty and neglect has also been found in other countries such as Canada, Australia and the USA (National Clearing House on Child Abuse and Neglect, 2001; Trocmé *et al.*, 2005; Sedlak *et al.*, 2010). This link is not surprising if one considers the findings from the Joseph Rowntree Foundation study (2010a), which identified groups of children and families at particular risk of poverty. The factors that make children vulnerable to poverty are very similar to those of children at risk of neglect (Spencer and Baldwin, 2005; Daniel *et al.*, 2011). These included workless households and those consisting of part-time workers, families with more than three children, children living with a disabled adult and children of teenage mothers. The Joseph Rowntree Foundation also explored the impact on children of living in poverty and found that children growing up in poverty are 13 times more likely to die from unintentional injury and 37 times more likely to die from exposure to smoke, fire or flames; six times more likely to be obese; and more likely to be born premature and have low birth weight or die within their first year than other children. They are also less likely to attain basic school-leaving qualifications. Ghate and Hazel (2002) found that living in very poor neighbourhoods also means living with exposure to crime and drugs. And DePanfilis (2006a) notes that children who live in impoverished and dangerous neighbourhoods have been found to be at greater risk of neglect than children living in safer neighbourhoods. Bearing in mind the impact of neglect on a child, which is explored in Chapter 3, the combination of neglect and poverty is a toxic mix seriously affecting a child's life chances. What is also of note is, irrespective of country, children are all too aware of the impact of poverty on their daily lives, such as exclusion from friendships, play, leisure and community activities (Walker *et al.*, 2008).

Stevenson (2007, p. 20) argues that when professionals encounter neglect in cases of very obvious poverty and deprivation then it is all too easy to focus on trying to improve the family situation through the use of material resources without an 'ecological understanding' of what will work for that particular family at that time. For example, in the Anytown study, one family was given two washing machines in the space of four years and another family four stair gates. In both cases the goods were left to rust in the outside yard because there were family issues beyond poverty that were affecting the ability of the parents to meet the needs of the children. In the case of the family with the washing machine, the mother was depressed and did not have the energy to wash the clothes. Regarding the stair gates, the issue of lack of supervision was far more about the mother's attitude towards her children than the steep stairs the young children were climbing unsupervised.

Reading the case study about Gemma and her two boys, one gains a picture of a young mother who is socially isolated with the few relationships she has being unsupportive. Cash and Wilke (2003) found that positive social interaction, including opportunities for childcare, is a protective factor against neglect in families with substance misuse problems. In addition, Zolotor and Runyan (2006) found that as a family becomes more isolated, neglect and psychologically harsh parenting is more likely to occur. Families from ethnic minority groups are particularly likely to have few social supports. Thoburn *et al.* (2000), for example, found, in a UK study of family support in cases of emotional maltreatment and neglect, that ethnic minority families were less likely to be in touch with family members and had fewer social supports than white families.

There are a range of social supports that can help parents with child rearing. A common source of support for many parents is their own parents. However, comparative research by Coohey (1995) found that whilst neglectful mothers may live near to their own mother, the quality of relationship, as in the case of Gemma, is likely to be poor, with fewer positive 'exchanges' between them. This is hardly surprising, bearing in mind that neglectful parents are more likely than other parents to have received poor parenting from their parents. Rose and Barnes (2007) noted that this relationship can be further complicated in some cases. In their overview of serious case review reports, they found the neglectful parents acquired responsibility for caring for a disabled elderly parent which detrimentally affected their own parenting capacity.

Another potential source of support is a live-in partner. However, as discussed earlier in this chapter, there is a strong correlation between single-parenthood by mothers and child neglect (Connell-Carrick, 2003). If these mothers do have partners they are often shadowy figures in the household who do not contribute positively to either supporting the mother or caring for the children (Daniel and Taylor, 2001; Daniel and Baldwin, 2002). Neglectful mothers are also vulnerable to engaging with dominating men who are often violent and abusive towards them and may undermine their already limited sense of self-esteem. Gudjonsson *et al.* (2011), building on the research of others, found that early life experiences of maltreatment, particularly neglect, make some adults more vulnerable to pressure from others and to the demands made on them by others. This may explain why, as will be discussed in Chapter 11, domestic violence is common in cases of neglect.

Friendships are also a source of informal support, but as neglectful parents often lack the social skills to develop and maintain relationships, as with Gemma in the case study, the relationships are often weak, unsupportive, unstable and volatile. When they break down the parent can be left feeling more isolated and alone (Gaudin, 1993).

A further type of support is the community. However, the impoverished communities that many neglectful families live in are associated with limited support and social contact (Ernst *et al.*, 2004), but the situation may be exacerbated by neglectful families viewing their communities as less supportive and helpful than other families do (Gaudin, 1993). The limited support available may be denied neglectful families, who may be excluded and shunned because of the visible signs of neglect: the rubbish outside the house and lack of attention to the appearance of the home; children out in the street unsupervised and uncontrolled; the police and other professionals visiting routinely. This can be exacerbated for the family from an ethnic minority group by racism or harassment. Harassment may also be a feature of family life for parents with a learning disability (Spencer and Baldwin, 2005). Alternatively, the community may accept poor parenting, violence, drug and alcohol misuse as the norm, thereby giving the family a distorted perspective of good enough parenting.

Conclusion

One of the most significant challenges when deciding how best to intervene in cases of child neglect is identifying what is required to meet the needs of the child and their family. Unfortunately – as is evident from the case example of Gemma, Dylan and Ethan – there is no simple solution: neglect is multifaceted in relation to factors that can contribute to neglectful parenting and the effects these can have on children. In order to identify the most effective interventions, practitioners have to dig deep and go beyond the presenting problem to explore the specific parental behaviours that are causing concern and consider the needs, desires, capacity and beliefs of the parent that are informing those behaviours. Moreover, there are a diverse range of potential influences informing neglectful behaviours, such as the parent's ability to understand the needs of the child, the parent–child relationship; the carer seeing the child as a problem; carers' stress levels; parental self-esteem and parental emotional responses and self-control. Family and environmental factors – such as their own experiences of being parented, poverty, poor housing, lack of social support, drug and alcohol misuse and mental health issues – all have a part to play in shaping parenting behaviour.

Chapter 3

Impact of Neglect on Children and Young People

Case study 3.1: Dylan

My name is Dylan. I am six years old. I live with my mummy and baby brother Ethan. We have to climb lots of stairs to get to home. It is smelly. Mummy says people pee on the stairs. I get really scared when I go up the stairs as there is a funny man who comes out his door and shouts at us. Our house smells too. Mummy says it is damp. I know what that is: it is the black stuff on the walls. On a good day Mummy wakes me in the morning and then I get up and go to school for breakfast club. I like that as everyone is nice to me and I love the cereal and toast. My teacher Mrs Hunter is nice but the children in my class are not nice. They say I smell and have dirty clothes. It is not my fault and they won't let me play their games. I got so mad one day I hit one of the boys and then I got into trouble. I also got told off for saying words Mummy uses but Mrs Hunter told me they are naughty words. I have one friend Jason but he is like me and does not go to school every day. I like reading and sums but I'm no good, Mrs Hunter says I'd be better if I came every day. She gives me books to read at home with Mummy but Mummy is too tired and gets cross when I ask her to read to me. Sometimes I sleep in lessons, it is so nice and warm in my classroom, and then I get laughed at. I love the school dinners and if anyone leaves theirs I'll try and eat up what is left. The others call me a pig. One boy told me he has another dinner when he gets home. I wish I was him. I get bags of crisps and a bottle of pop. I get worried when we get to going home time as I hope Mummy will be there for me. She came on Monday and walked and smelt funny. She shouted at me and Mrs Hunter told her off so she hit me when I got home. I hate it when I get home. Mummy says she's tired and sleeps on the settee and tells me to look after Ethan. He cries a lot and I can't stop him so Mummy shouts at us both. I watch TV and sometimes I fall asleep on the floor or Mummy will tell me to go to bed. I wet the bed sometimes. The sheet might be dry when I go to bed. If not, I keep my clothes on. Sometimes if I've wet the bed and got no dry clothes Mummy gets cross and I can't go to school and I watch TV. I don't like that as there is nothing to do, and Ethan cries a lot and Mummy shouts at us. Sometimes Mummy lets me go to the shop for her. I hate going past the scary man but I like being out and I know you have to look for cars before you cross the road. There is a nice lady in the shop and sometimes she'll give me chocolate.

Hildyard and Wolfe's (2002) summary of the literature on child neglect stresses, as is apparent when considering Dylan's life, that neglect affects all aspects of children's development – physical, socio-emotional, cognitive and behavioural. This finding is supported by a study of frontline practitioners' experience of neglect (Action for Children, 2009). The practitioners indicated that in their experience neglect impacts on poor attainment at school, emotional and mental health problems, poor social skills, isolation and poor physical health. The effects of neglect continue to manifest themselves in adolescence and can persist into adulthood, having a wide-ranging impact. For example, the study by Currie and Widom (2010) of the long-term consequences of child abuse and neglect highlights that neglected individuals were more likely than a control group to be unemployed or in menial or semi-skilled jobs, with women being particularly vulnerable.

In this chapter I do little more than provide a brief overview of the different ways in which neglect affects the development of children and young people. For those who wish to learn more see Horwath (2007), Stevenson (2007) and Daniel *et al.* (2011). Whilst I will explore neglect, in this chapter, by focusing on the different ways it affects the different developmental needs of the child, it is important not to compartmentalize these needs without recognizing the cumulative impact of neglect on the miserable daily lives of neglected children such as Dylan.

Neglect and brain development

In order to appreciate why neglect affects every aspect of the child's development it is necessary to understand the impact of neglect on brain development (Twardosz and Lutzker, 2010). The early experiences of a child affect brain development and can have lasting effects on children's cognitive, emotional and behavioural development (National Clearing House on Child Abuse and Neglect, 2001; Heim *et al.*, 2010). 'Global' neglect, which is sensory deprivation – including lack of exposure to touch, language and social interactions – not surprisingly has the most significant and dramatic effect on brain growth (Perry, 2002, p. 92). Work by the National Scientific Council on the Developing Child at Harvard University (2007) has highlighted how experiences shape the architecture of the developing brain. The infancy period and early years are a time when the foundations are laid for all future development, and each developmental layer or 'scaffolding' is dependent on the last. Without a good base, it will be harder for children to learn and to reach their full potential. Their work also highlights the significance of the quality of children's attachment and relationships to brain development, as it is through the interaction between primary carer and child that the 'scaffolding' of children's brains is further developed and more complex skills learnt.

Whilst neglect in early years can have damaging and long-term effects, this is exacerbated by further experiences of abuse *and* neglect (Perry, 2002). This combination has a negative effect on the parts of the brain that control cognition, problem solving, empathy, aggression, anxiety, self-regulation, hyperactivity and impulse control. It is therefore not surprising, as discussed in Chapter 11 and 12, that young people who have experienced abuse and neglect in early childhood are more likely to have problems with aggression, violence and mental health issues in later life. Although the right environment for early brain development is of critical importance, recent research at the American National Institute of Mental Health indicates that brain development is still a work in progress in adolescence. Their research, although still in its early stages, would appear to indicate that adolescent brains continue to develop and change. Between the ages of six and 13 there are growth spurts in the parts of the brain that specialize in language and understanding spatial relations. Between puberty and adulthood, changes occur in the parts of the brain that are responsible for self-control, judgement and emotional regulation (ACT for Youth, 2004; Dahl, 2004; De Bellis, 2005; National Institute for Mental Health, 2010).

Physical development

Brain growth is, in part, dependent on adequate nutrition. Severe malnutrition not only impedes brain growth, it also affects bone development and physical growth. Inadequate nutrition, such as the poor diet described by Dylan, results in vitamin and mineral deficiencies and affects preschool- and school-aged children's behaviour, cognitive development, academic achievement and activity levels (Mackner and Starr, 1997; Kerr *et al.*, 2000; Polonko, 2006). For example, DePanfilis (2006a) notes that iron deficiency, the most common form of malnutrition in the USA, can lead to cognitive and motor delay, anxiety, depression and problems with attention. An inappropriate diet may not only lead to malnutrition but also result in obesity, which has implications for children's longer-term health and development because it is linked to diabetes, respiratory problems, sleeping disorders, cardiovascular diseases and gastrointestinal problems (Sabin *et al.*, 2004).

There has been much debate, however, regarding the extent to which neglect can be linked to weight problems in children. Whitaker *et al.* (2007) studied a cohort of 24,000 three-year-olds who were part of the American Fragile Families and Child Wellbeing Study. They found the odds of obesity were 50 per cent higher amongst children whose mothers had reported neglectful behaviours in the previous year. This finding persisted after adjusting for maternal obesity and multiple socio-economic factors. Bennett *et al.* (2010), in contrast, took as their sample 185 children in urban American communities, 91 of whom had a history of neglect. They saw the children when they were between four and six and again between seven and nine. They found similar body mass indexes (BMIs) between the two groups of children, although both had BMIs significantly greater than the norms for age, gender and ethnicity. In terms of low BMIs, neglect chronicity did predict lower BMIs but only at ages eight and nine. The authors conclude that neglect per se does not appear to predict weight problems.

Focusing on factors associated with weight faltering or failure to thrive – a consumption of insufficient calories – the following have been found to be contributory factors: poor intake and accompanying feeding difficulties; the inherent appetite characteristics of the child; and the child being a fussy eater or having a small appetite. The way in which the mother responds may also play a part, and a mother struggling with parenting may find the baby's avoidant reactions to food, such as spitting out food, crying and screaming when fed, turning away or closing their mouth when offered food, particularly difficult. Moreover, experiences of stress within and beyond the family may also play a part (Wright *et al.*, 2006; Batchelor, 2008). Some of or all of these issues may be present in neglectful families but are not exclusive to these families. What is important is to establish where the problems lie, the parents' ability and motivation to address these issues, and to take these into account when considering interventions. For example, in some cases, dietary advice may be sufficient; in others it may require more intensive home-based work if part of the problem is the interaction between the parent and child. Brandon *et al.* (2011), for example, drawing on a sample of children who had died as a result of abuse and neglect, found that some of the parents found ways of switching off from their children and, as a consequence, did not feed babies, restricted their food intake or made feeding time a distressing experience for the child.

Although there does not appear to be evidence that neglect can predict weight problems, we need to consider another issue. Is a parent neglectful if they fail to address professionals' concerns about the weight of their children? In recent years there has been a debate in the media as to whether allowing a child to become obese is a form of neglect. For example, in 2007, Cumbria Council received attention from the press for taking an obese child into care. Other councils in England and Scotland have since received publicity for taking similar actions. Viner *et al.* (2010), from the Institute of Child Health, brought the issue to the fore when, in the *British Medical Journal*, they argued that parents who do not assist their obese children to lose weight are guilty of neglect. They have a responsibility to change their lifestyle and seek outside support through weight management initiatives like those recommended below. But this is not easily achieved. For many obese children living in neglectful families, the failure to seek treatment and change lifestyle forms part of a wider picture of neglect, linked to poor hygiene, lack of understanding and an inability or lack of motivation to meet the physical needs of the child. In a small minority of cases this lack of engagement with services raises questions as to when obesity turns into a child protection issue.

Physical development is not only dependent on diet, it is also dependent on the stimulation required to ensure the development of gross motor skills, such as running and jumping, and fine, hand-to-eye coordination skills. Studies indicate that the development of basic skills, such as crawling, walking and running, require practice in order to ensure the physical system is working (Daniel, Wassell and Gilligan, 2010). Neglected children may be denied opportunities to physically explore their world, and acquire and practise these skills – for example, as a result of being left strapped in a buggy all day, day in and day out, leaving the child apathetic, withdrawn and abandoning efforts to investigate the environment around them (Skuse *et al.*, 1994). Alternatively, the child may become frustrated through lack of stimulation, and display this frustration through restlessness, head or fist banging or out-of-control play (Horwath, 2007).

Cognitive development

A child's cognitive functioning is more negatively affected by neglect, particularly physical neglect, than any form of maltreatment (Kendall-Tackett and Eckenrode, 1996; Polonko, 2006). Iwaniec (2006) notes that teachers of neglected children highlight limitations in their problem solving and basic literacy skills, which are compounded by poor concentration and attention spans. School-age neglected children have also been found to perform at a lower level and have more discipline problems than their non-neglected peers (Egeland *et al.*, 1983). Bearing in mind the impact of neglect on a child's cognitive development, it is not surprising that a recent UK study by Action for Children (2009) found that poor attainment at school was the most commonly cited issue for neglected children, and Egeland *et al.*, in their American study, found neglected children required remedial teaching and were failing in one or more subject area. Nolin and Ethier (2007) note that whilst neglect is detrimental to cognitive function, the impacts increase when combined with physical abuse. Moreover, children assessed as suffering from *both* neglect and faltering weight gain or failure to thrive are more likely to experience deficits in cognitive functioning than those diagnosed as suffering from neglect *or* failure to thrive (Mackner and Starr, 1997).

Language development from an early age can also be affected by neglect (Gaudin, 1999; Hildyard and Wolfe, 2002). Neglected children may have poor speech and struggle with using expressive and receptive language if their carer does not actively engage with them and encourage speech and language development. Language development is fundamental to further learning as it fosters the development of cognitive processes. Sylvestre and Mérette (2010), in a review of the literature, identify a number of factors that have been associated with language delay. These include weaker cognitive development; prematurity; alcohol and drug misuse during pregnancy; parents having had language problems themselves in childhood; poor economic environment; being less well educated; having a lack of knowledge about child development; parents providing limited stimulation and having an inappropriate interactive style; living in a large family; being a boy; having untreated hearing problems; and having a mother with depressive symptoms. Sylvestre and Mérette wished to ascertain whether language delay in severely neglected children under three years of age was better explained by specific risk factors or the cumulation of the various factors. They studied 68 severely neglected French-speaking children in Canada and their mothers: all were receiving services because of concerns about neglect – information was not gathered about the fathers. The children were between 24 and 36 months old, and over a third had language delay identified through standard tests. Using multivariate logistic regression, they established that the child's delayed cognitive development, the mother's own physical and emotional abuse experiences as a child, and the mother's low acceptability level towards the child are linked to language delay in severely neglected children, as opposed to the cumulative environmental risk factors. Whilst this was a small-scale study, what the researchers have done is highlight the importance of the mother's psychological availability, and her attunement and sensitivity towards the child.

Socio-emotional development

Quality attachments in the early years are essential for the acquisition of emotional understanding and regulation (Bowlby, 1979; Howe *et al.*, 1999). Where carers are 'in tune' with the child's signals for food, safety, emotional security and closeness, and respond with consistency, acceptance and sensitivity, the child develops a positive attachment and is likely to have a positive self-image, seeing themselves as lovable and worthy of attention. This internal working model, or mental representation of worthiness, provides the basis for children's feelings and beliefs about themselves and about how they are likely to be treated by carers and other people. This gives the foundation for secure attachment relationships in which children regard others as being available and responsive to their stresses and anxieties.

Neglect can contribute to insecure attachments as children struggle to make sense of, and find a way of surviving in, their particular caregiving environment (Howe, 2005). Where carer responses are inconsistent, children have to manage the unpredictability generated by not knowing what their carer will do. They learn that emotional displays, for instance, crying, whining and being overly demanding, are more likely to elicit a response. However, when the carer does respond, the infant's reply is one of ambivalence: she or he wants the contact, yet, simultaneously, is uncertain about being able to rely on the carer's psychological availability. In turn, this gives rise to more erratic responses from the carer. The infant learns to count on emotional behaviour, such as clinginess or angry, disobedient reactions to gain attention, and is unable to explore the world or develop a sense of competence. Children with such anxious/ambivalent or resistant attachments are likely to have an internal working model of themselves as ineffective, dependent and unworthy of attention, whilst others are neglectful, unreliable and unpredictable.

Alternatively, when carers are indifferent to or rejecting of the child's signals and offer no empathetic response, the child protests initially. If the response is negative, she or he learns to contain emotions and not to demonstrate the need for comfort. Children with these anxious/avoidant attachments become emotionally independent, self-contained and compliant. Their internal working model is that they can only rely on themselves, as others are rejecting and intrusive whilst they are unlovable. As a result, such children understand social relationships on a cognitive rather than an emotional level, leaving them ill equipped to forge intimate relationships.

Crittenden and Ainsworth (1987) identified that some neglected children display anxious/avoidant attachments, whilst others show anxious/ambivalent ones towards their mothers. Egeland *et al.* (1983) observed that physically abused and physically neglected children showed predominantly anxious/ambivalent attachment whereas emotionally neglected children tended to demonstrate anxious/avoidant attachments. Severely physically neglected children may see themselves as helpless and appear to be apathetic and listless, having developed a passive, depressed dependence. This leads to a decreased need for their carer to engage with them, creating a 'cycle of decreasing stimulation' (Howe *et al.*, 1999, p. 93). Occasionally these children may try to provoke stimulation through frenzied bouts of hyperactive behaviour.

Thus, children who have experienced neglect in the first three years of life are likely to experience problems with emotional and social functioning, alongside other issues such as behavioural and cognitive problems (Scannapieco and Connell-Carrick, 2005). This is borne out by the findings of the large-scale Minnesota Longitudinal Study of High Risk Parents and Children. Elementary school-age, emotionally neglected children were found to be socially withdrawn, unpopular with peers and exhibited internalized problems. They were found, however, to be aggressive and less attentive. Physical neglect was also found to impair the child's socio-emotional behaviour, with these children ranking lower than the control group on peer acceptance and emotional health ratings (Erickson and Egeland, 2002; Maxwell *et al.*, 2012). Part of the problem for these children is that past experiences mean that they do not have the emotional knowledge to discriminate expressions and understand emotional contexts, which makes it difficult for them to interpret the behaviour of others and respond appropriately (Bentovim *et al.*, 2009). The consequences of these issues are not just restricted to relationship problems, but limited interactive skills are likely to lead to low self-esteem and affect physical and mental wellbeing as well as educational achievement (Carter, 2012). Shipman *et al.* (2005) found neglect may interfere with the normal acquisition of emotional understanding and emotional regulation skills amongst children. They conclude that children who have been physically neglected show less emotion towards their mothers, expect both conflict from their mothers and little emotional support. DePanfilis (2006a) drew together common themes from a number of studies and concluded that it is not only with regard to relationships with mothers that neglected children struggle. These children have problems with emotional understanding and regulation, such as difficulty displaying empathy or emotional awareness, and struggle finding appropriate strategies to manage anger and sadness. She also found that these children are more distrustful of others, and demonstrate a lack of confidence and impaired social cognition, which can make interactions with others stressful.

Social presentation and rejection

The combination of limited academic ability and poor social skills can leave neglected children socially isolated and excluded from peer activities in and outside of school. Such rejection may be fuelled by perceptions of neglected children as dirty, smelly or inappropriately dressed, and is compounded by their 'lower levels of emotional understanding, fewer adaptive emotional regulation skills and less effective coping strategies' (Shipman *et al.*, 2005, p. 1023) than their non-neglected peers. It is not surprising, therefore, that a survey of 3,000 primary school-aged children highlighted that neglected children were likely to be bullied, laughed at, talked about or ignored (Action for Children, 2010). The impact that this can have on a child is evident in Dylan's story.

Antisocial behaviour

Antisocial behaviour describes: aggression to people and animals; property destruction; deception; theft and serious rule violation (Daniel, Wassell and Gilligan, 2010). Research findings, largely from the USA, indicate that a history of neglect can be associated with antisocial and risk-taking behaviour as the neglected child becomes an adolescent (Koenig *et al.*, 2004; Stewart *et al.*, 2008; Stein *et al.*, 2009). Polonko (2006), for example, found child physical neglect is associated with aggression and arrests for violent behaviour. Kotch *et al.* (2008), in a USA study of 1,318 children perceived to be at risk of maltreatment, conclude that only early neglect was significantly associated with high aggression scores; neglect that occurred later in life and other forms of abuse were not significantly predictive of aggression. Dubowitz *et al.* (2004), in another study, found that by the age of three years psychological neglect was already associated with aggressive behavioural problems in some children, whilst others showed signs of depression. Neglected young people do not appear to have developed the same levels of self-control as other youngsters (Duke *et al.*, 2010; Lazenbatt, 2010). This is most evident in adolescence, when impulsivity and immaturity can lead to difficulties at home and school, with carers and teachers describing their behaviour as being out of control (Howe, 2005). The combination of these behaviours, together with a dearth of relationships with caring individuals who set appropriate boundaries and sanctions for wrongdoing (Koenig *et al.*, 2004; Stewart *et al.*, 2008; Duke *et al.*, 2010; Lazenbatt, 2010), and few, if any, positive social relationships add to these young people's vulnerability and increase the likelihood of engagement in antisocial activities (Chapple *et al.*, 2005). It is not surprising, therefore, that in adolescence the neglected child is also likely to become involved in heavy drinking, drug use and truanting, and eventually drops out of education (Erickson and Egeland, 2002). These young people, particularly young women, are also vulnerable to sexual exploitation and becoming young parents themselves. Antisocial behaviour and neglect are considered further in Chapter 12.

The neglected adolescent

Much has been written in the past few years about the lack of attention paid to adolescent neglect; indeed this was recognized by the (then) Department for Children, Schools and Families (DCSF), which commissioned a literature review on the subject to establish exactly what is known about neglect amongst young people between the ages of 11 and 17 (Rees *et al.*, 2011). Arguably, the reason that neglect amongst this age group has not received much attention is that the young people are not perceived as neglected adolescents in the same way that we consider neglected younger children; rather, they are labelled by their presenting behaviour. Therefore, the teenager who frequently has cognitive, behavioural and emotional problems as a result of neglect (Hildyard and Wolfe, 2002) is often labelled by the manifestation of these problems – the drug user, the young offender, the runaway, or the victim of sexual exploitation.

Rees *et al.* (2011) note that we should distinguish between the problems encountered by young people as a result of their cumulative experiences of neglect and problems associated with the continuing neglect of the adolescent child by their carer. Unfortunately, both parents and professionals can make assumptions that the adolescent is old enough and sufficiently resilient to take care of him- or herself and therefore minimize ongoing neglect. Moreover, the relationship between parents and adolescents normally changes as the young person becomes more independent and begins to challenge their parents. This, together with poor parenting skills and the externalization of problems by the young person, is a toxic mix and it is therefore not surprising that many social workers will have had the experience of parents contacting them in desperation and demanding that the child is removed because 'they cannot do a thing with them'. This is supported by the findings of a study of 831 young people in the USA. Simmel (2010) found that conflictual relationships between parents and young people, often accompanied by youth behaviour problems, were a primary reason for child welfare agency involvement with this age group. Another concerning study completed by Ritchie and Buchanan (2011) in the UK took a community sample of 391 13- to 15-year-olds and found that high percentages of the young people reported parents often being angry, to the extent that at times the children were frightened, and that the parents lacked warmth and affection in their interactions with their children. Moreover, they found that particular negative parenting styles in one parent are likely to be found in the other. This raises questions about the level of neglect and emotional abuse amongst the teenage population. What is also important is to recognize that self-neglect may also be an issue amongst adolescents: low self-image and a poor sense of self-worth can result in these neglected young people neglecting themselves through, for example, poor physical care, self-harming or placing themselves in vulnerable situations. And, as was briefly discussed above, the teenage brain continues to develop, with changes taking place to functions such as self-control, judgement, emotions and organization. Without appropriate parenting this could, in part, explain why young people, particularly those whose development has been affected by maltreatment, are prepared to engage in risky behaviours such as alcohol or drug misuse (ACT for Youth, 2004).

Disabled children and children with special needs

There is much debate as to whether children with special needs are more vulnerable to neglect or whether the families are likely to be involved with professionals on a more routine and regular basis and are therefore under more scrutiny. Sullivan and Knutson (2000), in a study of 50,278 American schoolchildren, concluded that disabled children are 3.4 times more likely to be abused than non-disabled children. However, Govindshenoy and Spencer (2006, p. 552), in a systematic review of population-based studies, found the evidence base for an association between maltreatment and disability was 'weak'. They found only limited evidence that physical disability predisposes a child to maltreatment. However, they noted that psychological and emotional problems and learning disabilities amongst children appeared to be associated with abuse and neglect. But they argue that this might be explained by a shared, common aetiological pathway. DePanfilis (2006a) argues, however, that disabled children are more vulnerable to neglect because the parent may be overwhelmed by the needs of the child, particularly ongoing and complex medical needs, and respond by being irritable and inconsistent in their care, or negligent. Also, as the children may appear unresponsive or have limited communication ability, it may make developing an appropriate parent–child attachment more difficult.

It is worth noting that neglect may have contributed to the disability – for example, neglect during pregnancy, as discussed in Chapter 1, is associated with premature births, which can increase the risk of birth abnormalities.

Conclusion

If interventions are to be effective, then practitioners should consider how the daily lived experience of each child in the family is affected by neglect so that interventions can be put into place to improve the quality of their lives. Neglect, particularly in the early years, affects the developing brain of the child and can have a devastating and long-lasting effect on all of the child's developmental needs. As the child develops and the root cause of the neglect is unchecked, the child is more likely to exhibit behaviours such as aggression, language delay, poor cognitive and interactional skills, and antisocial behaviours that bring them to the attention of professionals. As is evident from Dylan's story at the beginning of this chapter, the lives of these children become progressively more bleak and miserable and the harm caused more cumulative. Moreover, as the children become adolescents they display many of the problem behaviours that make parenting even more challenging. Practitioners, therefore, need to work with the child and their family to break the cycle, improve the quality of parenting and ensure the children have their needs met so that they, in turn, can become good enough parents.

Part 2

Assessing the Potential for Change and Planning Interventions

Chapter 4

Assessing Readiness to Change: The Neglected Assessment Task

Introduction

Irrespective of whether one is identifying emerging concerns or risk of significant harm in cases of child neglect, the fundamental purpose of an assessment is to understand how the safety of the individual child and their health and wellbeing are affected by the neglect. Drawing on this knowledge, practitioners can then determine how to intervene to ensure the needs of the child are met. In the UK each nation has its own assessment framework. The *Framework for the Assessment of Children in Need and Their Families* (DH *et al.*, 2000), commonly known as the Assessment Framework, is used in England and Wales; in Scotland it is *the My World Triangle*; and in Northern Ireland *UNOCINI* (Understanding the Needs of Children in Northern Ireland). All of these frameworks are underpinned by an ecological perspective that recognizes that the development of the child is influenced by both the capacity of the parent or carer to meet their needs and the environment in which the child is brought up (Bronfenbrenner, 1979). This means that practitioners, whether identifying emerging concerns about neglect or assessing the risk of harm to a child, should consider: the developmental needs of the child; parenting capacity to meet those needs; and the family and environmental factors that affect family life. An ecological approach towards assessing the needs of children is also taken in Canada, Romania, the Russian Federation, Slovakia, Sweden, Ukraine, Malta, Croatia, the Republic of Ireland and some parts of the United States of America and Australia (Daly, 2007; Rose, 2010).

In the last ten years there has been significant attention paid, both in the UK and internationally, to improving the quality of these assessments, and there is evidence that assessments are now much more focused on identifying the needs of the child and the factors that contribute to their needs being or not being met than in the past (Cleaver *et al.*, 2004; Holland, 2011; Davies and Ward, 2012). One of the consequences of this emphasis on assessment, however, is that identification and assessment of neglect can be viewed as an intervention in their own right. For example, professionals who participated in the Action for Children (2009) study of neglect described the identification of neglect, referral to an agency, assessment of the child and family needs all as interventions. There is no doubt that an assessment is, at one level, an intervention into the life of the family, but the assessment alone does not necessarily lead to sustained change. Assessment is not a stand-alone activity: in order to ensure it leads to improved outcomes for children it should be inextricably linked to planning, intervening and evaluating progress (DH *et al.*, 2000).

In my previous book on neglect I explored assessment in cases of neglect in great detail. For readers who would like more information about how to identify and assess neglect using an ecological framework, I refer you, therefore, to *Child Neglect: Identification and Assessment* (Horwath, 2007). There are other books that also pay attention to this topic (Dubowitz, 1999b; Taylor and Daniel, 2005; Daniel *et al.*, 2011). In this book I am going to focus on one aspect of the assessment process that is frequently neglected and yet is crucial to effective engagement in interventions to improve outcomes for children: parental readiness to change. In the Anytown neglect study (see Box 0.1 and Appendix), for example, the majority of participants acknowledged that they do not pay specific attention to assessing parental capacity to change; rather 'the hope is that this [the assessment and conference] will be a sort of a wake-up call to the parents and they will want to engage and there will be change' (social worker 2).

Millar and Corby (2006), in their study of 34 sets of parents, found that the assessment process did highlight for some parents why they needed to change their behaviour. Unfortunately, this is not always the case and the negative consequences of just relying on the assessment and conference as a 'wake-up call' for parents is apparent in the findings of a small-scale study completed in the USA involving 16 mothers (Sykes, 2011). These mothers were engaged, involuntarily, with child protection services because of concerns about neglect. Sykes interviewed the mothers and their caseworkers and found that despite both assessments that provided evidence of neglect and plans designed to improve the quality of parenting, the mothers' attitudes towards the concerns indicated that they were not ready to change. Sykes identified four different responses:

- *The good mother:* the mothers often described themselves positively in relation to parenting and stated that they were either misunderstood by child protection services or the allegations against them were unfounded or grossly exaggerated. If they did acknowledge poor parenting, this was rationalized as occurring because of factors beyond their control, such as being depressed or experiencing financial hardship.
- *Associational distancing:* mothers taking this stance argued that they had been randomly and unfairly identified as neglectful by

professionals, and they knew other parents who were worse parents and, in contrast to themselves, were not involved with child protection services. These mothers drew on media reports and examples from their community to identify parents who were far worse than themselves. They also distanced themselves from the neglect, arguing that their children had experienced 'accidents' and it was unfair to label these as neglect.

- *Institutional distancing:* the mothers who used this approach questioned the standards applied by child protection professionals. By arguing the standards were too high and unreasonable they were able to maintain their positive parenting identity. The mothers tended to use institutional distancing when it came to standards of cleanliness and hygiene, questioning the harm of, for example, dirty dishes. Taking this stance, they argued that all parents leave dirty dishes around at some time or have a dirty, untidy house, therefore why should such an innocuous act lead to so harsh a response from child protection professionals?
- *Resistance:* these mothers resisted the label of neglect and therefore could not appreciate why they needed to change their behaviours. The mothers who took this stance feigned engagement in plans in order to get the child protection professionals out of their lives. This response is discussed in more detail in Chapter 5.

Similar responses that demonstrate a lack of readiness to change were found amongst 32 mothers in Australia who were interviewed about their experiences of child protection assessments (Harris, 2012). If interventions are to be effective, then parents' willingness to accept the concerns, recognize the need to change and consequently engage meaningfully with interventions is crucial. Thus, an essential part of any assessment is for practitioners to determine a parent's readiness for change.

Pathways to change

The majority of participants who participated in the interviews and focus groups in the Anytown study, whilst recognizing that parents need to change behaviours, were vague as to how to assess readiness for change. A minority did, however, make reference to a model developed by Prochaska and DiClementi (1982). This model was originally developed to assess readiness and engagement with change amongst adults misusing substances. It was originally adapted for use in child welfare by the late Tony Morrison (1998) with further adaptations by myself and Tony Morrison (Horwath and Morrison, 2000, 2001; Morrison, 2010).

The model, as shown in Figure 4.1, draws on this more recent work. Five stages of change are considered:

Stage 1 – pre-contemplation: at this stage the parent is unaware that they are failing to meet the needs of their child. Alternatively, they may have some awareness (for example, through a health visitor or teacher expressing concerns about a child), but the parent is not thinking seriously about the need to change behaviours and attitudes towards the child.

Stage 2 – contemplation: the parent becomes aware of a problem. This awareness may result from a professional indicating to a parent that they are failing to meet the needs of their child. Contemplating change does not, however, necessarily require external input; the parent themselves may realize they are not meeting the needs of their child. At this stage the parent may, however, have difficulty understanding the cause of the problem and what needs to change.

Stage 3 – preparation or determination: at this point the parent is not only aware of what needs to change but also recognizes that they must do something, themselves, to change their problematic behaviours.

Stage 4 – action: here the parent begins to make changes to their behaviour and possibly to their environment in order to meet the needs of the child.

Stage 5 – maintenance: changing behaviour alone is not enough; the parent has to be able to sustain these changes and adapt to meet the ever-changing needs of the child.

At any of these different stages the parent may exit the change process, or indeed they may fail to engage in the process at all. Alternatively, they may

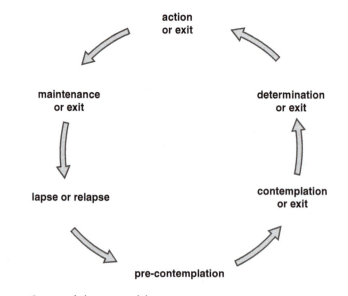

Figure 4.1: Stages of change model

Source: Horwath and Morrison (2001) (adapted from Prochaska and Diclementi (1982))

change their behaviours and establish new ways of functioning only to revert back to old ways; Prochaska and DiClementi refer to this as 'lapse' if they subsequently return to the new behaviours and 'relapse' if they do not. Lapses and relapses are most likely to occur at times of crisis and stress when it is all too easy to revert to old, familiar ways of managing a situation.

Neglectful parents are often expected by professionals to make significant changes to their lives. Bearing in mind what is expected of them, there are a number of factors that practitioners should take into account. First, it is unrealistic to expect change to be straightforward: every change one makes in one's life has gains and losses attached to it. It is only when the individual perceives that the benefits of change outweigh the losses that change is likely to take place. Senge *et al.* (1994) have noted that in the main people do not resist change, but they resist being changed. If workers, therefore, make arguments for or persuade parents to change without parents understanding why change is necessary or desirable they may become resistant to change (Forrester *et al.*, 2012). Alternatively, parents may be afraid that if they do not accept what professionals say then they will be perceived as uncooperative and may potentially lose their children, which can lead to feigning compliance with plans (Harris, 2012). Second, changing the entrenched behaviours associated with chronic neglect takes time. Therefore, professionals should not withdraw or reduce their involvement and support before the changes have bedded down. Third, lapse and relapse are a recognized part of the change process; some parents may have a number of attempts at changing behaviours before finally being successful. For example, Davies and Ward (2012), commenting on the *Significant Harm of Infants Study*, noted that some parents were eventually able to change their lifestyle sufficiently to provide an environment that met the needs of their child after having had a number of children removed from them. Moreover, lapse is common in cases of chronic neglect as the behaviours that need to change are often so entrenched that they are hard to change; without support these lapses can become relapses.

Miller and Rollnick (2002) have contributed to our knowledge and understanding of the change process by recognizing that what is crucial to engagement in the change process is that the individual, in this case the parent, is motivated to change. They developed the concept of Motivational Interviewing, which is based on the notion that resistance to change is normal and needs to be addressed. The role of the worker, therefore, is to explore and support the service user considering change, and begin to resolve the parent's feelings of ambivalence about changing current problematic behaviours. Motivational Interviewing requires workers to listen empathetically to the parents, and understand their point of view and their reasons for resistance in order to assist the parent in resolving any resistance or ambivalence to change.

Whilst the Prochaska and DiClementi model is a useful way of thinking about change, there are a number of factors that practitioners should take into account (Girvin, 2004). Rates of change vary. Thus, parents may find some changes to their parenting and lifestyle easier to make than others. This means the parent may be at one stage of the change process with regard to one particular behaviour, and at another stage in relation to a different behaviour. Alternatively, they may change some behaviours but not others, or they may be so overwhelmed by the number of changes they are expected to make that they are paralysed into inactivity. In addition, change may be hindered because of factors beyond the control of the parent. For example, the parent, whilst motivated to change, may not have the resources or support necessary to make and maintain the changes. Finally, parents may appear to engage in the change process but the quality of life for the child does not improve because their commitment to change is not to meet the needs of the child; rather, it is to ensure child protection professionals leave the family alone.

Assessing the needs of neglected children: establishing parental willingness to change

Davis and Day (2007) argue that everyone constructs the world differently: in cases of child neglect the construction of the neglect and the part played by the parents in changing behaviours and addressing any professional concerns will be significantly influenced by the interactions between professionals and the family. These constructions are not necessarily conscious or verbalized but may become apparent through engagement or lack of engagement with the child protection process and the plan. Therefore, if workers are to be effective in terms of ensuring parents understand professional concerns and the rationale for interventions, they need to take the following principles into account:

- Everyone takes in and processes information for meaning:
  'They say I am not disciplining Mylah properly. I am not sure I know what I'm doing wrong but they say she is having problems at school 'cos she swears at the other children like I swear at her.'
- Everyone constructs a model of the world, which helps them anticipate and adapt to the world:
  'I really don't think I'm doing wrong but if I don't change then I might lose her.'
- Constructions develop from previous experience and are unique to the individual:
  'I'm confused. My mum treated me like that and I see my friends doing the same.'

- Constructions are subject to a constant process of testing, clarification and change:
  'I saw a programme on TV last night and they showed a child of Mylah's age being naughty and how to deal with it.'
- Social perceptions, interactions and feelings are influenced by the constructions of others:
  'I've discussed the programme with my social worker and she gave me some ideas as to how to discipline Mylah next time she is naughty. I'll give it a go.'

Drawing on these principles, in order to engage the parents meaningfully in the process of change it is important to 'read the family's way of interpreting the situation' (Hoskins and White, 2010, p. 41). This can be accomplished during the assessment by listening to family members, attempting to understand their perspectives and highlighting congruence between their views and those of the professionals (Platt, 2007). In most cases, congruence can be achieved by agreeing that both parents and professionals want what is in the child's best interests. There are, however, a number of assessment practices that prevent practitioners both 'reading the family's way' and assisting parents in recognizing the need to change. These are considered below.

Failing to look beyond the presenting problem

When practitioners are overwhelmed by the complexity of a case they can ignore the more difficult issues and focus on assessing the presenting problem, often proposing a practical solution (Cleaver *et al.*, 2004). By focusing purely on the presenting problem, it is all too easy for practitioners to identify quick-fix solutions. In these situations more deep-seated and difficult issues may be ignored. The consequence can be that professionals fail to take into account the behaviours that need to change if the quality of life for the neglected child is to improve significantly. Moreover, parents can remain at the pre-contemplation stage: they do not need to change their behaviours or lifestyle as the problem lies elsewhere. For example, in the Anytown study, concerns about lack of supervision of a two-year-old within the home resulted in the provision of a stair gate with no additional services provided. The child was re-referred to children's social services within months. In this case, workers had failed to look beyond the presenting problem to consider the reason why lack of supervision was occurring and whether it was possibly symptomatic of other parenting issues, which is what Zielewski *et al.* (2006) found in their American study of poor parental supervision of children.

For many neglectful families the complexity of their daily lives means that they lurch from crisis to crisis: a bill needs paying; benefits have not come through; a child has been excluded from school; a partner has been arrested. It is all too easy, when assessing the needs of children in these families, for practitioners to find themselves drawn into addressing these immediate concerns. This focus on immediate crises is referred to as the 'misdirected gaze' (Akister, 2009, p. 12) as the crisis or presenting problem deflect the attention of professionals from the more concerning problems.

Ignoring past engagement with the child protection system

Families where chronic neglect is an issue are likely to have had experience of a diverse range of assessments and services over years of involvement with child welfare agencies. Much can be learnt, therefore, from family case files and chronologies about the parents' past engagement with services and their ability and motivation to change their behaviours. Findings from the Anytown study, however, indicate that the focus of many assessments appears to be the parents' current verbal commitment to change and their demonstration of this commitment during the assessment, rather than a comprehensive analysis of past engagement. For example, there were concerns raised in one assessment, included in the case review, about the lack of appropriate adult supervision of the children in the evenings. The assessment analysis indicated that the social worker had made clear to the parents that the children should not be left with 'inappropriate' babysitters. The practitioner believed that the parent understood that better quality supervision was required and had agreed the children would be adequately supervised in the future. The case was closed without the practitioner taking into account that there was a past history of lack of supervision and professionals attempting to address the concerns. This scenario raises questions, however, as to whether a verbal commitment to change is sufficient demonstration of motivation and commitment to sustained changes of behaviour that seem to be well established.

Whilst ignoring past involvement with agencies can be an issue, paying too much attention to this history can also act as a barrier to change. Families where chronic neglect occurs are likely to become labelled: Thoburn *et al.* (2009, p. 13), for example, refer to groups of families with complex needs, including those that are difficult to engage and 'hard to change'. The individual families and their labels are likely to be known to practitioners and their agencies. The parents in these families, in turn, are likely to be very familiar with the way in which child welfare agencies function and practitioners operate. This can lead to the 'I know what you are like' effect. When this occurs, the practitioner may prejudge the parents and the outcome of the assessment negatively, based on what they know about the family history from the file or their own experiences of working with the family. The message to the parents when this happens is, 'You have not changed before. Why should it be different this time?' This approach does not take into account that attitudes towards change alter over time, and on this occasion the parent may be sufficiently motivated and ready to change (Miller and Rollnick, 2002). The 'I know what you are like' effect can also work the other way, with parents knowing what practitioners expect of them and consequently providing the answers to the assessment questions that they believe practitioners want to hear. This is one of the downsides of a standardized assessment format for children in need: parents who have experience of assessments will know the questions they are likely to be asked and the answers practitioners want to hear to allay their concerns. The parents' motivation in providing particular answers to questions may be to prevent further interference by practitioners in their lives rather than a genuine commitment to meet the needs of the child.

Failing to consider past family history

It is not only past involvement with agencies that will influence parents' approach to change. Parents' own past history, their experiences of being parented and of being a parent in their own right will also have a considerable impact, not only on their parenting capacity but also on their motivation and ability to change. In the Anytown study practitioners recognized, for example, 'mother has experienced abuse and neglect as a child', 'father spent time in care', 'mother has a history of depression'. There was, however, very little detail included in the assessment reports about the impact of these experiences on current functioning. Yet these past experiences, as discussed in Chapter 2, can affect the way in which the parent approaches the parenting of each child in the family, their feelings towards the child, and their motivation and ability to change the way they interact with the child (Howe, 2005).

Failure to consider past history can be a particular issue when working with families from ethnic-minority groups, particular first-generation immigrants. Maiter and Stalker (2011), in a Canadian study of South Asian immigrants involved with child protection services, highlighted some important points which reinforce the findings of other studies, such as that completed by Chand and Thoburn in the UK (2005). The participants in the study indicated that workers had not taken into account reasons why families had immigrated and the changes of status that resulted from immigration and how these impacted on parenting. For example, in their home countries many of the immigrants had been professionals who employed staff to undertake household tasks; parents felt inadequate and frustrated that now they could not find appropriate employment. Moreover, many of these parents described losing their support network as a result of immigration. Some of the participants also described workers failing to explore, and therefore not understanding, different approaches to parenting and the cultural values that underpinned some of their child-rearing practices.

Superficial information sharing

It is routine practice for the social worker leading the assessment and other professionals to discuss their assessment reports with the parents and children prior to the child protection conference. However, as is evident in this quote from a parent who had experience of the child protection system, sharing report content is not always undertaken in a meaningful manner:

> We have been to lots of case conferences, but we always got the report when we arrived. We were already nervous, and then we had this report to read. It was so much better when we got the report the week before the meeting. We could take it all in, understand what they were worried about. We didn't necessarily agree with it, but at least we were prepared. (Office of the Children's Commissioner, 2010, p. 42)

There are a number of reasons why meaningful sharing of information may not always occur. First, the reports are often complex and confusing and are written using professional terminology and abbreviations, which may mean little to family members. This confusion can be exacerbated if the parents have literacy problems or English is not their first language. Second, stress and anxiety about report content may mean that parents struggle taking in information, as highlighted in the quote above. Third, the findings from the Sykes (2011) study indicate that parents may find it hard to acknowledge that there are aspects of their parenting that professionals consider are not good enough. This is likely to be exacerbated if the concerns are general, such as 'the parent does not provide sufficient boundaries and guidance' with little detail as to ways in which the parent is failing to provide these boundaries and guidance. Fourth, insufficient time and attention is given to discussing the assessment report and analysis by practitioners. Hard-pressed practitioners who find they do not have the time to discuss and explain the content of the report at the parents' pace may draw parents' attention to what the professionals themselves consider important. When reports and assessments are not shared properly, parents are likely to feel that change is being foisted upon them and, as discussed earlier in this chapter, may resist the proposed changes. Moreover, under these circumstances, it is all too easy for parents to dismiss concerns and for professionals to be left with the impression that the parents do not accept there is a problem.

Going through an assessment report in a manner that is meaningful to parents can provide the parent with an opportunity to begin to understand exactly why practitioners are concerned about their behaviour and what needs to change. This is most likely to take place if the reports are written in plain English, with specific examples of concerns and strengths in relation to the various dimensions of parenting capacity and the developmental needs of the child.

Ignoring the voice of the young person

Cossar *et al.* (2011) interviewed 26 children who had experience of the child protection system. The children reported that what concerned them was not necessarily the same as either what had brought them to the attention of the professionals or what concerned the professionals. If parents are to meet the needs of their children it is important that they, together with professionals, have an understanding of the child or young person's perceptions of the issues and what the children would like to change. This requires practitioners to listen carefully to young people. In the Anytown study there were notes on the files indicating that workers had asked the children about their wishes and feelings as part of the assessment. These were recorded as generalized comments such as: 'Sheldon would like mother to stop drinking'; 'Jordan wants dad to stop hitting mum'. There was, however, very little evidence of information being gathered from children about their daily lived experiences within the family. For example, what is life like on a daily basis for Sheldon living with a mother who is misusing alcohol? The brief account of Dylan's life, at the beginning of Chapter 3, highlights the miserable existence this child experiences day in day out, and what needs to change, in a way that 'I want mummy to sleep less', for example, does not.

Conclusion

Assessment is the foundation from which plans and interventions are constructed. If an assessment is to inform effective planning to meet the needs of the child then it is important that practitioners consider parents' attitude towards the professionals' concerns and their willingness to engage meaningfully in a process to address these concerns. The following list of questions is designed to assist practitioners not only to assess parental readiness to contemplate change but also to ensure they are providing them with the support necessary to engage meaningfully in the change process.

- How have I expressed my concerns about the neglect? Have I identified strengths as well as issues?

- Have I provided sufficient information to the parent/s so that they can understand why I am concerned? For example, do they realize why continual failure to clear up animal faeces in the house can result in serious physical damage to their child?
- Do I have a comprehensive understanding of the lived experience of each child in the family and what they would like to see change in their daily lives?
- To what extent have I considered past family history, patterns of behaviour, and so on, and the way they may influence the parents' response to the concerns?
- Have I shared the findings of my assessment in a manner and at a pace that is appropriate for this parent? Have I taken into account their anxieties and ability to absorb the content of my assessment or report?
- What is the parent's or parents' attitude towards current and ongoing concerns? Do they accept the need to change?
- If they are challenging or showing resistance, have I explored with them the reasons for this?
- Have I provided them with opportunities to share their feelings and experiences of previous engagement with child protection and other services and discussed how this is influencing their current attitude towards change?

Chapter 5

Identifying a Pathway for Change: The Child Protection Conference

Introduction

In Chapter 4, I considered ways in which the assessment process can facilitate or inhibit parental acceptance of the changes they may be required to make in order to meet the needs of their child. Readiness for change, however, as Prochaska and DiClementi (1982) argue, is only the first step in the change process. Once parents have recognized the need to change they have to work out how to make the necessary changes. In the novel *A Cupboard Full of Coats*, the main character reflects on her ambivalent relationship with her young son and, whilst accepting the need to change, concludes:

> I did not know how to change it. It felt like something needed to happen inside me. But I was not a magician. There was no quick-fix abracadabra available to change me into anybody else. (Edwards, 2011, p.35)

Unfortunately, all too frequently professionals within child welfare agencies are expected to act as magicians and work with parents to identify and implement a 'quick-fix abracadabra' solution that changes the way in which a parent feels and behaves towards their child. Yet practitioners cannot wave a magic wand to bring about change: there are rarely quick-fix solutions in cases of neglect but all too often systems are set up for these types of responses (Munro, 2011a, 2011b; Platt, 2012).

In the UK, decisions about parental changes necessary to protect a child at risk of harm are usually made at a child protection conference. At this meeting professionals and family members, including the child if they are considered of sufficient age and ability, discuss concerns and identify the best way professionals can work with the family to address these concerns (Stafford *et al.*, 2011). In this chapter I consider how decisions are made and plans formulated in these forums, and question whether the child protection conference promotes or hinders parental engagement in the change process.

Whilst the focus in this chapter is on the child protection conference, the points made are applicable to any meetings that involve professionals and family members making decisions about neglect, such as case planning meetings designed to promote the health and development of a child and address emerging concerns.

Family participation

Parents in the UK are routinely invited to attend child protection conferences, alongside children if they are considered of a sufficient age and understanding. The chair has a critical role in facilitating the involvement of both the family and professionals. This means they need to recognize the emotions that members of the conference may be experiencing and take account of their potential impact on proceedings. For the parents the atmosphere at the conference is emotionally charged and they are likely to experience a range of feelings including anger, hostility, distress and resistance. Professionals too may be nervous and anxious and, as a consequence, may revert to using professional jargon and abbreviations. Stressed parents are likely to find this frustrating and bewildering. This, in turn, can lead to withdrawal, aggression, or resistance on their part to recognition of the issues and engagement in any plans. Alternatively, professionals can become so concerned with engaging parents that the focus of the conference can shift from the needs of the child to the needs of the parents (Bell, 2007a). This can be a particular issue in cases of chronic neglect, as the parents are likely to be needy with numerous problems in their own right. This was evident in the Anytown neglect study (see Box 0.1 and Appendix), a social worker participant commenting that professionals can be 'so busy trying to work with the parent and get the changes in the parents, sometimes they don't always filter through to oh, okay, what, you know, what it's like for the child, what's the impact on the child?' (social worker 4).

If the conference is to serve a purpose in identifying ways in which parents should change in order to protect the child from harm, then both task and process must be meaningful to family members, particularly parents. Thus, by the end of the meeting the parents should:

- recognize and understand professionals' concerns
- understand what changes are required of them and why
- appreciate the rationale informing the content of the plan
- be aware of the particular actions included in the plan
- know what specific actions are required of them and why
- be aware of the way in which professionals will support them make the necessary changes
- understand what they need to achieve in relation to improved outcomes for their child or children in order for the plan to be discontinued
- understand what will happen to their children and their family if they do not make the necessary changes.

Child participation

One of the participants in the Anytown study who chairs conferences said: 'There is nothing more powerful than a child coming to Conference...they may just come for ten minutes, but there's nothing more poignant than a child coming in, agencies actually being able to see that child and listen to that child's voice' (chair 5).

Whilst parents routinely attend conferences, attendance by children, even older children, is variable. Yet if plans are to meet the needs of children, it is important they have a voice. Cossar *et al.* (2011), in their study of young people and children involved with the child protection system, judged that 78 per cent of the children under 12 and 25 per cent of those over 12 did not understand the purpose of the conference. The researchers concluded that workers often struggle making decisions – both as to how much information to share with children regarding the child protection process and conferences, and whether the young person should attend the conference.

When children are not actively given a voice at the conference, as with the assessment, members of the conference are dependent on indirect information from family members and the professionals (Prince *et al.*, 2005; Cossar *et al.*, 2011). Helm (2011) argues that this means professional analysis is based on partial and, in some cases, flawed evidence. In these circumstances it is also easier to minimize the uniqueness of each child in a family or fail to piece together a day in their life (Cm 5730, 2003). This was evident in some of the reports submitted to conference in the Anytown study, where the same information was provided for each child in the family even though their circumstances, ages and abilities meant they had different needs. The respondents in the Anytown study also recognized there were other ways of ensuring that the child has a voice at the conference even if they are not present, such as through the use of child advocates. The chair can also play a part in focusing attention on the child. As one chair who participated in the study put it: 'I do use phrases such as, you know, can we think what it would be like, you know, for Johnny experiencing this?' (chair 2).

Towards a plan: sharing information, analysing and making decisions

By the end of the conference professionals should have constructed an outline plan that indicates the actions that will be taken by the family members and the professionals to safeguard the child from harm and meet their needs. These decisions will be informed by the parents' recognition of professional concerns, their willingness to accept these concerns and their commitment to engage in a series of actions to safeguard the child and promote their welfare. In terms of the model of change discussed in Chapter 4, this means that by the end of the conference the parent will be expected to demonstrate that they have moved through the first three stages of the change process: from pre-contemplation through contemplation to not only determining how to change but also being ready to take action after the conference. Yet, in the UK, parents have very little time to make these transitions. The conference, if it takes place in Northern Ireland or Wales, is expected to occur within 15 working days from the decision to commence the assessment of significant harm, and in Scotland no later than 21 days from notification of concerns (DHSSPS, 2003; Welsh Assembly Government, 2006; HM Government, 2010; Scottish Government, 2010). In England, at the time of writing, it is proposed that 'the timing of the conference must meet the needs of the child and the nature and severity of the harm' (DfE, 2012, p. 20) Thus, most practitioners at the conference may be working with parents who are still only in the early stages of contemplating change whilst at the same time being expected to take actions to safeguard their children. Moreover, some of these actions may require significant life changes on their part, such as leaving a partner who is abusive towards the child. If the parent has not had sufficient opportunity to consider the implications of these decisions and determined for themselves that the gains of the change outweigh the losses, then meaningful change that benefits the child is unlikely to occur. Yet practitioners cannot wait limitlessly for parents to accept the need to change, as change must take place at a pace that ensures the child is safe and their health and wellbeing are promoted. Thus, a balance has to be achieved between setting parents up to fail by expecting too much too quickly and allowing parents too much time to engage with the change process, which may result in case drift, discussed further in Chapter 6.

Sharing and analysing information

In order to make judgements about risk of harm and decisions about future actions, conference members share and analyse information (Holland, 2011). The participants in the Anytown study indicated that this takes up two-thirds, or approximately 50–80 minutes, of conference time. Time spent sharing information, however, was viewed as important and inevitable in cases of chronic neglect.

Although practitioners are generally able to gather relevant information, they find making sense of this often complex information challenging (Barlow *et al.*, 2012). This was evident in the Anytown study, with most respondents noting that professionals are 'very good at information sharing and saying this is what's happened, given sort of factual information, but they don't tend to get so much involved in like say the analysis and, and thinking about change' (social worker 6).

In cases of chronic neglect there are a number of issues that make the analysis process in cases of neglect particularly challenging. First, the amount of information that professionals have to share on various members of the family can be overwhelming. Munro (1999) argues that one way in which this is managed is to focus on the verbal information presented. When this occurs, it is likely that the factors that are of most concern, or are considered most significant by the different professionals, are emphasized. As a consequence, the more positive or routine, yet often significant, information is marginalized. When this occurs it is all too easy to understand how the parent believes they are being labelled the 'bad' parent, as described in Chapter 4. Second, in cases of neglect it can be difficult being really specific about the concerns. As Burgess *et al.* (2012, p. 15) put it, neglect 'is a collection of phenomena which are unpredictable'. On some days the needs of the child might be met; on others this will not be the case. This unpredictable care can lead to lengthy discussions at the conference as to whether the threshold for significant harm has been reached. Third, Bell (1996) found practitioners can struggle when considering what allowances should be made with regard to the impact of poverty and material deprivation on family life. It is not surprising that parents witnessing these discussions may become confused as to the actual concerns. This, in turn, can result in institutional resistance: 'If the professionals themselves cannot agree on the concerns and a reasonable standard of care, why should I take this seriously?' Finally, the chair plays a crucial role in influencing the way in which the conference analyses information. Bell (2007a) warns that an over-directive chair can lead to decisions being made that do not reflect the views of the professionals and therefore can affect their engagement with the plan. Moreover, when this occurs, parents may fail to understand professionals' concerns or feel they are being told what to do and therefore resist these changes. On the other hand, a chair who takes a laissez-faire approach can leave both professionals and family members confused as to the nature of the concerns. The chair, therefore, needs to facilitate discussion that is sufficient to make meaningful, child-centred decisions.

Sharing and analysing information concerning sibling groups

It's the mass of information but it's the fact that there is [sic] so many children as well... you're having to do things so swiftly really, are you fully robustly looking at everything? And then when you put on the parenting capacity issues on top of that, it becomes, it becomes quite massive to get your head round. (Chair 1)

The participants in the interviews and focus groups in the Anytown study were divided about their ability to identify the needs of individual children in a sibling group. Some respondents expressed concerns that there were difficulties identifying the separate needs of a large number of siblings in the two-hour time slot usually allocated for conferences. Conferences involving large sibling groups were reported to go on far longer in order to ensure that the needs of each child were considered: 'I mean the initial conference went on for, especially five kids, went on from, for the best part of five hours' (social worker 1). When this occurs, not surprisingly, the chairs found it a challenge keeping both professionals and families engaged and focused, particularly if the practitioners are not involved with all of the children. Others raised concerns about the size of the conference for large sibling groups: 'I've worked with a family of nine who are all on the Register ... there was, pretty much seven, different education establishments for the nine' (social worker 11). One chair acknowledged:

> well inevitably really you have one or two children in a family who have more needs than the others. So invariably, you know, you tend to waffle on about those children and you know, then you're trying to scoop up the other children and I think it's really difficult. (Chair 3).

This situation can be exacerbated if families choose to focus on one particular child for their own reasons and obscure information concerning a different child. Or it may be that the worker is intimidated and therefore does not elicit information regarding individual children:

> If they're quite uncooperative or hostile, you get social workers who are intimidated by that, who will then merge each child as one, and I think that can sometimes, that's more difficult. And equally parents who may prefer one to another, that can, you know, that can also affect it. (Chair 6).

From analysis to planning

Drawing on the analysis of the information shared at the conference, members of the conference must decide whether the child is at risk of significant harm and what interventions are required to protect the child. This is a difficult task. Dorsey *et al.* (2008, p. 378), for example, in a study of decision making regarding risk of harm by caseworkers in 2,139 cases in the USA, found that workers' identification and assessment of children most at risk was low, with their assessment being 'only slightly better than guessing'. Barlow *et al.* (2012) conclude, having completed a systematic review of models for analysing significant harm, that structured professional judgement making is a promising method for assessing risk. This involves drawing on structured guidelines to identify family strengths and weaknesses and children's needs, and to assist in the classification of risk of harm. These guidelines and tools do, however, have their limitations; many do not allow for particular features of individual cases and exclude factors that have insufficient research evidence to support inclusion (Barlow *et al.*, 2012). Thus, practitioners need to consider the relevance of the findings for each case and make judgements bearing in mind the unique features of each child and family.

Barlow *et al.* (2012) have identified two frameworks developed in England that show promise in providing structured guidelines, although the current data on their effectiveness is limited. These are: the *Safeguarding Assessment and Analysis Framework* (Bentovim *et al.*, 2009, pp. 228, 229) and the *Graded Care Profile* (Srivastava *et al.*, 2003). What is particularly useful about these two tools and the others summarized below is that they facilitate the analysis of information in such a way as to focus on both family strengths and weaknesses. This goes some way towards helping parents appreciate that their parenting is not all 'bad' whilst identifying what needs to change. Moreover, most use diagrams or other visual methods, which can be far more effective in retaining and making sense of information than just listening to what is being said.

Safeguarding Assessment and Analysis Framework (SAAF)

Information obtained from the assessment is collated to develop two cycles. One focuses on positive parenting, the other on harmful parenting, as shown in Figures 5.1 and 5.2. Each cycle consists of three circles: the inner circle focuses on family and environmental factors, the middle one on the various dimensions of parenting capacity and the outer one on the impact on the child's development. This enables practitioners to map links between the provision of positive and harmful parenting to each dimension of the child's developmental needs. By undertaking the analysis in this way, it becomes possible to develop a profile of harm. This profile can be used to begin to identify the parental level of difficulty in meeting the needs of the child in relation to each aspect of parenting, the parent's recognition of the difficulty and their willingness to work with professionals to address these problems. Drawing on the findings from this profile of harm, practitioners can begin to develop plans to meet the needs of the child. Depending on the level of concern and the parents' willingness to engage with professionals, this may mean working with parents as part of a child protection plan or removing the child from the home (Bentovim, 2010).

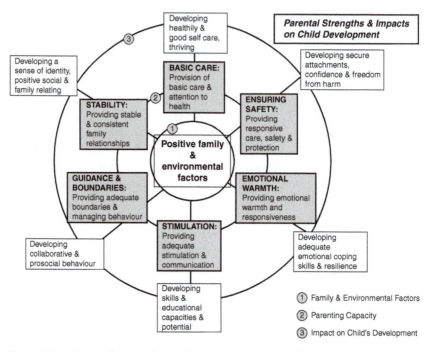

Figure 5.1:   Parental strengths and impacts on child development
Source: Bentovim *et al.* (2009)

Grade Care Profile (GCP)

The *Graded Care Profile* (GCP) scale (Srivastava *et al.*, 2003; Srivastava *et al.*, 2005) has been specifically designed to assess child neglect. It seeks to provide an objective tool for 'grading' the care of a child by their carer. As part of that process the tool enables practitioners and the family to identify strengths and difficulties and the effort made by the carer to meet the needs of the child. The GCP focuses on four 'areas' of care – physical care, safety, love and esteem – which are assessed against predetermined criteria. These areas are broken down into 'sub-areas' and specific 'items'. For example, under 'love' a sub-area is the carer's approach, which is broken down further into different components or 'items'. One of these is the 'sensitivity' of the carer to the child. To complete the assessment the practitioner grades each item on a five-point scale. For example, 'sensitivity' is graded from 'anticipates or picks up very subtle signals – verbal or non-verbal expression or mood' through to 'insensitive to even sustained intense signals or aversive' (Srivastava *et al.*, 2005). Each point on the scale has a description, enabling the practitioner to rate what they have observed and for parents to self-score. The scores are then recorded for all the items and areas

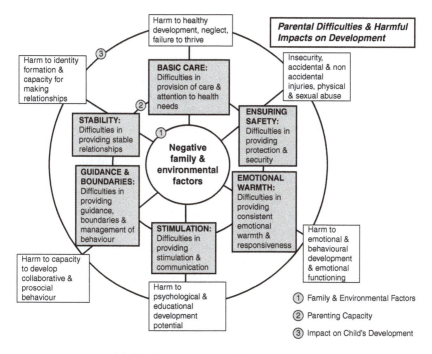

Figure 5.2:   Parental difficulties and harmful impacts on development

Source: Bentovim *et al.* (2009)

of strength and difficulties identified. Scoring care in this way provides a baseline against which practitioners and parents can make judgements about the quality of care the child is receiving, what needs to change, services designed to support these changes and how progress will be tracked through changes to scores. Any variation in scores between practitioners and family members can be discussed to identify differences in perception and to assist the conference in reaching a shared understanding as to what needs to change.

Whilst Barlow *et al.* (2012) considered the GCP to show promise in assisting practitioners analyse risk of significant harm, there has been no rigorous study to date. A small-scale study by Carter (2012) found that practitioners indicated that using the GCP added greater criticality to their observations, highlighted parental strengths as well as concerns, brought more clarity to vague concerns, and promoted positive engagement with families. Parents in turn indicated that the GCP gave them a greater understanding of professional concerns. However, as in the study by Sen *et al.* (2012), Carter found that training in the use of the GCP was essential for its effective use.

Capturing the daily lived experience of the parent and child or children

This tool, developed by the author, is currently being piloted by a number of local authorities in England. Underpinning the tool is a belief that decisions about safeguarding children who are neglected should be based on an understanding of the daily lived experience of the child (Cm 5730, 2003). In order to ensure that is the case, drawing information together in relation to the daily lives of children and families is a useful method for making decisions. As information is shared by various members of the conference, it can be interpreted and collated to provide members of the conference with insights into 24 hours in the life of each child and parent. Take the case of Leah. The head teacher notes in her report that 'Leah routinely arrives at school hungry'. In order to make sense of why this is occurring and the impact this has on Leah, members of the conference and family members consider this statement in the context of what is happening to the child on a routine basis. For example, what happens to the child, in terms of feeding regimes, when she returns home from school, during the evening, before she goes to bed, and in the morning before school? How is hunger affecting the way in which Leah behaves at school and at home, her attitude towards food, her ability to engage in physical activities and so on? This information can be used to identify what the daily lived experience of the child or children in the family is like and how aspects of their lives can be improved.

It is particularly useful to consider the information about the child's daily life alongside that of the parent's. Collating information in this way can provide insights into strengths and weaknesses in relation to parenting capacity. In Leah's case, the collated information highlighted that her lone parent mother suffers depression and is unable to get herself out of bed in order to prepare breakfast for the child. In the evenings she is exhausted and finds her medication (which she takes in the evening) makes her tired and lethargic, so she does not have the energy to prepare food for her child. This information can then be used to consider what interventions can address the specific issues. In this case, a change in terms of the mother's medication and the time when it was taken had a significant and positive effect on the child's situation.

A clock drawn on a whiteboard, which is filled in as information is shared at the conference, is a visual way of collating what is known about the daily lives of the child and other family members. Making sense of information about the family's daily lived experience is user friendly and can be meaningful to both parents and children, most specifically enabling parents to identify changes necessary to improve the lived experiences of their children. What should be taken into account, however, is that these families are likely to have good and bad days (Burgess *et al.*, 2012). Therefore, differences between the two types of days need to be explored.

Practitioners have also found that obtaining information from children about their daily lives is easier than asking vague questions about their wishes and feelings, as this participant in the Anytown study notes:

> I've done a task where, you know, I've gathered lots of, everyday photographs, well pictures then...uniform, going to school, having baths, watching telly, eating meals, it's all of those things and the child will tell me from all the different pictures he picks of what his day starts with, you know, wake up to an alarm clock or Mum wakes me up or whatever, you know, and they take you through their day, and that's really good because you can tell how often they're watching telly, how often they're eating sweets, whether they're having the meal. I've had children tell me, no we don't have cooked meals in our house, we don't have cooked meals on a Sunday at Nana's house. That's significant in telling me what life is like for them. (Social worker 4)

Resilience matrix

This is represented as a two-dimensional diagram, which can be used to map the child's experiences, focusing particularly on child and family strengths and the pressures the child is encountering. The aim is to provide a visual matrix of risk and protective factors as shown in Figure 5.3 (Daniel, Wassell and Gilligan, 2010). Four factors are mapped out with information that is shared at the conference:

- *Resilience*: the characteristics that enhance normal development.
- *Vulnerability*: the characteristics of the child, family and community network which might threaten or challenge healthy development.
- *Protective factors*: aspects of the child's environment which act as a buffer to the negative effects of adverse experiences.
- *Adversity*: life events or circumstances that pose a threat to healthy development. (Aldgate and Rose, 2008)

Signs of Safety

This model draws on a solution-focused approach, seeking to build safety rather than eliminate danger and risk alone. It has been developed by Turnell (2012) and is used in a range of jurisdictions, most notably Australia and the UK. The approach requires workers to find strategies for engaging and working effectively with families, using critical enquiry to gather infor-

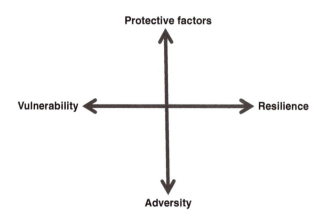

Figure 5.3:   The resilience matrix

Source: Daniel *et al.* (2010)

mation and obtain evidence, thereby reducing the potential for bias. The information is then 'mapped' and analysed under the following headings:

- *Danger/harm*: this includes past harm, current and future concerns, complicating factors.
- *Safety*: the focus is on existing strengths that have been demonstrated as protective of the child over time.
- *Agency goals*: the professionals' required outcome.
- *Family goals*: the family's desired outcome.
- *Immediate progress*: what are the indicators that some small but positive changes have been made?

Finally, using this information, collaborative planning between family and professionals is completed in order to address dangers and risks through protective care. Decision making and planning are undertaken using a one-page assessment and planning protocol that maps harm, danger, complicating factors, strengths, existing and required safety, and a safety judgement when children are considered at risk of harm. This judgement involves practitioners producing a quantitative assessment of risk using two scales – safety and context – each being rated on a ten-point scale with certain reoccurrence graded as 0 through to sufficient safety to close the case graded as 10. Tools have also been developed to promote the engagement of children and young people in the process.

Gardner (2008) believes that the Signs of Safety model can be particularly useful in cases of child neglect because of the focus on safety rather than risk. Moreover, it encourages professionals to be clear about their concerns and provide supporting evidence in such a way that parents can appreciate these concerns. The use of a scale enables parents to appreciate the degree to which professionals consider current issues are a danger to the child.

Whilst these tools have been considered in the context of analysing information at the conference, they were originally developed to assist individual practitioners make sense of information they had gathered about a child and their family. Therefore, they can also be used in this way.

Outline plans: determining a pathway for change

If the plan is to assist parents in determining a pathway for change then they need to understand the rationale behind the plan, appreciate what is expected of them and why, and feel confident that they can engage with the plan as required by professionals. This is a time-consuming task and is not easily achieved. Some of the challenges encountered by the practitioners and family members in constructing a plan that determines a pathway for change are considered below.

What is an outline plan?

One of the most significant challenges for conference participants is determining how to keep the child safe and what should be achieved through the implementation of the plan. A common understanding as to the purpose of the plan may be presumed but may not actually exist. For example, participants in the Anytown study held very different views regarding the aim of the plan. Some professionals, for example, were clear that they were looking only at reducing risk of harm, whereas others appeared to have a more all-encompassing approach, including improving the developmental outcomes of the child. This lack of clarity can create confusion amongst both practitioners and family members in terms of identifying the outcomes to be achieved in order for the plan to be terminated.

Members of the conference may also have different ideas regarding the detail that should be included in the outline plan, as opposed to the more comprehensive plan developed later by the core group of professionals and family members who implement the plan. Some participants in the Anytown study felt that they needed very clear aims, objectives, actions and agreed timescales, whereas others wanted more flexibility so that there was greater ownership and discussion at the core group: 'I like a very simple kind of [plan], a few points that we need to work with and then we draw out other things as we go along and, and amend and stuff as we go along' (social worker 2). If plans are very vague, however, parents will leave the conference unsure about what is expected of them.

It is all too easy at the end of a lengthy conference to just summarize plan content with brief statements such as these from the Anytown study:

'Father not to consume alcohol in family home. If father presents as intoxicated, mother to take appropriate action.'
   'Regular visits from social worker with children's bedrooms to be seen on three occasions.'
   'Attend family centre to address concerns of conference and thus reduce risks.'
   'For Charlie to be supported to reach his full potential.'
   'For Mia to be a happy child with good emotional behaviour.'

For many professionals this is a form of shorthand and whilst they may have some understanding of the logic underpinning these actions, for family members the connections are not so easily made. For example, the language used in these examples is open to interpretation: what is meant by 'appropriate action' or 'support'? In some cases, the link between aim, outcome and action is vague, as is evident from this Anytown study example: 'Aim: children's health needs to be met. Planned outcome: children to have good health. Action: mother to keep appointments.' In this example it is not clear exactly what the health needs are, what 'good health' would look like, how it will be measured and how the mother merely keeping appointments leads to better health. Surely there are other factors that should be taken into account, such as ensuring children follow recommended medical interventions.

The outline plan should, therefore, contain sufficient detail to enable the family members to understand the concerns in terms of the impact of their behaviour on the child; know what needs to change; appreciate how the interventions will support the changes; and be aware of the consequences of not adhering to the plan. If the plan does not appear relevant at this stage then the parent may fail to make the transition from contemplating and determining how to change to engaging in actions to facilitate change.

Time allocated for planning at conference

The findings from the Anytown study indicated that the time actually spent constructing the outline plan at a conference may vary between 5 and 25 minutes. The time and focus on the plan appeared to be influenced significantly by the chair rather than the needs of the child or children, or the parents. Three different approaches were taken. First, plans that are constructed: 'by the chair more than anything I would say, at the end and that's usually, ooh I don't know, about probably fifteen minutes, fifteen minutes, something like that' (social worker 5). Second, planning as a group activity so that: 'when you leave a conference, you leave with the responsibility of a plan and that you own that plan along with every other agency' (chair 5). Third, some chairs devised the plan after the conference, drawing on the analysis and recommendations of conference members. One chair explained why they took this approach: 'I really think everybody's had enough by the end and I can't marshal my thoughts quick enough' (chair 4). This chair makes a point, which raises questions as to how effective meaningful planning can be in the conference arena when so much time is spent sharing information and making decisions as to whether the child is at risk of significant harm and requires a plan.

Agreeing on the content of the plan

Munro (1999) and Farmer and Owen (1995) argue that there is often a drive at a conference to reach consensus as to whether the child has suffered or is likely to suffer significant harm and on the content of the multi-disciplinary child protection plan. When this occurs, the professionals with most status and professional influence can dominate decision making, with other members deferring to their judgement. Reder and Duncan (1999) refer to this as exaggeration of hierarchy. The key role the social worker plays in informing the need and content of the plan was evident in the Anytown study, with other professionals deferring to the social worker's views. This finding is commensurate with that of other studies. This issue was evident in the study conducted by Prince *et al.* (2005), with conference chairs indicating that they had difficulty in obtaining the views of all group members present as some dominated discussions. What is of note is that it is often the practitioners with the least status – the learning support assistant, the family support worker – who are most likely to know the child and family best and who make the least contribution to planning.

A further issue for members of the conference, in terms of plan content, is recognizing what is required to safeguard the child whilst at the same time being aware that the parent must engage with the plan in order to make the necessary changes. Their views may be very different from those of the professionals as to the best way in which to meet the needs of the child (Akister, 2009). In some situations the gap between what the parents feel able to do and what is required of them to keep the child safe is so great that it raises questions as to whether the child will have their needs met by the parents. Under these circumstances it is important to be realistic and to be prepared to make the decision that the child will be at risk of harm if they remain with their parents. Alternatives such as placement with extended family and care proceedings should then be considered. (This option is explored further in Chapter 13.) Alternatively, the members of the conference may agree that the parents should be given an opportunity to work with professionals to meet the needs of the child. It is always important that conference members have a contingency plan if parents do not engage with the child protection plan, but in these cases it is essential.

Without this in place, the situation may be allowed to drift, placing the child at risk of harm.

Overlooking children in the family

It is not surprising that the child in a sibling group who is overlooked during the assessment, as discussed in Chapter 4, may also be overlooked when planning interventions. This was evident in one of the cases in the Anytown study involving a sibling group, where the needs of the middle child, who was 'shy and withdrawn', were ignored because of the significant concerns about both an older and a much younger sibling. One of the social worker respondents gave an example of the consequences of failing to consider the needs of individual children in the family:

> [At the conference it was agreed that] it was important to keep these five siblings together and we managed to find a placement to, to make that happen. Which is, which was – everybody was high fiving that fact, for want of a better term yeah. Really they didn't consider the individual child and subsequently we know, we now know that some of those children should be separated. (Social worker 1)

Start again syndrome

Professionals can be so overwhelmed by the complex and multifaceted needs of the family that it is all too easy, when making decisions with limited time available, to focus on the current concerns and begin with a clean slate: what is known as the 'start again syndrome' (Brandon *et al.*, 2008). When this occurs, previous parental responses to service interventions and the parents' motivation and ability to change may be ignored. The consequence is that families are provided with services that have not been found to be effective in the past and, if parental circumstances and motivation have not changed, are likely to set parents up to fail again. For example, in the Anytown study there was one striking example of a plan being constructed that was a replica of a plan that had failed to protect the child four years earlier. In this situation no consideration was given, according to the conference minutes, to why the original plan had failed, what had changed and why conference members thought it would work now.

A list of actions

The outline plan can become a 'to do list' for both parents and professionals. When this occurs, little time is spent ensuring that parents understand why these actions will be of benefit, how the actions complement each other and the priority that should be given to each action. A further issue with the production of a list of actions is that they do not take into account that some changes will be easier for parents to make than others. When such a list of actions is constructed, it is all too easy for professionals to forget how difficult making changes to parenting capacity and lifestyle can be and for the parents to interpret the plan as no more than a set of tasks they need to complete in order to get professionals out of their lives.

'Cover our backs' plans

> It's like the outline plan was for this man to attend pattern changing [for a drink problem], which was unrealistic...even though I said, look...I know he can't do it, yet it still went ahead, still, that was still in the plan, so this man should if he wants to change...he should have to take seven Fridays off [work]. (Social worker 1)

Some plans can be constructed more to allay the anxieties of the professionals than address the needs of the child, as is the case in this example. In these situations, parents can be overwhelmed by the demands and expectations placed on them, with professionals being over-optimistic in terms of what can be realistically achieved. For example, in one Anytown study plan designed for parents of six children, the professionals' concerns regarding the chronic neglect of the individual children were such that, in addition to meeting the complex health needs of two of the children, the parents were expected to: improve the living conditions; ensure the children were at school regularly and on time; attend a parent and toddler group, a parenting programme, a pattern-changing group for domestic violence; meet the health needs of one of the other children; work with the social worker; and, in addition, the father was to attend literacy classes. Plans such as this are more likely to set the parents up to fail rather than meet the needs of the children. It is not surprising, therefore, that in response to such a plan a mother in the study completed by the Office of the Children's Commissioner indicated that she felt overwhelmed: 'We were told we that we must do everything they told us to do and if we didn't we were not thinking about the kids. Yet it was impossible to do it all. It just depressed me to look at it all (Office of the Children's Commissioner, 2010, p. 35).

Focusing on one issue

In contrast to an overwhelming list of actions, some plans focus on just one issue or problem. Whilst this may be appropriate on occasion, it can also be the result of the whole conference being affected by the 'misdirected gaze' described in Chapter 4. This may occur because the parent encourages the professionals to focus on one particular issue, indicating a simple solution: 'I just need rehousing'; 'help to clean the place'; 'my benefits sorted'; 'an appointment at the child psychiatrist's for Jessica to sort her out is what's needed'. Alternatively, it may happen because professionals concentrate on the one particular issue that is causing the most concern or anxiety to the members of the conference, such as domestic violence or alcohol misuse. When this takes place it is easy to minimize the other issues that need addressing if the child is to be safe.

Plans driven by resources

The content of outline plans will inevitably be driven by available resources. Identifying appropriate services and resources can be a difficult and frustrating process, particularly if the resources are not available or there is a lengthy waiting list for services (Munro, 2002). The consequence of this can be that the same services are used time and time again because nothing else is available and professionals take the view any intervention is better than none. This lack of resources can be disheartening for both practitioners and families, particularly if the services do not meet the specific needs of the child and family. A study undertaken by the Children's Commissioner highlighted another issue related to scarce resources, which is encapsulated in this quote from a practitioner who participated in their study:

> If the actual need [of the family] meets the service, the family are very responsive, but if the need doesn't meet the service they're going to have it anyway, hence resistance, because the service offered doesn't make sense to the family. (Office of the Children's Commissioner, 2010, p. 30)

Is the child protection conference a suitable forum for making decisions about significant harm in cases of neglect?

Many of the points made in this chapter echo the findings of a study completed by Corby *et al.* (1996). They noted that many parents found the conference emotionally challenging and too proceduralized. In addition, they felt overwhelmed by the number of professionals present and thought they had little influence over decisions, which were often made in a rush. Whilst the conference provides a structure for making difficult, joint decisions, both Munro (1999) and Farmer and Owen (1995) questioned, at the end of the last century, the suitability of the conference as a forum for analysis of concerns and discussion of plans. It would seem, in the second decade of the twenty-first century, this remains a pertinent question. Sharing information, making decisions and constructing outline plans in child protection conferences, as has been discussed above, is fraught with difficulties for both professionals and family members. Yet, it is important these tasks are completed in a meaningful manner so that parents appreciate what needs to change and why. So, is there an alternative?

An alternative that originated in New Zealand in 1989 is the family group conference (FGC). The conference brings together professionals, the immediate and extended family and other key people of significance to the family in a meeting to address collaboratively issues of childcare and, in some jurisdictions, such as New Zealand and Queensland Australia, child protection concerns (Holland and O'Neill, 2006; Darlington *et al.*, 2012; Morris and Connolly, 2012). The FGC is characterized by:

- an independent coordinator who prepares the family and is responsible for facilitation of the meeting
- private family time, without professionals present, when family members have time on their own to consider how to keep the child safe
- professional commitment to respect the family plan unless the child is placed at risk of harm.

This approach appears to have a number of benefits if one considers the factors that promote and inhibit parental engagement with change. Doolan (2006) argues that child safety and wellbeing are enhanced when family groups and professionals collaborate and work in partnership. In addition, greater commitment and engagement to child protection plans and high satisfaction levels with the process have been noted in a number of studies (Morris and Connolly, 2012). The notion of private family time is particularly useful in this regard as it provides the family with an opportunity to consider the nature of professional concerns and what they can do to address the concerns, weighing up the advantages and disadvantages of potential strategies for change.

Whilst FGCs show promise, Healy *et al.* (2012), drawing on the findings of a small-scale study of their use in cases where children are considered at risk of harm, found, as did Doolan (2006), that the family's ability to make decisions is curtailed by the power imbalance inherent in many child protection systems. Practitioners are both investigators of maltreatment as well as supporters of child and family. That is, the adversarial relationship between state and family, which underpins the forensic system used in many countries including the UK, does not fit easily with the democratic ethos of FGCs.

Healy *et al.* (2012) conclude, however, that the FGC can be used as a more inclusive approach to decision making in child protection cases if:

- the parents and family members are prepared adequately
- a balance is secured between the number of professionals and family members attending
- both family members and professionals have a shared understanding of the purpose of the meeting and the roles and responsibilities of those present
- there is a written agenda to promote transparency
- the conference takes place in a setting that is welcoming and conducive to family participation, accessible and culturally appropriate
- the child's views are taken into account through their presence or other means
- opportunities are created to encourage the family members to have a voice
- private family time is assured.

Reflecting on this list, it seems that – irrespective of whether the decisions are made in a child protection conference, FGC or at a children in need planning meeting – if these fundamental principles are applied, they go some way to creating the conditions necessary to support parents identify pathways for change.

Conclusion

The primary task for members of the child protection conference is to assess information and plan how best to safeguard and promote the welfare of the child. However, if the child is to remain with their parents, then it is important that parents understand how they need to change in order to meet the needs of their child. The conference serves a secondary purpose, therefore, and that is to ensure that the parent understands what needs to change, why the changes are necessary and how they can make these changes. If the parents do not appreciate the need for change and are not ready to make these changes then interventions are unlikely to keep the child safe from harm.

With these two tasks in mind, when analysing the information that is shared at the conference and constructing the plan, professionals should pay attention to the following questions:

- Do professionals have a shared understanding of the nature of the concerns?

- Are the parents aware of, and take ownership of, the behaviour and attitudes that are concerning professionals? Do they acknowledge the impact these are having on each child in the family?
- How have parents' past experiences influenced their current construction of the problem?
- Has child's/children's and parents' expressed needs, wishes and feelings been considered?
- Is there an understanding of what a good and bad day is like in the life of the child?
- Are expectations regarding parental engagement in the plan clear and are contingency arrangements in place if parents do not engage?
- Has consideration been given to the allocation of new workers to assist with plan implementation and the impact that this may have on parental willingness to engage in the plan?
- Do parents and professionals have a shared understanding of what will happen next?

Chapter 6

Plans to Safeguard Neglected Children from Harm

In this chapter, having considered the assessment process and the initial child protection conference, I move to the next stage of the child protection process: implementing the child protection plan. For professionals implementing the plan there is a tension to be managed between care and control. Professionals have to collaborate with and empower parents to change behaviours, lifestyles and attitudes in order to meet the needs of the child. At the same time both the professionals and the family are aware that parental non-engagement can lead potentially to the removal of the child from the family. The way in which professionals manage this tension can have a significant impact on securing the engagement of parents in the implementation of the plan (Turney, 2012). Ferguson (2011) argues that effective management means being clear with parents about professionals' authority but also identifying opportunities to maximize the influence of the parent over the plan.

I begin by considering what is required of both parents and professionals if meaningful engagement with a plan is to be achieved. I move on to explore the reasons why either the family or professionals, or indeed both, may not engage with the plan in a manner that achieves better outcomes for children. As part of this exploration I reflect on planning processes and discuss ways in which they can promote or inhibit effective engagement.

What follows is as relevant for plans designed to meet the needs of children where there are emerging concerns about neglect as for neglected children at risk of harm. However, I will focus on planning where there are child protection concerns, particularly cases of chronic neglect, as these, according to the participants in the Anytown neglect study (see Box 0.1 and Appendix), can be the most challenging group to engage with plans.

In Chapter 5 I considered how an outline plan is constructed at a child protection conference. In the UK, alongside developing the outline plan, members of the conference identify a multidisciplinary 'core' group of professionals. This group will work with the family to develop the plan into a detailed working plan, which they are then expected to deliver. The core group are also responsible for any ongoing or further assessment, regularly evaluating the progress and reporting back to the review conference on this progress. The role of the review conference, which has a similar membership to the conference, is to consider whether the child should continue to remain the subject of a child protection plan. The review conference meets at regular intervals during the lifespan of the plan (DHSSPS, 2003; Welsh Assembly Government, 2006; HM Government, 2010; Scottish Government, 2010).

Taking action to promote better outcomes for children

Engagement with the plan requires both effort and commitment from parents, as illustrated in Figure 6.1. If parents are prepared to make the commitment and put in the effort to improve outcomes for their child, they are 'walking the walk and talking that talk'; if they appear to be committed but are putting no effort into change, then we have surface static or a parent who is 'talking the talk'. Other parents may, however, appear to be making an effort but are not genuinely committed to making change; this means they are superficially complying with the actions included in the plan or just 'walking the walk'. Finally, there are parents who are not prepared, or are unable, to make the commitment or effort to change and therefore disengage from the process. Disengagement is, not walking the walk or talking the talk, a manifestation of resistance to change.

Walk the walk and talk the talk: meaningful engagement

In order to assist practitioners understand what is required of parents if they are to engage meaningfully in the plan, Platt (2012) has taken the

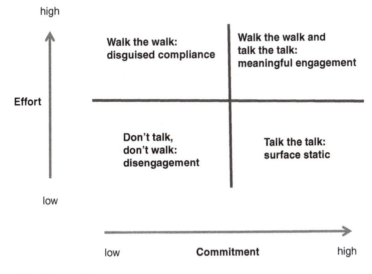

Figure 6.1:   Parental engagement

Multifactor Offender Readiness Model MORM (Ward *et al.*, 2004) and considered its application in the context of statutory child protection practice. MORM is based on the concept that engagement is required at both behavioural and attitudinal levels. At a behavioural level this means that the parent should be: keeping appointments, open about concerning problems, using workers' support, demonstrating a commitment to completing the required tasks, prepared to make sacrifices in order to meet the needs of the child, and beginning to take the initiative in managing family life more effectively. Attitudinal engagement means maintaining a 'working alliance' (Platt, 2012, p. 141) between the members of the core group and the parents. Parents should feel trusted and respected, agree on the goals to be achieved and the ways in which they will be achieved. Platt goes on to argue that the level of engagement at both levels will be influenced by individual parental factors, such as their ability and motivation to change, and their levels of confidence and self-identity. However, external factors, such as the circumstances under which the plan is being delivered, the support and approach of workers and the resources available will influence the level of engagement.

Walk the walk: superficial compliance

This occurs when parents appear to engage with the plan and undertake the tasks that are expected of them but the daily lived experience of the child does not improve. In this situation the parents are often putting effort into getting professionals out of their lives rather than meeting the needs of the child. Dale *et al.* (1986, p. 91), in the classic text *Dangerous Families*, describe this approach as 'passive-aggressive resistance', whereby superficial compliance may conceal feelings of anger and antagonism towards workers. This response to professional interventions has been noted in a number of studies with regard to child neglect (Horwath, 2007; Brandon *et al.*, 2008; Davies and Ward, 2012).

Superficial compliance has frequently been observed amongst clients who have previous experience of the child protection system and know what they need to do and say to satisfy practitioners. Recent serious case reviews, such as that of Peter Connolly and Victoria Climbié (Cm 5730, 2003; The Lord Laming, 2009), have highlighted that behind the veneer of engagement parents can be manipulative and continue with the maltreatment. Arguably, with increased attention paid since the mid-1990s to the need to work in partnership with parents, it can be both unpalatable and challenging to practitioners to recognize and address the fact that beneath a guise of pleasantness and engagement can be devious parents. Therefore, it is important that practitioners always keep an open mind and a healthy scepticism when parents appear to comply with the plan, particularly if lit-tle seems to be changing that benefits the child (The Lord Laming, 2009).

Some of the parents who walk the walk may be the emotionally neglect-ful parents discussed in Chapter 2 (Crittenden, 1999). These are parents who find relationships difficult and do not wish to enter into a working alliance; thus, professionals are kept at a distance. Although they feign compliance with plans they do not internalize these changes or change the way in which they respond emotionally to the needs of the child; rather, they try to suppress their negative and often hostile feelings towards work-ers. However, on occasion they may find this impossible and outbursts of verbal and physical aggression may occur.

What is crucial in these cases is that practitioners go beyond verbal asser-tions of change to consider tangible, sustained evidence that the quality of life has improved for children in the family. Moreover, this evidence should not be merely the completion of practical tasks, such as ensuring regular attendance at school, but also evidence that children's emotional needs are being met.

Talk the talk: full of good intentions?

The parents who talk the talk may appear to be full of good intentions: they mean to engage with the plan and may even be enthusiastic about the help that is being offered, but some crisis or event always seems to prevent them from taking action. Dale *et al.* (1986, p. 92) consider this to be a form of 'passive-hopeless resistance'. The parents whom Crittenden (1999) describes as the disorganized neglectful may engage in this way. The prob-lem for practitioners can be that these parents often appear to be sincere and want to engage and address the concerns. They may be tearful and genuinely upset that they are unable to make the most of the help on offer. In this situation it is all too easy for professionals to go into 'rescuer' mode and to give the parents chance after chance to demonstrate that they can put the effort into changing. This response can result in drift; whilst there are signs of good intentions nothing comes to fruition in a way that makes a positive difference to the lives of the children in the family.

Disengagement

Disengaged parents are those who do not make a commitment to, or put any effort into, change: they do not comply with the plan; physically or emotionally the parents are walking away. This disengagement may, in part, be due to a lack of understanding about professional concerns. It may also be associated with depressed neglect (Crittenden, 1999), which is described in Chapter 2. In these cases the parents are so preoccupied with their own issues they are unable to engage in a process that requires effort and commitment to look beyond these to the needs of the child. Parents who have serious addiction to drugs and alcohol or have mental health issues may present in this way.

Parents who are not prepared even to consider change may use a variety of fight or flight behaviours. Flight behaviours are the strategies adopted by parents to keep professionals at bay. These include avoiding meaningful engagement with professionals by moving from one area to another, not keeping appointments, stage-managing visits, limiting what the practitioner can see and who they speak to, and coaching children (Ferguson, 2011). The most common forms of disengagement, however, are what Dale *et al.* (1986, p. 91) refer to as 'hostile resistance', or fight behaviours. Parents exhibiting these behaviours may be verbally and physically antagonistic towards workers, refusing to take concerns seriously, or they may become confrontational and provocative, challenging practitioners to make them change, making threats such as, 'I'll get my solicitor onto you', or intimidating workers – 'I know where you live. You take my child and I'll take yours.'

Forrester *et al.* (2012) have identified five causes of resistance to change. These are: social structure and disadvantage; the child protection context; parental resistance; denial and minimization of abuse or neglect; and the behaviour of the worker. Whilst the latter three are considered elsewhere in this and the previous chapters, it is worth exploring the influence of context. Most neglectful parents have low socio-economic status and have experience of disadvantage and poverty. They may feel disempowered as a consequence of this. These feelings may be exacerbated if they are also, for example, members of minority ethnic groups or have a learning disability. Many of these parents will also have experienced abuse and neglect. These experiences are likely to lead to a sense of lack of control over their lives, with professionals such as social workers, police officers, probation officers and others in authority being perceived as having played a significant part in controlling them in the past. In these situations it is easy enough to understand how some parents respond by resisting engagement and demonstrating fight or flight behaviours.

Making plans work: professional engagement

Forrester, Kershaw *et al.* (2008) studied 24 taped interviews between a social worker and an actor playing the part of a parent. They found that the factor that most strongly influenced client response was empathy. When the worker was empathetic the simulated client was more likely to disclose information and was less resistant. All too often, however, they found that social workers asked closed questions and focused on issues rather than identifying positives and allowing the parent time for reflection. This lack of empathy was also reported by parents in the study conducted by the Office of the Children's Commissioner (2010). The parents complained that workers did not understand what life was like for people they worked with, and the result was they often applied textbook solutions without recognizing the family's lived experiences. This study highlights that the approach of the worker can influence client engagement. Indeed, there is a growing body of work that emphasizes that the qualities of the worker combined with the service user's perception of their ability to help are as important to effecting change as the parent's ability to change and the selected interventions that are used (Lambert and Barley, 2001; Harnett and Day, 2008).

Barlow and Scott (2010, p. 62) argue that parents who have experienced insecure attachments in their own childhood, which would appear to be the case for many parents who neglect their children, require an 'emotionally corrective relationship' which includes a supportive therapeutic approach that is based on acceptance, empathy, genuineness and trust. This forms the basis for a partnership between the worker and parent to identify and meet some of the parent's unmet needs and, in turn, to meet the needs of their children. Thus, the relationship between the practitioner and the parent is crucial in terms of positive engagement by the parent in the change process. The workers implementing the plan, therefore, have to demonstrate to the parent that they, as professionals, are prepared to make the effort and show the commitment to assist the family to change: that is, professionals need to 'walk the walk and talk the talk'. This means ensuring that they not only engage meaningfully in the actions ascribed to them as part of the plan but that they do this in partnership, establishing a relationship with, and working alongside, the parent. This does not mean they ignore their professional power; rather, they need to be clear about their authority and the consequences for the family of not engaging with the plan. This approach will assist in establishing and maintaining the working alliance described by Platt (2012) that is necessary for parents to engage meaningfully with the plan.

All too often, however, whilst practitioners may intend to engage meaningfully with the family, they may find themselves 'walking the walk' – in other words, going through the motions of compliance with their part of the plan. 'Seeing the child', 'monitoring the situation' or making fleeting visits to check 'all is well' are behaviours that indicate the worker is engaging in superficial compliance or creating surface static. This can occur if practitioners are uncertain about what is expected of them or are cynical about the plan being effective. A more aggressive and detrimental version of walk the walk takes place when workers are directive and, at worst, browbeat or bully parents into completing tasks outlined in the plan (Ferguson, 2011).

'Talk the talk' may also occur amongst practitioners. This is evident when workers make promises to visit which are then cancelled, fail to return phone calls from parents, offer to write letters or obtain resources for the family and forget to do this or do not provide feedback to the parents. Such behaviour is exemplified in this comment by a parent: 'She said she would make the referral for him. But the next time I saw her she still hadn't done it. This went on for weeks and weeks' (Office of the Children's Commissioner, 2010, p. 35).

Finally, fear and anxiety about working with particularly hostile or difficult parents or complex cases can lead to professional disengagement and a lack of focus on the needs of the child. In these situations, disengagement may take the form of avoiding certain family members, not visiting at all or rationalizing a reduction in visits: 'They seemed fine last time I called. I'll leave it this week.' Alternatively, workers may visit but fail to ask pertinent questions or engage meaningfully with the child and other family members because of fear of the parents' aggressive reactions (Stanley and Goddard, 2002).

If a parent is committed to change but interacts with workers who are not fully engaged or committed to making the plan work, then the task for the parent is going to be made much more difficult. If, however, both parent and workers are engaging in superficial compliance then it will be all too easy to make presumptions that the child is safe when, in fact, this may not be the case. Moreover, situations where professionals and parents do not go beyond the surface static can result in the case drifting, with little change for children in the family. Arguably, the most concerning situation is where parents have disengaged and show hostile or challenging resistance, and workers are frightened and intimidated and, in turn, do not engage with the parents, or engage with them on the parents' terms and, as a result, the needs of the child are ignored.

Organizational influences on professional engagement

In exactly the same way that the working alliance between the worker and the parent affects the implementation of the plan, the relationship between the worker and their supervisor will affect the worker's approach towards the child and their family (Morrison, 2007). For example, a practitioner whose supervisor is both committed to providing high quality supervision and ensures that it takes place is likely to provide the worker with the support and guidance necessary to work effectively with the family. So, what is high quality supervision? This is supervision that goes beyond managerial processes, such as checking the worker has complied with organizational requirements, to providing opportunities for critical thinking and reflection as well as offering emotional support (Hawkins and Shohet, 2000; Wonnacott, 2012). All too often, however, supervision is no more than superficial compliance with organizational expectations. In these situations, the focus is likely to be on the worker adhering to policies and procedures, such as whether the worker has visited as outlined in the plan, kept records of core group meetings, and 'seen' the child. In these situations the worker has little opportunity to explore their concerns regarding the case and their anxieties and feelings about working with the family. It is all too easy to see how inexperienced or stressed workers can mirror the attitude of the supervisor in their work with families and 'walk the walk'. Alternatively, supervisors may spend considerable time discussing how the worker feels about the case: 'talk the talk'. If this occurs and the supervisor provides no opportunities for the supervisee to critically reflect on these feelings and concerns and to consider the implications for practice, the focus on the child and their needs is lost. Supervisors may also disengage from providing meaningful supervision, either by continually cancelling arranged sessions, allowing sessions to be constantly interrupted or just providing supervision 'on the hoof' (Horwath, 2007).

It is not only supervision but also the organizational context or work environment that is significant in relation to outcomes for children. In pioneering studies undertaken by Glisson and his team in the USA over the past ten years, the researchers have found that poor organizational environments reduce workers' capacity to help maltreated children because they increase workers' stress, depersonalize the relationships between worker and client and contribute to high staff turnover (Glisson and Hemmelgarten, 1998; Glisson and Green, 2011). In the most recent study, Glisson and Green found, unsurprisingly, that the long-term outcomes for maltreated children are more positive if the children are served by agencies with a positive organizational climate – that is, the workers are clear about their roles and responsibilities, are not overloaded and do not feel they are working in a stressful environment, even though the nature of the work might be stressful and anxiety provoking. In this climate workers believe they are able to undertake worthwhile tasks successfully, they remain involved in their work and are concerned about their clients. In other words, they are 'walking the walk and talking the talk'. This environment provides a firm foundation, enabling workers to build that all-important working alliance with families.

Engaging fathers

Both Harlow and Shardlow (2006) and Milner (1993) found fathers are invisible and do not actively engage in core groups and, if they do attend, they tend to be aggressive and non-compliant. (In this context 'fathers' refers to any man who is responsible for the care of a child. This includes live-in partners and stepfathers as well as biological fathers.) Engaging with male caregivers can become even more challenging if practitioners are working with multiple fathers to children in the family and a number of men who, over the time of engagement with statutory services, may live in the family home as partners of the mother.

There may be a number of reasons why these men are marginalized by workers or why they avoid professionals. Scourfield (2006) found, in his ethnographic study of a child protection team, that workers tended to prioritize physical neglect and, as women are traditionally held responsible for managing the physical care of the home and their children, the focus of assessment and plans is on mothers rather than fathers. Ferguson (2011) argues that workers may believe that men do not have the capacity to talk about feelings, relationships and intimate topics. In addition, Maxwell *et al.* (2012) conclude that men are often perceived of, and labelled by, workers as being either a 'risk' or a 'resource', and the potential for them to be a mixture of both is not explored sufficiently. Moreover, if they are considered a risk, workers may marginalize them or construct plans that place the mother in the role of protector of her children rather than work with the man on the source of the risk. The mothers themselves may be unwilling to identify the men who participate in caregiving, out of fear of intimidation from the man, of losing him, losing their children or possibly losing benefits (Maxwell *et al.*, 2012). Maxwell *et al.* (2012) also found that men, in turn, may avoid engaging with workers, perceiving the issues to be associated with mothering and failing to understand that they too might be contributing to the problems. Scourfield (2006) notes that many of these men are socially marginalized and may themselves be damaged as a result of abuse and neglect. This will also affect their willingness to engage. Yet, if a plan is to make a difference to the lived experience of the child, then the child should benefit from, and if necessary be protected from, both parents. This will be meaningfully achieved only if both carers recognize their strengths and weaknesses, are actively committed to changing negative behaviours and make the effort to meet the needs of the child.

Maxwell *et al.* (2012) reviewed research between 2000 and 2010 on the engagement of fathers and have drawn on the findings to identify the following strategies as showing promise when promoting the engagement of fathers and caregivers:

- Early identification and engagement of fathers in the process ensures that from the start fathers understand the nature of the concerns and what is expected of them.

- Making services available and relevant to fathers. (In the following chapters consideration is given to interventions that meet the needs of fathers.)
- Using a client-centred yet directive style, such as motivational interviewing, which seeks to enhance motivation and reduce resistance. Cognitive-behavioural approaches that enable fathers to understand the impact of their behaviours on their children appear to be beneficial.

Engaging parents with a learning disability

Cleaver and Nicholson (2007) found that social workers made considerable effort in working with families where the parents had a learning disability. However, prejudice and lack of understanding can lead to children of parents with a learning disability coming to the attention of child protection services indiscriminately (Lamont and Bromfield, 2009; Tarlton and Porter, 2012). Moreover, the learning disabled parents who participated in the Office of the Children's Commissioner's study (2010) felt that social workers from children's services did not see them as individuals but as a problem. They believed the workers did not spend sufficient time explaining their concerns in a way that made sense to the parents. In addition, they felt unable to trust social workers because the workers made assumptions that they could not parent: 'They have a view about you, they think just because you find reading and writing hard that you must be a bad parent' (p. 24). It is not surprising that these experiences can affect their engagement with child protection plans (Traustadottir and Sigurjonsdottir, 2010). In order to promote engagement, the Office of the Children's Commissioner's study (2010) highlighted the importance of ensuring that services provided as part of a plan meet the particular needs of the parents and their family. For example, one mother who participated in the study described how she was expected to attend a parenting group. She found the other mothers did not talk to her, she could not understand the programme content and did not appreciate the relevance of the content to her situation. These learning disabled parents also spoke about the importance of workers recognizing that they need more time to work on issues than other parents. A key theme from the study was that many of these parents felt helpless. This feeling extended to their children, who thought that workers did not pay sufficient attention to the impact of bullying and harassment on family life when a parent had a learning disability: 'We had it every day, throwing bricks, calling names, shouting at me. My mum was scared. I was scared but we got no help, none at all' (p. 25).

Lamont and Bromfield (2009) argue that the extent to which a learning disability affects parenting will vary depending on the nature and degree of disability, and the risk and protective factors. Thus, an assessment of parenting capacity should consider not only how the learning disability is affecting parenting but also the stressors and the support available. When constructing a plan for these families Lamont and Bromfield (2009), drawing on themes from research in this field, conclude that family-centred packages provided over the longer term are most beneficial. These packages, as discussed further in Chapter 11, should focus on strengths rather than deficits, include participatory rather than relational elements of practice, and concentrate on learning and applying knowledge and skills in the home environment rather than just learning abstract concepts.

Creating an environment for meaningful engagement

It was evident, in both the interviews and focus groups included in the Anytown study, that many practitioners were unsure about the purpose of the core group: is it just to intervene to protect a child from risk of harm or should it go further and ensure the needs of the child are met? Moreover, as noted in other studies (Horwath and Calder, 1998; Harlow and Shardlow, 2006), there was a lack of clarity regarding roles and responsibilities. As a consequence of this confusion professionals tend to defer to the social worker and view the core group as social services' roadshow.

It is not only professionals who lack understanding of the task and process associated with core groups. In the study undertaken by the Office of the Children's Commissioner (2010) into families' perspectives on the child protection system, it was evident that many parents – and, as discussed further below, children and young people – did not know what a core group was either. This lack of shared understanding, together with the complex nature of implementing child protection plans in cases of neglect, can affect parental and indeed professionals' engagement. Calder and Horwath (1999) argue, therefore, that at the first core group meeting members should establish a common and shared understanding of the core group tasks and the roles and responsibilities of the individual members, including family members. There are, however, additional challenges encountered by those delivering the plan as part of a core group that make 'walking the walk and talking the talk' both complex and challenging, as is discussed below.

Membership of the core group

Baxter and Print (1999) recommend that the group delivering the plan should not exceed six professional members, if it is to be a functional and supportive working group that does not overwhelm the family participants. A particular issue in cases of chronic neglect, however, is that the multifaceted nature of the concerns means that a significant number of professionals may be actively working with the family. In the Anytown study, for example, core groups usually had a specified membership of between six and ten professionals plus the parent or parents and, on rare occasions, young people. The core group exceeded these numbers, however, if a sibling group was considered together in one core group.

The participants in the Anytown study indicated that core groups routinely included the social worker, teachers, health visitors, family support workers, family centre staff and, in a significant number of cases, professionals from adult services. However, sustaining this level of membership was a challenge. First, professionals from adult services did not appear to be regular attenders, despite parenting issues having a significant impact on parenting capacity in many cases. This lack of engagement by professionals from adult services was also noted in the study of core groups completed by Harlow and Shardlow (2006). The participants in the Anytown study indicated that the lack of engagement occurred because the adult practitioners were reluctant to share information about their 'client' or believed:

> that's a parenting issue, it's not for us to get involved in, but we need [their] specialist input to know how to work with this, to understand how to teach them to parent, what their learning style is, you know are they able to change? Are they able to learn? We need their input – I guess they're fearful of it I suppose. (social worker 7)

Second, studies of core group practice, including the Anytown study, indicate that attendance by professionals is high immediately after the initial child protection conference but that as professionals' concerns are abated the level of attendance reduces, with core groups of between three and four professionals and the parent or parents routinely taking place (Horwath and Calder, 1998; Harlow and Shardlow, 2006). Third, professionals appear to absent themselves from the core group if they have not seen the family between core group meetings, believing they have nothing to report. Fourth, it appears that a large core group can lead to disengagement and marginalization of certain professional members who do not feel they have a central role and therefore do not attend or only attend if they have something significant to contribute. This, in turn, can affect the way in which parents view the core group and its tasks: 'If professionals do not take it seriously then why should I?'

The lead social worker

In the UK the child's social worker acts as lead professional, coordinating the interagency work undertaken in the core group. This can be a particularly challenging role as the social worker is not only leading the work of the core group but also attempting to generate ownership by other members of the group, ensuring their meaningful engagement with the plan and its delivery (Firth, 1999). Members of the core group, however, often have different expectations from the social worker of what 'lead' means. For example, they may expect, as indicated in the Harlow and Shardlow (2006) study and also found in the Anytown study, the social worker as 'lead' to take responsibility for practical tasks such as chairing the meeting, organizing the venue, and preparing and circulating the minutes, whilst the social worker feels aggrieved that other professionals are not prepared to share the responsibilities. In addition, Harlow and Shardlow (2006) found that social workers also felt they were the sole container for emotions, having to deal with any aggression from the parents or voicing any concerns that may bring professionals into conflict with parents. These tensions, if played out in the core group arena, do not make for a conducive atmosphere in which to promote change, and allow other practitioners to take a back seat, giving the family the impression they are not actively committed or engaged in delivering the plan. A conference chair, interviewed as part of the Anytown study, summarized most effectively what is required of practitioners if they are to engage in a meaningful way within the core group:

> It comes back to each agency taking responsibility and ownership of the core group so that there isn't this expectation that a social worker has to manage chairing the core group, managing the dynamic of the core group, minuting the core group, getting those minutes out to the core group, because actually that's just agencies relying on another agency, isn't it? So somehow link to each, you know, everybody walking away from the Conference with a sense of, this is my responsibility, I own part of that plan and this is how I'm going to implement it and this is how we're going to discuss it, I think it's all one and the same thing in some respects. (Chair 5)

The participants from a range of disciplines who contributed to the focus groups in the Anytown study, as did the participants in the Harlow and Shardlow study (2006), identified a number of issues that prevented social workers from 'walking the walk and talking the talk'. First, a significant turnover amongst the social work personnel who acted as lead professionals meant that the family and practitioners did not have the opportunity to establish the important working alliance (Platt, 2012) before the worker changed again. Second, they found the inevitable sickness, leave and crises on other cases meant that workers were late, appointments changed and, at worst, cancelled with no notice. A parent in the Office of the Children's Commissioner's study (2010, p. 34) put it well: 'How does she think her [the social worker's] constant lateness makes me feel? Worthless? Unimportant? Yes. If I am late – well that's different. They do not understand that.'

Finally, a number of local authorities have systems in place that mean there is a change of social worker after the initial child protection conference or at the first core group meeting. A change of worker at the point where many parents have begun to contemplate change and considered how to achieve this can seriously disrupt the process and add to the parent's sense of loss and unwillingness to trust. As a parent put it: 'I am sick of telling new people the same old things' (Office of the Children's Commissioner, 2010, p. 34).

Engaging with children and young people

Cossar *et al.* (2011), in their UK study of children's experiences of the child protection process, asked young people about their experiences of attending child protection and core group meetings. Only ten of the 19 who answered the questions recalled attending meetings. Some of them had not wanted to attend but were not aware of alternative ways in which their views could be made known to the meeting. Of those who had attended, they found the meetings difficult, although eight did speak at the meeting. They thought they were only partially listened to and felt awkward being asked difficult questions in front of their parents.

Only five of the 19 recalled seeing their child protection plan. However, a few young people did discuss the advantages of having a plan, associating it with getting extra help at school or being given priority for services. In the main, however, they thought there were also negative aspects, particularly with regard to social work involvement. They described feelings of intrusion and stigma and increased stress in the family.

Findings from the Anytown study indicate that children and young people are not routinely engaged in core groups, even if the plan requires the young person, rather than the parent, to make significant changes to their behaviour. For example, one plan addressed the needs of a neglected 14-year-old who had problems of aggression and antisocial behaviour within school and was misusing drugs and alcohol. Progress was reported back to the core group through the staff working with her but her voice was missing.

Cossar *et al.* conclude that engaging children in child protection meetings, such as core groups, needs to be handled sensitively, with professionals recognizing the emotional impact on the child. Meaningful participation requires adequate preparation of the child before the core group, support throughout the meeting and feedback afterwards. In addition, young people should be given a choice of ways in which they can make their wishes, feelings and experiences known, over and above actual attendance at the core group. If the plan is to make a difference to the lived experience of the child then it is essential that every effort is made to give the child or young person an autonomous voice rather than depending on the interpretations of others (Aubrey and Dahl, 2006).

The child protection plan

As indicated above, one of the key tasks for the core group is to develop a full-blown, working, child protection plan from the outline plan constructed at the conference. This detailed plan should specify exactly what each family member and professional should be doing, why they are expected to do it, what the intended input should achieve and how this will be measured. The case example below highlights the detail that is required.

Case study 6.1: Carla

Carla lives alone with her daughter Freya. Freya is seven years old. An assessment highlighted that Freya does not have a set bedtime and usually stays up to keep her mother company in the evening, as Carla gets lonely. They watch adult DVDs together, usually in silence, with Carla shouting at Freya if she talks or interrupts her mother's viewing. Freya often falls asleep during the evening or becomes 'whiney', which irritates Carla; therefore she leaves her on the sofa all night in her day clothes and then Freya goes to school in the same clothes. Freya rarely has a wash and her hair has not been shampooed for months. The assessment also indicated that Carla finds Freya a 'difficult and unfriendly' child. Freya has no regular mealtimes and Carla often forgets to buy any food for them, so Freya is irritable, hungry and lethargic when she is at school. She is falling behind and there is particular concern about her poor literacy skills. In addition, the other children in her class are frightened by the tales Freya tells them based on the DVDs she's watched. This, in addition to her being dirty and smelly and verbally aggressive towards the other children, means they do not want to play with her.

What would it look like if Freya's needs were being met each evening?

- A meal when she gets home from school.
- Carla spending time with Freya so Freya can practise reading the books she brings home from school.
- A snack before bed.
- A set bedtime.
- A bed for Freya to sleep in, with bed linen, changed weekly.
- A washing routine prior to going to bed, including a change of clothes into nightwear.
- Fresh and clean clothes in the morning, which she puts on after a wash.
- A 'settling down for the night' routine in her bedroom including a bedtime story, a cuddle and time for a chat with her mother.

- She only watches children's DVDs or TV programmes early in the evening before going to bed at 7.30.
- She arrives at school on time, is clean and tidy and ready to learn.
- Her academic performance improves.
- She has friends and interacts as would be expected of a child of her age and ability.

What does Carla need to do to achieve this?

- Learn how to establish what is appropriate for a seven-year-old in terms of watching DVDs, bedtime and feeding regimes by attending the parenting programme at the Family Centre every Friday morning for the next ten weeks.
- Understand how she can support Freya develop her literacy skills by meeting with Freya's teacher once a fortnight to discuss what books Freya will bring home and how she can read with Freya at home.
- Discuss with the social worker why she feels as she does about Freya, why she is lonely and needs to have Freya with her during the evenings.
- Identify and discuss with the social worker the challenges she will encounter in changing her routines and working on the plan.
- Meet with the family support worker twice weekly to discuss her difficulties in managing bedtimes and then work with the family support worker, applying what she is learning at the parenting programme to develop a bedtime routine with Freya.

What will the other members of the core group do?

- The coordinator of the parenting programme will ensure that the issues Carla is having with bedtimes and so on are covered by the parenting programme.
- The family support worker will initially visit twice a week in the early evening to help Carla establish a bedtime routine as described above and work with her on planning meals for both of them.
- The head teacher at the primary school will provide information on any changes to Freya's appearance and behaviour in school. She will arrange for Freya to attend a school-based programme designed to improve her social interactions and for Carla to be given the advice and support she needs to assist Freya develop her literacy skills.
- The social worker will explore with Carla ways of improving her relationship with Freya, reducing her sense of social isolation, and she will work with Carla on addressing any barriers to change.
- The social worker will spend time with Freya every three weeks to establish how her daily lived experience is changing.

How will we know if our actions are making a difference?

- In six weeks' time Carla should have an understanding of what she will need to do to both establish a bedtime routine for Freya and support her in developing her literacy skills. We will know this is achieved because Carla will appreciate why Freya needs support with learning, a regular bedtime routine, feeding after school and before bed, and why she should not watch adult DVDs.
- By the first review conference Carla should be spending some time listening to Freya read, getting Freya ready for bed after she has had a meal, changing her clothes, ensuring she has had a meal, had a wash, brushed her teeth and, twice a week, washed her hair. We will know that this is effective because an improvement in Freya's physical appearance should be noted by the school. Moreover, she should not be so lethargic and she should be more engaged in learning and social activities at school. Freya should also be indicating that her daily lived experience has improved through her discussions with the social worker.
- By the second review conference Carla should be spending some time listening to Freya read, getting Freya ready for bed after she has had a meal, changing her clothes, ensuring she has had a meal, had a wash, brushed her teeth and, twice a week, washed her hair. But in addition Freya should be going to bed routinely at the agreed time, with Carla following a night-time routine of reading a story, giving her a cuddle and having a chat, as outlined in the plan. We will know this is effective because Freya's social presentation should have improved, and she should be performing better at school with more positive interactions with other children. Moreover, Freya should be indicating to the social worker that she is feeling happier at school, she is emotionally more secure and the quality of her relationship with her mother has improved.

Whilst this is a time-consuming task, it provides both family members and professionals with a shared understanding of what needs to be achieved, by whom and what the plan seeks to accomplish to improve the daily lived experience of the child.

Part of developing the plan involves practitioners being very clear with the parents about what is and what is not negotiable. One of the issues identified by Ferguson (2011) is that practitioners themselves may not be able to agree what aspects of the plan are negotiable. If this is not clear it may affect the parents' engagement with the plan: 'They said I must attend the parenting programme every week, I've not gone for a month and nothing has happened.' Thus, a task for the core group is to agree on and include in the child protection plan a clear statement about all the negotiable and non-negotiable areas, being clear about the consequences of not engaging with the non-negotiable elements. In the case example above, ensuring Freya does not watch adult DVDs, that she sleeps in her own bed, has a change of clothes and has a washing routine may be some aspects of the plan that are non-negotiable. How many times her hair is washed, whether all her clothes are changed daily, and the timing of her evening meal may be areas subject to negotiation.

As discussed in Chapter 4, if the outline plan is vague, professionals who were not at the conference may struggle making sense of the plan, which is then open to misinterpretation. On occasion, professionals may fail to develop the outline plan further in terms of particular actions, believing they are self-explanatory. For example, with regard to Freya and Carla, the detail could be summarized as: 'Carla to establish a bedtime routine'. What would not be clear would be the rationale behind this action, what a good enough bedtime routine would look like and how it should make a difference to the child. If plans are to be an effective vehicle for bringing about change then it is important that both family and practitioner members of the core group agree on these criteria.

There are a number of other factors that can influence the effectiveness of plans. These are considered below.

Matching needs and services

Child protection plans in cases of chronic neglect normally require parents to engage in services such as parenting programmes. Whilst it may seem obvious to practitioners that these services will address concerns about parenting and the parents should attend, it is also important that parents are motivated and prepared to make the effort to attend. Webster-Stratton and Reid (2010) found that in the USA 50–80 per cent of parents involved with statutory child welfare agencies who commence a parenting programme do not complete it. Both Webster-Stratton and Reid (2010) and Gardner (2008), referring to the UK context, identify some of the reasons why parents may not engage with these programmes. They include:

- stressful life circumstances and other parenting issues, such as mental health concerns affecting the parent's or parents' ability to absorb or engage with the programme
- lack of motivation or resistance to being 'told' or mandated to attend
- projection of problems from parents to external factors and therefore not recognizing the need to attend a programme
- lack of faith in parenting programmes as a means to address their specific problems
- reluctance to engage in group activities

- requiring one-to-one rather than group support because of particular needs
- feeling isolated within the group, such as parents from ethnic minority groups.

Recognizing the challenges of engaging parents, Webster-Stratton and Reid (2010) have identified strategies that practitioners can use not only to involve parents but also to sustain their involvement in parenting programmes. These include a focus on collaboration and parenting strengths, as well as a non-blaming, non-confrontational approach when introducing the parent to the programme, and providing weekly support and guidance through calls to parents from group leaders outside of the programme. In addition, they found 'buddy' schemes, whereby the parent is linked to another parent in the group, helpful as the parents can complete specified assignments together. Addressing practical issues to secure engagement is also valuable by, for example, providing food, transportation and child-care.

Resources

One of the issues encountered by many practitioners and managers when identifying services to meet the needs of the family is that resources are very limited, and whilst it is often relatively easy to ascertain the appropriate resource, it may not be available in the area. The result can be that services that have been used previously are provided once again, even though they do not appear to have made a difference to the parenting of the child. In the Anytown study, for example, this appeared to be the case, practitioners taking the view that something is better than nothing. In a number of cases, this led to disengagement by the parents, who felt the service had not helped them in the past, and it was not clear to parents, and indeed in some cases to workers, what re-referral would achieve. Jonson-Reid *et al.* (2010, p. 279), however, found in a study of in-home child welfare services, that the notion of 'we've tried it before and it didn't work' requires further exploration in each individual case. They found that sometimes increasing the level of service to already chronically neglectful families can be fruitful. Thus, practitioners need to be clear as to why the service could make a difference on this occasion.

It was a common component of plans in the Anytown study to include referral to services, such as Child and Adolescent Mental Health Services (CAMHS), community mental health and disability services. Referrals, however, were on occasion rejected by the service as the case was not deemed to meet the necessary threshold. Moreover, when referrals were accepted, professionals and family members were often confronted with lengthy waiting lists. By the time a place became available the parents' motivation had reduced. When this occurs, there is a mismatch between the parents' readiness for action and the availability of services to support that action. In this situation it is all too easy for parents to disengage from the change process (Morrison, 2010).

Setting realistic timescales

One of the tensions, in terms of child protection planning in cases of chronic neglect, is that change needs to take place at a pace that meets the needs of the child. Whilst this may be the case, it is also important that unrealistic expectations are not placed on the parent or parents in terms of pace of change as this will only set the parents up to fail. These unrealistic expectations were most evident in the Anytown study when it came to improving the home conditions. For example, one set of parents were expected to clean out a very filthy four-bedroomed house in two weeks. In this situation the enormity of what was actually required of them had been given insufficient attention, and under these circumstances it is not surprising that little change took place, with parents reporting that they did not know where to start and felt overwhelmed. In some Anytown plans, however, an incremental process was taken, which was more effective in terms of bringing about permanent change. For example, one plan, concerned with addressing a filthy house, had clear and realistic targets such as: 'parent to clean up the bathroom and remove all rubbish from there in the next fortnight'. In this plan the parents were expected to clean additional rooms in the house as the weeks progressed, alongside maintaining cleanliness in the rooms that had already been cleaned. In another family, the house was so filthy that the children had to go and live with relations whilst the parents worked on cleaning up the house. In this case, the parents were set specific and achievable cleaning tasks, and it was made clear to them at what stage of the cleaning process the children would be returned. This plan was an example of recognizing and meeting the needs of the children, whilst at the same time facilitating change at a pace the parents could manage.

Failing to keep appointments

A possible sign that parents are not engaging in the change process to meet the needs of their child is demonstrated in a failure to keep appointments. However, this lack of engagement cannot be presumed without exploring with the parents why they had not attended the necessary appointments. For example, in one case there was a long history of concerns about the hearing, sight and dental care for a family group of young children, with a pattern emerging of parental failure to keep appointments, new appointments being issued which were not kept, and eventually a withdrawal of services. Each core group appeared to start again in terms of attempting to get these health needs met by making further appointments without considering the past history and the current reasons why the parents were not taking the children for appointments. The result meant additional delays in getting the children the medical attention they needed.

Influence of changes in the household

One of the most striking features regarding parenting amongst the albeit small case sample in the Anytown study was the influence of live-in partners on the quality of parenting. In some cases the quality of parenting improved dramatically with the arrival of a new partner; in other cases it reduced.

The ever-changing relationship between parents, particularly when domestic violence was an issue, also had a significant influence on the quality of parenting. When the parents were experiencing a 'honeymoon' period the parenting improved, but then declined as the parents' relationship deteriorated. Whilst in many cases there was an acknowledgement of the change in the quality of parenting capacity associated with changes in the household, the extent to which it had an impact and the presence of contingency plans to address these fluctuations in relationships were not always evident.

Plans for siblings

The Anytown study also highlighted the challenge of developing plans for large sibling groups. Often members of a sibling group were considered at the initial child protection conference and all made the subject of child protection plans. Whilst each child appeared to have their own plan, these plans lacked focus on the individual children, with many plans grouping the actions for the children together. For example, 'parents to ensure children attend school regularly'. In one family the reasons varied as to why the different siblings were not attending school but this was not evident in terms of the actions expected of the parents. Moreover, planning should take into account that timescales for children vary and the pace at which the parent is changing may meet the needs of one child but not of another child in the family.

A significant issue for the core group is managing the delivery of child protection plans for a whole sibling group. Not only are these core groups large – for example, three teachers from three different schools may be present – but it is relatively easy for the needs of a particular child to become marginalized. This was most evident if one or two children in the family were exhibiting externalized behaviours that challenged both parents and workers. When this occurred, the needs of the children who were internalizing their responses to neglect, such as being very withdrawn, were marginalized.

Evaluating effectiveness

If the content of the plan is vague, such as 'establish a bedtime routine', then generalized phrases are more likely to be used to describe progress. The following are some of the terms included in reports to the core group and in the minutes of core group meetings in the Anytown study indicating progress:

'No concerns'
'Everything going well'
'Everything at home fine'
'Mother and father cooperating with the Dept'
'Undertaking work around DV'
'Children appear happy and well'
'Drinking at an acceptable level'
'Making progress'
'No issues arising'
'No concerns raised'
'School nurse offered support'
'Behaviour issues'
'Struggling to cope'
'Engaged with services'
'Acceptable home conditions'
'Behavioural problems'
'Mental health issues'

Without any elaborating statements or evidence, it is difficult for members of the core group to appreciate why the professional has reached the conclusions described in these statements. The situation is further exacerbated if these comments are included in reports to the core group in lieu of professionals' attendance. A lack of clarity regarding proposed outcomes can also result in professionals working on the plan using a variety of different thresholds to measure success. As a consequence, parents may be given mixed messages about progress: one professional tells them they are doing well, another that it is not good enough. Moreover, a failure to be specific about expectations, as well as lack of shared indicators of progress, can result in a failure to recognize and acknowledge the efforts made by parents to improve parenting. This, in turn, can leave parents feeling frustrated, angry and disillusioned. In time, this can affect relationships with professionals and result in disengagement, with the parents reverting to old behaviours (Harnett and Day, 2008). Finally, all too often, busy practitioners can become focused on measuring progress by concentrating on parents completing tasks. However, as noted above, parents may complete the tasks required of them: they may 'talk the talk' but with little changing to improve the quality of life for the child.

Measuring effectiveness

If practitioners are to monitor progress effectively, the fundamental question they need to be asking is: 'Has the daily lived experience improved for this child?' Therefore, measures should be child focused, relating to changes that directly or indirectly improve the lived experience of the child, such as those in the example of Freya above. As has already been discussed, change is a process, and therefore incremental indicators of progress should be identified and progress against these measures should be monitored regularly. An effective way of measuring effectiveness is to consider how a day in the life of a child, hour by hour, is changing for each child in the family as the plan progresses. Discussing daily life with the child and parent can be a more effective way of gaining an understanding of whether meaningful change has occurred for the child than just 'seeing' the child or ascertaining their wishes and feelings. Moreover, it can provide an effective vehicle for practitioners and parents to gather and make sense of the information shared at core groups.

Making the decision that insufficient progress has been made and that the plan is not keeping the child safe is always going to be difficult. Making this decision is going to be much harder if:

- the outcomes of the plan with regard to improvements to the health and development of the child are not clear
- different professional perspectives regarding measures to indicate the child is safe from significant harm are not identified and addressed
- the focus of the plan is on actions and task completion rather than child-focused outcomes
- members of the core group do not routinely monitor progress in terms of the impact of the plan on the child's daily lived experience
- the needs of the parent marginalize the needs of the child
- professionals allow parental superficial compliance or surface static to go unchecked

- the plan drifts due to lack of resources, waiting lists or lack of engagement by service providers.

If, however, the plan has clear, detailed child-focused outcomes, indicators that signpost progress is being made towards achieving these outcomes, then professionals have evidence that the plan is or is not being effective.

The review conference

It is not only members of the core group who evaluate progress; progress in the UK is also considered by members of the review conference. The review conference meets at regular intervals whilst the child remains the subject of a plan and has a wider membership than the core group, usually consisting of the same people as attended the initial child protection conference. The tasks for the review are to establish whether the child is continuing to suffer, or is likely to suffer, significant harm, and whether the child is making developmental progress against child protection plan outcomes. Based on these conclusions, the members of the review make a decision as to whether the child continues to be safeguarded from harm through the child protection plan and whether the existing plan should continue or be changed. Each professional in the core group is expected to produce a report for the child protection review. The report should provide an overview of the work undertaken by family members and professionals, and evaluate the impact on the child's welfare against the planned outcomes set out in the child protection plan.

One of the most difficult decisions that members of the core group and review conference have to make is that the child is not being protected from significant harm and that the child is unlikely to be safe with their immediate family even if the child protection plan is altered. Under these circumstances, commencement of care proceedings and out-of-home care have to be considered. This is discussed in detail in Chapter 13.

Managing endings and maintaining change

Arguably, the most challenging stage of the change process is maintaining change (Prochaska and DiClementi, 1982). Anyone who has tried to make significant changes to their behaviour or lifestyle will know that there can be a honeymoon period when the change seems easy to make. This is often followed by a period when the enormity of sustaining these changes becomes apparent, and it is all too easy to lapse back into the original, familiar behaviours and, without support, relapse into these old behaviours. The way in which the child protection system operates in the UK encourages plans to be terminated if there are indicators that the risk of harm has been reduced, but without ensuring that the new behaviours that are keeping the child safe are embedded into family routines. If the plan is terminated too early, without alternative services being provided, then parents who encounter a crisis, a challenging situation or periods of stress are likely to revert to the old, concerning behaviours. This is most common if they do not have the supports available to assist them manage these challenges. Thoburn *et al.* (2009), in their review of the literature, conclude that high-intensity family preservation services are more likely to be effective in preventing long-term family breakdown if they are preceded or followed by other services, such as the lower-intensity targeted services described in Chapter 9. However, these are not always on offer. Ward *et al.* (2012), for example, in a study of infants suffering or at risk of suffering harm, found that despite the parents having a past history of children being placed for adoption and encountering complex problems, their often intensive child protection plans lasted just a few months. This surprised many of the parents who, in some cases, requested that the plans continue in order to have continuing support. The professionals did not think this was necessary as the parents could contact social workers if they had problems in the future, but this did not occur because the parents feared that their babies might be removed if they asked for help once the case was closed. What was of note was that the parents felt that contacting a health visitor was not so threatening. Davies and Ward (2012, p. 82), referring to this study, conclude that 'too little attention is paid to processes by which children and families might be referred back to less intensive services when social work cases are closed'.

Abrupt endings to plans can also result in parents feeling abandoned and can have a negative impact on any future engagement with workers. It is important to bear in mind that, as discussed in Chapter 2, these parents are likely to feel they have been let down by their own parents and will be particularly vulnerable to feelings of loss and bitterness if practitioners suddenly end contact. They may feel they trusted the practitioners and attempted to work with them only to be set aside. One parent commented, at a review conference in the Anytown study, that she felt abandoned now that the child protection plan was complete and the case closed. Another noted that as concerns about the family diminished visits became more spasmodic and she did not know if she could still contact workers when she felt the need.

Conclusion

Bringing about parental change that safeguards and promotes the welfare of children in cases of neglect is a dynamic process that requires commitment and effort from both parents and professionals. If this does not exist, both parents and professionals are in danger of superficial compliance with plans or merely articulating good intentions that do not lead to change. It is inevitable that some parents will not engage with the change process as they do not recognize the need, or are not yet ready, to change and may exhibit fight or flight behaviours to avoid engaging with the plan. In addition, professionals who have inadequate supervision, or work in an organization that is not conducive to working with these cases, may struggle to engage in a meaningful way with the plan.

If family members and professionals are to implement the plan in a manner that keeps the child safe and leads to improved outcomes then the following questions need to be considered, ideally at the first core group meeting:

- Is there a shared understanding of the aims and objectives of the plan and what the outcomes for the child should be?
- Are we sure we have identified and addressed the needs of the different children in the family?
- Have we made serious attempts to ensure that the voice of the child informs our discussions and decisions?
- Have we identified realistic actions that take account of limited resources and service waiting lists?
- Have we distinguished between actions and outcomes?
- Are we clear which aspects of the plan are negotiable and which are non-negotiable?
- Have we set realistic timescales that recognize both the needs of the child and ways in which change takes place?
- Have we agreed how we will monitor progress?
- Do we have a contingency plan if this plan is not effective? For example, what is our response to parents failing to keep appointments? How will we manage changes to household membership?
- Have we considered whether services should be provided and from whom when the plan is terminated?
- Are core group members clear about their roles and responsibilities in delivering the plan?
- Is the size of the core group such that it is a functional and supportive working group?
- Are the relevant professionals from adult services actively engaged in the work of the group?
- Do we share the practical tasks amongst the group so that they do not all fall onto the lead social worker?

Part 3

Intervening: What Works?

Chapter 7

Interventions: When and How?

Thus far in this book I have considered the needs of neglected children and their families and ways in which professionals can assess and plan to meet those needs. In the previous chapters I have paid particular attention to the importance of trying to develop plans that not only improve the daily lived experience of the neglected child but also support parents in making changes to behaviours and attitudes necessary to ensure they meet the needs of their child. The quality of the plan will inevitably depend not only on parents' engagement in the change process but also on the services that are available to families and the way in which these services are delivered. In the third part of the book, therefore, the focus shifts to consider the range of interventions available to assist families where there are concerns about neglect. In this chapter I consider different levels of need and explore the factors that influence receipt of services at the different levels.

Different needs, different interventions

In order to make sense of the diverse range of services that are available to meet the needs of children, Hardiker *et al.* (1996) developed a hierarchical framework categorizing four different levels of children's need and related interventions designed to meet the particular needs. This framework has been used and adapted in a number of nation states, including England, Northern Ireland and various federal states in Australia, to classify the types of interventions available to different groups of children (Hardiker *et al.*, 2002).

Level 1: Universal or population-based services for children with no additional needs

Universal or population-based services are services that all children require in order to maximize their developmental potential. Interventions at this level include education services, from preschool through to further education and training, and health provision, including health visiting, the services of midwives, general practitioners, hospitals and professionals allied to medicine. Services at this level should be available as and when they are required. Children and young people who only require these services are usually making progress in all areas of their development with no additional support.

Level 2: Targeted or early help services for children with additional needs

These services are for children and young people who have been assessed as having additional needs that cannot be met purely by universal provision. That is, there are indications that without the provision of these additional services the child's needs or circumstances may be affected detrimentally. With regard to neglect, these would be children and families where there are signs and indicators that the parents are unlikely to meet the needs of their child without some additional support. Additional support may be provided to prevent neglect occurring, for example targeted antenatal services to ensure vulnerable mothers know how to meet the needs of the baby. Alternatively, the services may be designed to address emerging concerns related to health, social or educational issues. Engagement with services at this level is likely to be on a voluntary basis, with families working in partnership with professionals to address an identified need.

Three different types of services fall into this category: first, services for children in targeted areas, such as those for families in socially and economically deprived communities, for example local early years provision; second, services for children and families with identified needs, such as special educational needs, speech and language delay and support for disabled children; third, services for particular families who require early help to prevent circumstances arising that will lead to a failure to meet the needs of the child. The services may be provided by one agency or a number of agencies, with staff working together to support the family and address the identified needs.

Level 3: Specialist services for children with complex needs

At this level children and young people have additional, complex needs; they may be at risk of harm or their health and development may be impaired without the provision of services. They require targeted and enhanced support to address their needs. In cases of neglect at this level, there is usually evidence that the parents are failing to meet the developmental needs of the child and this failure is affecting the child. The service response is very likely to necessitate a multiagency approach and may include specialist provision. The services are, in the main, provided on a voluntary basis. However, some children and families where there is an identified risk of significant harm and the child is the subject of a child protection plan, as discussed in Chapter 6, may be receiving services on an involuntary basis to ensure family participation. Children who have a substantial and permanent disability or complex and permanent health needs will also have their needs met at this level.

Level 4: Specialist services for children whose needs are complex, prolonged or critical

Children receiving services at this level are at risk of having the poorest outcomes unless their needs are met as a matter of urgency. The needs of these children are often complex and usually result from exposure to significant harm. Cases of chronic neglect, where there is little evidence to date of the parents being motivated or having the ability to meet the needs of the child, fall into this category. Services at this level tend to be costly and resource intensive, such as out-of-home care. This level of intervention also includes the provision for complex health needs, such as residential or nursing care or in-patient psychiatric treatment. The different levels of intervention do not stand alone; rather, they reflect a continuum of different needs of children in any community, as shown in Figure 7.1.

For most children the desired outcome is that they only require universal service provision, yet many children will require interventions at higher

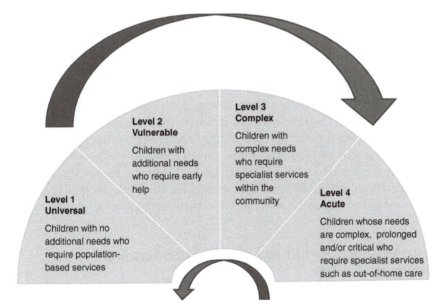

Figure 7.1:   Continuum of children's needs

levels at different times in their lives, depending on the way in which their family is able to meet their needs. This does not mean that they no longer require universal services; rather, they require these population-based services with additional services at the higher levels. What is also of note is that the different categories of need are not static but change depending on the government's approach towards child welfare. Take, for example, free preschool provision in England. The Conservative government in 1996 introduced a scheme allowing parents to use vouchers to partly fund any type of preschool provision for their four-year-old children, thus making part-time preschool provision for four-year-olds a universal service when previously it had been a level 2 service. The Labour government that followed continued to fund part-time places for all four-year-old children and in 2004 they extended this universal entitlement to all three-year-olds. The level of entitlement for both three- and four-year-olds increased under the Coalition government in 2011, with vulnerable two-year-olds able to access places from 2013, thus providing access to preschool provision at level 2 for some children. Governments that believe the family should be supported in meeting the needs of their child by the state are likely to provide a wide range of level 1 and 2 services. In contrast, those governments that believe in minimum state intervention in family life will provide very limited services, and these are likely to be for the most vulnerable in society and therefore only available at level 4 (Fox-Harding, 1997).

The Hardiker framework informs the public health approach to neglect advocated by Daniel *et al.* (2011). They argue that if neglect is to be addressed in a meaningful manner then the cause of the problem and changes to behaviours need to be addressed at a population or universal level: in other words, at level 1. They contend, using the vivid analogy of children in a river to represent the child welfare system, that practitioners tend to be positioned downstream and catch the children who are drowning – levels 3 and 4 – sometimes just watching those who are flailing and struggling – level 2. If the needs of children are to be met effectively and risk of harm prevented then practitioners should be positioned upstream, establishing why children are in the river, and based on this information preventing others from falling in. If children do fall into the river then practitioners should be positioned upstream along the banks so that the children are pulled out of the water to avoid them struggling and drowning.

Intervention: the influence of practitioners and service providers

One would expect, continuing the analogy of 'the river of child neglect' (Daniel *et al.*, 2011, p. 150), that even if the child is pulled out from the river downstream then practitioners would ensure that they do not fall into the river again. This, however, does not appear to be the case (Thoburn *et al.*, 2000; Brandon *et al.*, 2008). Rather, what seems to occur is an erratic and often inconsistent response from practitioners and service providers, which has the effect of children being rescued from the river only to be thrown back in when they are no longer in immediate danger of drowning. In other words, the services are often provided to safeguard the child from immediate danger of drowning but they are not of sufficient duration and breadth to ensure the parents know how to keep the child safe so that they do not fall into the river again. The result is that the child falls into the river again and once again is left to struggle, and it is only when they appear to be drowning again that they are rescued. This process may continue until the situation becomes so severe that the child may actually drown or be removed from the family. Alternatively, the child may find inappropriate ways of surviving in the river. For example, the child's problems bring them to the attention of other agencies, such as youth justice services.

There appear to be a number of reasons why this erratic response to intervening in cases of neglect occurs. These reasons are discussed in detail below.

Is my concern your concern?

As described in Chapter 1, working definitions of neglect are vague, open to interpretation and heavily dependent on the use of professional judgement. It is not surprising, therefore, that perceptions as to when and how to intervene in cases of neglect differ between professionals (Gardner, 2008). Moreover, Daniel, Taylor and Scott (2010) found a narrowing of definition the closer the child comes to professionals, most particularly those delivering child protection services. As a result, neglectful behaviours with potentially serious consequences for a child may be ignored or minimized if a specific professional does not appreciate their significance.

One of the issues, in having a system that is overly dependent on different levels of need and intervention is, in the words of Brandon *et al.* (2008, p. 8), that there is 'not only confusion and misunderstanding of thresholds, but also a preoccupation among agencies with eligibility criteria for services rather than a primary concern about the child or children with whom they were working'.

This preoccupation can have a significant influence on practice as the referrer attempts to access services and the recipient of the referral is concerned about the situation meeting the threshold for service eligibility. Reder and Duncan (2003) argue that both the information imparter and recipient give meaning to the content of an information exchange based on their personal values, beliefs and emotional state. For example, the recipient may think: 'I've received reports from that school before, they're always anxious and it's usually nothing.' In addition, agency context such as policies, workload and inter-agency relationships will also influence the communication, so the recipient may think: 'I've got such a backlog that if I accept this referral I'll never clear my desk and I want to leave on time, I've arranged to meet friends. Besides, it does not sound as if it meets our threshold.' The tone of voice, past relationships, the time of day, day of the week and the status of the referrer will also influence the way information is interpreted and, in turn, the thresholds: 'Typical she waits until 3.30 on a Friday, I know she only wants to have an anxiety-free weekend thinking she's passed her concerns on.' Munro (2002) has also noted that if referrers are concerned about a case they emphasize the worrying features in order to try to ensure the case meets the thresholds criteria, so the referrer may be thinking: 'I'm really worried about this child but I bet she's thinking it's a Friday she's dumping on me, so I'll just spell out my concerns, I won't mention that I think the grandma is around.'

The perceived or actual experiences of meeting thresholds for different levels of intervention, combined with workers' own anxieties about a case, can also influence practitioners' attitudes towards making referrals to other agencies or managing the situation themselves. In a study of professional practice in cases of neglect completed in the Republic of Ireland (Horwath, 2007), I found that anxiety was particularly evident in relation to practitioners' decisions as to whether to refer cases of child neglect to other agencies, particularly statutory children's social work services. The anxieties described by the participants included:

- A fear of looking foolish if concerns are dismissed by social workers or other professionals as insignificant.
- Concerns that families will experience considerable distress during the child protection referral and assessment process with no gain because of lack of services. This led, in some cases, to practitioners failing to report and trying to manage potentially high-risk situations outside the formal child protection system.
- Fear of repeating previous negative experiences of heavy-handed interventions into families or concerns about neglect being ignored. This behaviour results in professionals attempting to find ways of circumnavigating the challenges of negotiating the neglect threshold.
- Lack of feedback from those taking referrals, leaving referrers living with uncertainty and fearful of the response they can expect from carers as a consequence of making a referral.
- Fear of reprisal, including threats and intimidation from carers for making referrals, particularly to statutory child protection agencies. This was most apparent amongst practitioners in routine contact with families, such as teachers.

- Concerns about the way in which the community will perceive the referrer. This was prevalent amongst practitioners who work and live in the same community or run private enterprises.
- Anxiety about hitting the headlines if a child dies and therefore referring all cases to 'cover one's back'.
- Worries that making a referral is not in the best interest of the practitioner. Concerns included fear of complaints, going to court and damaging ongoing relationships with the carers.

These types of anxieties are likely to exist irrespective of statutory duties to report concerns. It appears that practitioners tend to use these concerns and anxieties to justify to themselves, maybe implicitly, reasons for not making referrals to other professionals, particularly statutory child protection services.

Daniel, Taylor and Scott (2010), in their systematic review, identified some key features that influence referral practice to services at levels 3 and 4. Over and above the personal and professional characteristics and experiences described above, they found that characteristics of the child and family, such as perceived maltreatment and the age of children, influenced the likelihood of referral as did legal requirements and absence of system barriers.

Even if the referral is accepted at levels 3 and 4 and an assessment of the needs of the child and risk of harm is completed, the Irish study, referred to above, highlighted significant inconsistencies in practice (Horwath, 2007). For example, the information gathered about the child and family, which in turn informed judgements, was determined by the ease with which social workers could make contact with different professionals. They frequently placed the onus onto professionals to return calls and provide the required information, on occasion not following up when this did not occur. Moreover, in the Irish study, some professionals, such as health visitors, were routinely considered more important points of contact than others, irrespective of the concerns about the child. This can result in distorted decisions made on selective information rather than a holistic assessment of the situation.

Differences in interpretation of concerns amongst professionals occur, not only in relation to identification and assessment but also at the point of intervention, evaluation and case closure, as was evident in the Anytown neglect study (see Box 0.1 and Appendix). Mardani (2010) uses the example of a question commonly asked of practitioners in relation to case closure, 'Is the child safe?' The notion of 'safety' is, however, open to interpretation, with different professionals taking different views – for example, do we mean physical safety, safe today or longer-term safety from harm?

Performance indicators and short-termism

The Labour government of the late 1990s and early 2000s took a new public management approach to managing the public sector in England. This approach led to an emphasis on quantifiable performance measures that provided information regarding service throughput rather than service quality and outcomes for children (Broadhurst *et al.*, 2009; Munro, 2010). As a result, agencies working with child neglect became more concerned with the organizational need to meet targets rather than the needs of the child. This led to a 'quick fix' approach, described in the previous chapters, as key performance indicators focused on the length of time children were subject to multidisciplinary child protection plans. A public management approach has also been used in various states in the USA, Australia and in New Zealand. A worker in New Zealand described the effects: 'We are a train station, not a destination, we have to move them on' (Mardani, 2010 p. 89). Thus, once the immediate presenting problem is resolved, the services are withdrawn with the underlying causes of the problem not being addressed. In other words, practitioners are preventing the child from immediate drowning. However, as the root cause of the problem is never addressed – the reason why the child has fallen into the 'river of child neglect' (Daniel *et al.*, 2011, p. 150) – the family is likely to present again with further problems.

Being overwhelmed or underwhelmed

Farmer and Lutman (2010, p. 1) suggest that 'there is a tendency over time for abuse and neglect to be minimized [by professionals], leaving children vulnerable'. In cases of neglect this means that professionals who have known particular families with deep-seated neglect problems for some time may become desensitized to the problems, so that the impact of the ongoing neglect on the individual children in the family is not recognized. Moreover, some practitioners, as was the case with participants in the Irish study (Horwath, 2007) and the Anytown study, are so weighed down by the complexity of a case that in their opinion small changes warrant case closure; others closed cases because they did not feel they had the necessary expertise to work meaningfully with these families and their multifaceted problems (Cleaver *et al.*, 2004). McSherry (2007) notes that in some cases of neglect perceived negatives, such as poor health and hygiene, are considered by practitioners to be balanced out by the positive aspects of the child's life, such as regular school attendance. When this occurs in highly pressurized systems more weight is likely to be given to the positive aspects and cases are therefore closed.

Professionals may also be underwhelmed by cases of neglect. For example, they may be prepared to accept low standards of care if carers are living in poverty and deprivation, if there are a number of neglectful families within the community or school and low standards of parenting are the norm.

Failing to make sense of the child's lived experience

The importance of making sense of the child's lived experience has been emphasized in the previous three chapters. Practitioners, however, can find it difficult to maintain a focus on the children's lived experiences, particularly if the needs of the parents are significant (Cm 5730, 2003; Platt, 2007; Holland, 2011). When this occurs practitioners may not fully appreciate the real impact on the child of living in a neglectful environment. A failure to focus on the individual experience of the child is likely to result in a standardized response to the situation or a 'one size fits all' response. As discussed in the previous chapters, children in a sibling group who are not obviously affected by the neglect – through, for example, acting-out behaviours – are likely to receive less professional attention than their siblings.

Lack of resources

Lack of resources will inevitably affect intervention pathways. For example, Brandon *et al.* (2008) found that all too often neglectful carers are threatened with children being removed, but then a lack of sufficient evidence for court, or lack of out-of-home resources, means that the child remains at home and the case is allowed to drift.

Whilst one would anticipate that child welfare systems are designed to meet the needs of children who enter that system, what appears to be the case is that the child and their family are in effect participating in a lottery, the particular mix of practitioners and agencies engaged with the child and family determining which neglected child gets what service and when. The result can be that some children and families receive services that are likely to meet their needs, and others will receive inappropriate services, if they receive services at all. Localism, at a time of austerity, is likely to exacerbate this situation.

Evaluating the effectiveness of interventions: determining what works

Having explored the different levels and types of interventions, the next question to consider is, what do we know about interventions that work in cases of neglect? Unfortunately, this question is not easy to answer because any available evidence that links specific issues, interventions and outcomes is very limited and therefore can act as little more than a guide as to what appears to show promise (Tanner and Turney, 2006; Moran, 2010).

Tanner and Turney (2006) have identified a number of limitations that go some way to explaining why it is so difficult to establish the efficacy of interventions designed to address neglect. First, as already considered in Chapter 1, neglect is not easily defined and there are a diverse range of definitions used by both researchers and practitioners. Second, there is very limited literature that focuses purely on neglect; most of the studies refer to both neglect and abuse. This lack of consistency, in terms of scope and definition, means it is problematic comparing the findings from the different studies of interventions. Third, many of the studies have been completed in the USA, with little empirical work in the UK or other nation states on effective working in cases of neglect. In relation to those American studies there are marked variations, not only regarding definition but also sample size and outcome measures and, as noted by Mikton and Butchart (2009), a paucity of randomized control trials or other rigorous research methods. Fourth, Tanner and Turney argue that the theoretical underpinning in much of the literature is not explicit. Thus, it is not clear what conceptual framework is informing the intervention. Fifth, it is not always evident to what extent the studies take account of ethnicity, class and gender. For example, it has already been noted in Chapter 2 that the majority of studies focus on neglectful mothers. Finally, what appears to work in a research setting may not be so successful in the real world of practice. Cross and West (2011) considered why this is the case and conclude that implementation fidelity, which can be broken down into implementer adherence and implementer competence, is the key. They argue that whilst many of the prescribed intervention programmes, such as the Webster-Stratton parenting programme (considered in Chapters 9 and 10), place considerable emphasis on the importance of trained and skilled facilitators following the programme to the letter, in the real world this can be both advantageous and disadvantageous. Adhering to the manual and programme content can be positive, but over-reliance and inflexibility can also reflect practitioners' lack of competence. The competence of practitioners implementing the programme is, according to Cross and West, reflected in their ability to be sensitive to the needs of the participants, their ability to deliver the content of the programme in a timely fashion, and their skill in communicating the content in a meaningful way to the programme participants. This point is developed further by Tyuse *et al.* (2010, p. 201), who argue that even if an intervention has been subjected to rigorous, controlled quantitative research, 'best empirical knowledge is necessary but not in itself sufficient for meaningful clinical intervention'. Practitioners must be able to adapt the intervention to the service user's particular situation.

Davies and Ward (2012) raise questions about the type of research that is completed in this field, arguing that many studies are not as methodologically rigorous as they may first appear to be. They argue that even randomized control trials (RCT), the gold standard for research, may be undermined by small numbers or high attrition rates. Researchers may also use a range of proxy measures rather than direct observation, and the diversity of outcome measures makes comparisons between studies challenging. They also query the justification of randomly assigning children to interventions for RCT, which could have long-term consequences for the child if there is some indication that the intervention may be effective. Taking these factors into account, it is not surprising that MacMillan *et al.* (2009) concluded, from a review of studies that evaluated interventions in cases of neglect, that there was insufficient evidence that neglect-specific programmes reduce the occurrence of neglect.

Barlow *et al.* (2006) offer a more optimistic outlook. They completed a systematic review of existing reviews of interventions to prevent or ameliorate child physical abuse and neglect. Whilst sharing many of the concerns identified by Tanner and Turney (2006), they found that there was evidence of some benefits in terms of improving a range of outcomes associated with maltreatment, including parental and family functioning. They concluded that:

- early interventions aimed at improving parenting practices have the potential to prevent many of the problems associated with abusive and neglectful parenting
- there is also scope for intervening to improve parenting practices amongst carers who have already abused or neglected their children
- in the main, the most effective interventions have multiple components that were adaptable and addressed the different facets of parenting resulting in maltreatment
- effective parent-focused interventions included home-visiting and behavioural parent-training programmes combined with cognitive behavioural therapy to help regulate emotional states
- multisystemic family therapy programmes, family casework and intensive family preservation services could also be potentially helpful.

These findings are supported by a subsequent review of reviews completed by Mikton and Butchart (2009) who specified that home-visiting, parent education, abusive head trauma prevention and multi-component interventions showed promise in terms of preventing maltreatment, including neglect, whilst home-visiting and parent education appeared to be effective in reducing risk factors. They note, however, that the evidence for effectiveness, irrespective of nation state, is weakened by methodological problems and paucity of outcome evaluations from both low- and middle-income countries.

Whilst taking into account the points made above, in researching and writing this book I read many research reports and accounts of practice which, whilst single-case or small-scale qualitative studies, often provide innovative examples of interventions that show some, albeit limited, promise. As these may be of interest to practitioners and managers wishing to develop practice I have included some of these. However, I recognize that they may be of limited validity, reliability and generalizability and I have therefore tried to provide some information about the nature of the studies so that the reader can decide for themselves the relevance of these findings.

Finally, it is worth emphasizing that the effective use of interventions with neglected children and their families depends on a diverse range of factors, such as context, knowledge and skills, funding and timing. When reading the next part of this book, therefore, it is worth having the following in mind:

> Deciding a service should deliver an evidence-based intervention is not like buying a ready-made meal. It is more like learning to cook by following a recipe. It requires systemic and systematic focus on developing the skills needed to ensure that the intervention is delivered as intended. This requires not only training but also on-going supervision focused on skills development and including observation of direct and recorded practice. It would also benefit from substantial investment in research and evaluation. (Forrester and Harwin, 2011, p. 188)

Conclusion

Different levels of need exist amongst children, and each level of need requires a different type of intervention. Thus, services for children where there are early signs that parents are struggling to meet their needs will be different from services for children who have experienced years of chronic neglect. The services available to these children and the ways in which they are delivered will depend on the approach taken by practitioners and their agencies to working with cases of child neglect. Theoretically, as the needs of the child fail to be met by level 1 (universal) and level 2 (early help) services, the child and their family should be able to access services at the higher levels, 3 and 4, until the needs of the child and family are met. This incremental approach towards meeting the needs of the neglected child does not appear to occur in practice routinely; rather, children seem to receive a more erratic response from service providers. This is, in part, attributable to: different interpretations of thresholds of need for the various levels of intervention; short-termism and a 'quick-fix' approach; practitioners being overwhelmed or underwhelmed by cases of neglect; ignoring the child's daily lived experience; and a lack of resources.

In terms of what interventions are effective, there is a lack of evidence that links specific issues, interventions and outcomes. Therefore, the evidence available should be used as a guide, which provides some steer as to interventions that appear to show promise in relation to addressing particular needs arising from neglect.

Chapter 8

Preventing Neglect: Population-based Services Pre-birth and in the Early Years

In the previous chapter I made reference to 'the river of child neglect' (Daniel *et al.*, 2011, p. 150) and to the importance of finding ways of preventing children falling into this river. Universal or population-based services should be designed in such a way that they not only prevent children falling into the river but keep them safe on the bank. These services are important because they are accessible to all and, therefore, use of these services should be non-stigmatizing for families (Davies and Ward, 2012). Yet whilst being of particular value to children at potential risk of being neglected, accessing these services can be challenging for their parents. In this chapter I consider the reasons why parents at risk of neglecting their children may struggle to make use of universal or population-based services and identify ways in which service providers can improve parental engagement. The focus will be on the take-up of services for parents-to-be and new parents, as universal services, particularly in the early years of a child's life, are important in terms of laying the foundations for a happy childhood, adult psychological and social wellbeing, educational achievement and an ability to make a positive contribution to society (Field, 2010; Allen, 2011; Munro, 2011a).

Throughout this chapter I use the term 'vulnerable parent' to describe parents who could potentially neglect their young child for the reasons outlined in Chapter 2.

Preparing parents-to-be: neglectful parents slipping through the net?

Most prospective parents have opportunities to learn about parenting before they actually become a parent. These include learning from one's own parents and other role models. Parents who are vulnerable to neglecting their children, however, may well have had poor role models, as discussed in Chapter 2. Field (2010), in his review into poverty and its causes in England, expressed particular concerns about poor parenting in deprived areas, the areas where neglect is most common, and argues that this could be addressed by the introduction of a qualification in parenting and life-skills. Advocating for such a qualification does, however, appear to be an overly simplistic solution. It ignores the point that learning only takes place if the individual is open to that learning (Kolb, 1988), and young people may not consider learning about parenting to be of immediate relevance to them. Moreover, the very young people who may benefit from learning about parenting are likely to be the ones who do not attend school sufficiently regularly or, indeed, do not remain at school long enough to obtain qualifications.

Interventions, such as the Canadian *Roots to Empathy* programme, have, however, been found to be effective with vulnerable young people. Young school-age children are taught how to parent infants by interacting with a parent and baby who regularly visits the classroom for a nine-month period. Through this experience they witness quality parenting and have a positive role model, which in turn informs their attitude towards parenting and skill development despite poor role models at home. This programme has also been found to foster empathy and reduce bullying in schools (Hosking and Walsh, 2010).

The time at which most prospective parents are likely to be open to learning about parenting is when it is of direct relevance to them, that is, when they actually become parents-to-be. In a recent systematic review of the research evidence on antenatal education, Schrader McMillan *et al.* (2009) found that antenatal education is associated with higher levels of satisfaction with the birth experience. There is also some evidence that it is of benefit in terms of health promotion behaviours, such as smoking and alcohol cessation, nutrition and exercise. Furthermore, group-based programmes that explore the transition to parenthood can be of benefit in terms of maternal psychological wellbeing, parental confidence, parent–infant relationship and the relationship between the couple. It also provides parents with the opportunity to meet and make friends with other parents-to-be.

Whilst many parents may be motivated to access antenatal classes, parents who are particularly vulnerable to neglectful behaviours may not be so motivated. For example, Siraj-Blatford and Siraj-Blatford (2009) and Nolan (1995) found mothers-to-be with high-risk factors associated with neglect, such as previous infant mortality, low birth-weight babies, smoking during pregnancy, being teenage mothers and suffering postnatal depression, have a low uptake of both ante- and postnatal services. If this is the case, can antenatal education be of value in preventing neglect amongst vulnerable groups?

Schrader McMillan *et al.* (2009) note that it is important that any antenatal package should take into account the developmental stage of the young mother, their coping strategies and any exposure to stressful situations.

With this in mind, they conclude that there is some value in providing multifaceted support and education to vulnerable, adolescent mothers, recognizing that they are unlikely to attend routine antenatal classes as they fear stigmatization. Packages that are designed specifically for this group, that are participative and continue into early parenthood, have been found to improve breastfeeding, health and maternal mental health, and child outcomes. They argue, based on their review, that integrated programmes that draw on a range of sources such as home-visiting, peer group provision and group learning can also be effective. NICE (National Institute for Health and Excellence, 2010) have recognized that the needs of teenage mothers differ from those of older women and recommend a flexible model of antenatal care provided in a variety of settings. They also recommend peer-based group work that is offered at the same time and same location as antenatal appointments. A successful example of this approach is the early notification of pregnancy system operating in Lancashire, England. Focusing on those parents-to-be who are identified as vulnerable in early pregnancy, support is offered through pregnancy using professionals working in local children's centres. The parents have reported feeling more supported and are more likely to carry on using the children's centres once their children are born (C4EO, 2010a).

Group-based social support during the antenatal and postnatal period can be effective in supporting women with mild symptoms of depression and anxiety, (Schrader McMillan et al., 2009). This is a group of mothers who, as discussed in Chapters 2 and 11, can be particularly vulnerable to neglect. Myors et al. (2011), in a review of effective services for this group, found that improved outcomes for both mother and child are likely if there is a collaborative approach towards care and support for the mother and child. This approach is necessary for timely treatment and the promotion of a positive maternal–infant bond in the perinatal period.

Another group who find it challenging accessing antenatal classes are parents from minority ethnic groups; the challenge is even greater if they are also vulnerable parents. These parents-to-be value culturally sensitive antenatal education and classes that address the potential differences between their own cultural mores and the routine messages usually provided in antenatal classes. This group have also been found to be more likely to attend relevant classes in their local community than in hospital-based settings (Schrader McMillan, et al., 2009; National Institute for Health and Clinical Excellence, 2010).

The perinatal period is an opportunity to engage young fathers in positive parenting. Yet Page et al. (2008) found that health professionals focus on mothers and marginalize fathers during this period. The consequence can be that vulnerable fathers get a message very early on that they are not central to child rearing. One way of ensuring that fathers appreciate their role and responsibilities and develop the appropriate skills is to engage them at the antenatal stage. Schrader McMillan *et al.* (2009) found that fathers benefit from engagement in men-only sessions within standard antenatal classes and teenage fathers gain from preparation-for-fatherhood groups. The needs of teenage fathers are similar to those of teenage mothers: they welcome opportunities to learn from experienced fathers and to focus on their own needs and experiences. Fletcher *et al.* (2008) found new fathers are drawn to information that links their role to active interaction with their infant. However, the focus of their study was on fathers from higher socio-economic groups.

Use of doulas

Schrader McMillan *et al.* (2009) found that doulas can be useful in supporting new vulnerable mothers. (Doulas are experienced women who offer emotional and practical support to a woman or couple before, during and after childbirth. For further information see Doula UK: http://doula.org.uk/content/what-doula) In the Netherlands this approach is a routine aspect of maternity care. The service, known as *kraamzorg*, provides a professional maternity nurse who looks after a mother and her newborn baby for eight to ten days after birth. The role of the nurse is to show parents how to care for the infant, such as bathing and changing nappies, and to support the establishment of a breastfeeding regime. Higher levels of support are offered to mothers with challenging home circumstances or those struggling with breastfeeding.

Creating firm foundations for a child's development

Once vulnerable parents have had their baby they need to learn how to care for the infant in a manner that ensures the needs of the child are met. Poor early care and lack of bonding with the baby are risk factors associated with a failure to meet the needs of a child (Siraj-Blatford and Siraj-Blatford, 2009), as discussed in Chapters 2 and 3. Thus, the quality of attunement between a mother and her baby during the first 18 months is crucially important (Hosking and Walsh, 2010). A key parenting task, therefore, during this period is for the primary carer, usually the mother, to bond with the baby and become attuned to identifying and responding to the baby's needs in order to create the conditions necessary for a secure attachment by the baby to the carer.

Breastfeeding is one of the most effective ways, but not the only one, to promote bonding between mother and child. The World Health

Organization (WHO) recommends that babies should be breastfed exclusively for the first six months, as breast milk contains all the nutrients for healthy development as well as antibodies to protect babies from childhood illnesses (C4EO, 2010a). Furthermore, a longitudinal, large-scale study of mother–child pairs found in children born at term that breastfeeding for four months or longer is associated with fewer parent-rated behavioural problems in children at five years of age. It is not clear from the research whether the finding is linked to the essential nutrients in breast milk or the attachment and early psychosocial nurturing resulting from the physical bond associated with breastfeeding (Heikkilä *et al.*, 2011). Unfortunately, breastfeeding is less likely in groups most vulnerable to neglect, such as mothers from the lower socio-economic groups and young single mothers, than other groups. For example, in a survey of breastfeeding in England only 32 per cent of women in routine or manual socio-economic groups breastfed beyond six weeks, with only a fifth of all mothers breastfeeding at the recommended six months (Boiling *et al.*, 2005). Some of these mothers may well try breastfeeding but are more likely than mothers from higher socio-economic groups to give up easily, resorting to bottle feeding (Hamlyn *et al.*, 2002).

Breastfeeding should be initiated as soon as possible after delivery, with sustained and ongoing support from health-care professionals or peers being of greatest benefit, but this level of support is often not available and parents are often just provided with written materials to promote breastfeeding, which on their own are not effective (Schrader McMillan *et al.*, 2009). In Denmark, one of the benefits of early postnatal support for breastfeeding is that parents are taught how to get to know the baby's cues and this in turn improves interactions with the baby (Hosking and Walsh, 2010). Yet in England, for example, there is a shortage of midwives, overcrowded maternity units, and only 10 per cent of hospitals reaching the standards developed by UNICEF and the WHO, such as establishing breastfeeding within half an hour of delivery (Boiling *et al.*, 2005). Without this level of support mothers, particularly vulnerable mothers, may fail to breastfeed and also have problems becoming attuned to their baby's cues.

A study completed in Northern Ireland emphasized the importance of recognizing societal and cultural approaches to breastfeeding (DHSSPS, 2004). The researchers found that many young people did not know about the benefits of breastfeeding. Many of the young mothers were unable to access information and sources of support, and whilst they received visits from community midwives they did not have the confidence to raise issues regarding breastfeeding. Exploring reasons why young women from low-income groups are least likely to breastfeed, Shaw *et al.* (2003) found that these mothers fear pain and are under the misconception that their babies will not gain sufficient weight from breastfeeding alone. In addition, they do not have positive role models as members of their family and their peer group are likely to bottle feed. Moreover, they are rarely exposed to a breastfeeding culture. For example, how many characters on UK soaps, which are watched my millions, breastfeed? Bottle feeding is the norm. Condon and Ingram (2011) found in their English study that there was a latent hostility in local poor communities towards breastfeeding. They argue that children's centres, which are described in detail below, have a part to play in supporting breastfeeding but found that the staff often lacked knowledge and skill to support breastfeeding.

Preventing shaken baby syndrome

Parents who do not have the parenting skills or motivation to manage the demands of a baby are not only more vulnerable to neglecting their child but also more likely to express their frustration by shaking the baby (C4EO, 2010b). Shaken baby syndrome or abusive head trauma can have serious consequences for infants, such as seizures, cognitive and physical disabilities, visual and hearing impairment and, at worst, death. A Scottish study indicates that shaken baby syndrome occurs with an annual incidence of 24.6 per 100,000 children under one year (Barlow *et al.*, 1998), whist the statistics for the UK indicate that at least 200 babies a year suffer non-accidental head injuries. Males, mostly from low socio-economic groups and often with a history of violence, are the most frequent perpetrators. It is therefore important that vulnerable parents who are at most risk of shaking their baby are made aware of the consequences in ways that they can engage with.

Many USA states have laws mandating education to new parents concerning the dangers of shaking their baby. The education programmes that appear to be most successful include bedside teaching of new mothers using different forms of media, such as videos and leaflets, describing not only the dangers of shaking but also strategies for coping with crying and inconsolable infants, emphasizing the normalcy of infant crying and, interestingly, a signed commitment by parents pledging not to shake their babies (Dias *et al.*, 2005). A variation of this programme is being piloted by the National Society for the Prevention of Cruelty to Children (NSPCC) in hospitals in the UK. When a mother's partner, if she has one, collects her and the baby they are invited to watch a short video by the midwife. The video focuses on the joys and stresses of a new baby and enforces the message to put the baby down in a safe and comfortable place and leave the room for a few minutes if the parent feels like shaking or hitting the infant (Boseley, 2012).

Staffordshire Children's Trust, in a project called 'Stop that Shake – Babies Break', developed resources for teaching secondary school-age children about the dangers of shaking a baby. Whilst they found that the teaching was effective, girls were far more likely to attend the classes than boys (C4EO, 2010b).

Population-based interventions to support vulnerable parents in the early years

The quality of parenting is in part influenced by the way in which information about child rearing is communicated to carers, both from professionals such as midwives and health visitors and also from family and friends. Vulnerable parents need opportunities to access information in ways that are comfortable to them, to have the information in formats that make sense to them and be supported to apply the knowledge to practice. In this section I consider how community approaches, new communication technologies, health visiting and family centres can assist in enabling vulnerable parents not only to access but also to make sense of and apply information about quality child rearing to practice.

A healthy community

Hosking and Walsh (2010) advocate a universal approach towards positive parenting that is designed to build a functional, healthy community. Parents raising children in this setting are aware of what is expected of them and feel supported as parents. It can be particularly useful for vulnerable parents as a key aim of this approach is to reduce social isolation. Social isolation, as noted in Chapter 2, can be associated with neglect. A positive example of this is the New Zealand government's *SKIP (Strategies with Kids, Information for Parents)* initiative. The aim of the programme is to to achieve a national cultural shift in parenting and ensure that good enough parenting takes centre stage within a community. It draws on the philosophy that it takes a whole village to raise a child. *SKIP* builds on the successful Swedish social model as well as knowledge about infant brain development and the importance of the early years. The emphasis is on encouraging parents and caregivers to bring up children with confidence and with the knowledge to manage their child's behaviour in a positive way without physical punishment. In addition, the child should experience a loving, nurturing relationship with the parent that provides the six things a child needs: love and warmth; talking and listening; guidance and understanding; limits and boundaries; consistency and consequences; and a structured and secure world. The messages are conveyed through highly visible materials, group activities and family days. *SKIP* is non-judgemental in approach, emphasizing what parents and children should do. Professionals, who take a partnership approach, put parents in contact with other agencies as appropriate. The *Healthy Child Programme* (in England) contains many of the elements described above. Health professionals and early years practitioners offer advice to expectant mothers and continue to provide each family with a programme of screening tests, immunizations, developmental reviews, and information and guidance to support parenting and child development (Allen, 2011; Easton and Gee, 2012). Hosking and Walsh (2010) note that whilst no quantitative reviews have been completed to demonstrate change using these types of initiatives, all those involved are enthusiastic, and feel it is successful in changing the culture and promoting positive parenting. The success is believed to be linked to the positive, universal and non-judgemental approach, a clear vision and genuine partnership with the community.

Use of different communication technologies to assist vulnerable parents learning about good enough parenting

As the use of the internet and smart phones increases so does consideration of them as a means of supporting vulnerable parents, by providing them with information regarding ways in which they can meet the needs of their child. When establishing such services Fletcher *et al.* (2008) conclude that tailoring general health promotion messages, such as caring for an infant, for particular demographic, psychosocial and behavioural characteristics is more effective than providing general information. It is more likely to be read, remembered, considered interesting and relevant, as well as being more often discussed with others.

Barlow and Calam (2011) drew on findings from a systematic review to consider what technologies can be used effectively to disseminate messages about quality parenting and the needs of the child to families who either do not normally access services or avoid them. Barlow and Calam (2011) found that self-directed, web-based or televised parenting interventions, such as storylines built into popular serials, were acceptable and often preferred by some parents. A good example of this is the *Driving Mum and Dad Mad* TV series aired in 2008 in the UK that was based on the first level of the *Triple P – Positive Parenting Programme* described in Chapter 9 (Sanders *et al.*, 2008). In a second series that was evaluated, Calam *et al.* (2008) found that it engaged parents who had not taken up parenting interventions before and was particularly popular with parents who used coercive parenting styles, demonstrated anger and were perceived to be dysfunctional. However, Barlow and Calam note that there is a significant drop-out before programme completion of many of these approaches.

An approach which would appear to have significant potential as a method for supporting vulnerable parents and identifying emerging concerns is the use of mobile phones. Lefever *et al.* (2008) used mobile phones in a research study to gather information about child neglect. They compared the information obtained through the use of these phones as opposed to using a landline, and mobile phones were found to be a very successful way of gathering both quantitative and qualitative information about parenting. Drawing on their experience, they believe the use of mobile phones has potential benefits as an intervention method targeted at hard-to-reach and vulnerable groups, such as teenage mothers. As part of their study they contacted mothers three times over three weeks at different times to gain a snapshot of parenting practices. They found that the mothers provided detailed information about parenting practices and responded well to open-ended questions, enabling the researchers to gain insights into the rationale behind particular parenting practices, parent–child interactions and issues. For example, one mother reported a particularly easy day with her baby, as the baby had slept all day, did not eat and had not had a wet nappy. This enabled the researcher to recognize that this baby was actually suffering from dehydration. The mobile phone is a method of communication that mothers are familiar with using; as it is portable the practitioner can make contact wherever the mother is. The mothers themselves did not find the use of phones in this way to be intrusive. Based on their experience, the researchers believe that using mobile phones is a cost-effective means of enhancing home-visiting programmes, whether at the universal level or for the early interventions described in the next chapter.

Health visiting

Health visitors have a crucial role to play in supporting new vulnerable parents and identifying signs that the parents or carers are failing to meet the needs of the child, particularly with regard to the parent not being attuned to the needs of the child. A systematic review of the international literature on health visiting, which included some British studies, completed by Elkan *et al.* (2000), found that health visiting was associated with improvements in: breastfeeding; parenting skills; the quality of the home environment and social support; some child behavioural problems, including sleeping behaviour; and intellectual development, especially amongst children with a low birth weight or failure to thrive. It was also found to be associated with a reduction in the frequency of unintentional injury and home hazards and better detection of postnatal depression. It is of note, however, that there was no evidence that home-visiting was effective in: improving children's motor development; increasing the take-up of immunizations; increasing the uptake of other preventive child health services; or reducing the use of both emergency medical services and hospital admission rates.

A recent Welsh survey of health visiting services provided to families identified as having potentially high needs, such as young parents and parents in workless households, found that these parents in the main welcomed the support from health visitors, and whilst the support provided was more than that received by parents with lower needs, the parents would have welcomed greater support. What was of note was that the parents facing multiple socio-economic disadvantages were less likely to say they wanted more support despite having fewer contacts with health visitors than average and greater support needs. The parents who had not found the support helpful cited the following reasons:

- the health visiting services had not been responsive to their needs
- they had experienced difficulty relating to or accessing their health visitor
- the health visitor had not been helpful
- lack of continuity of care
- inadequate staffing
- poor communication
- lack of information
- clinic opening hours had been inconvenient. (Ipsos MORI, 2011)

These findings really highlight the importance of the health visitor having the time and opportunity to establish a meaningful relationship with the parents that focuses on identifying and meeting their specific needs.

There has been much debate about the usefulness and timing of health visitors' face-to-face contact with families. Currently the focus is on the first few weeks, with ongoing regular contact, other than routine checks at the clinic, normally being offered to families where there are concerns about the quality of parenting or the child's particular needs. Wright *et al.* (2009) question the timing of routine checks and visits, arguing that problems may not become apparent in the first year. This finding was supported by Wilson *et al.* (2011), who conclude from their study of 549 families that a routine visit by health visitors when the child is 13 months is particularly useful in identifying the families who initially appear to be managing but begin to struggle as the child becomes more demanding. In this study the health visitors were asked to observe parent–child interactions, assess the psychological wellbeing of the primary carer and identify emerging parenting difficulties. They found the health visitors identified families in need of support who, without this visit, would have slipped through the service provision net.

Early years provision: children's centres

Additional universal services designed to support parents bringing up their young children are early years services such as nurseries and children's centres. Whilst this type of provision can have significant benefits for young children, parents who are vulnerable to neglecting their children may not seek out and use these services. In a recent study, Ben-Galim (2011) asked parents from low-income backgrounds why they rarely accessed nursery places beyond those available free for three- and four-year-olds. Whilst affordability was a key issue, she also found that most parents felt strongly that children less than two should be with their families, not in professional childcare facilities. If the child was left, in the main they preferred to leave them with family members rather than professionals or childminders. The parents used childcare primarily to support their child's social and educational development, including preparing them for school, and judged effective provision in terms of the child's happiness. When accessing childcare, location was a prime consideration, with the majority of parents wanting facilities that were close to their home, preferably in walking distance. Thus, when working with parents, encouraging them to access these services, it is important to establish their attitudes towards early years services.

One of the issues often encountered by staff in children's centres is associated with engaging families from minority ethnic groups; accessing these services can be particularly challenging if these parents are also vulnerable and struggling to meet the needs of their child. A small-scale study undertaken in Devon by Johnson (2010) highlighted some of the barriers that both staff and families from minority ethnic groups experience as barriers to accessing children centre services. These findings are commensurate with those of an early study of family centre use by black families (Butt and Box, 1998). These included:

- lack of awareness of the services available because, for example, such services do not exist within the country of origin
- social and cultural issues, such as being concerned that they will not fit in because of cultural or religious differences
- isolation, as few families from minority ethnic groups live in the area and they will therefore feel isolated within the centre
- language – fear of being the only non-English speaker
- location – services not well advertised and some distance away
- institutional – fear of the way staff in the centre will respond; concerns that the service is provided by figures in authority
- services not appropriate or useful, taking into account cultural needs.

Johnson concludes that a more proactive approach is required on the part of centre staff and other professionals in contact with these families to support them in engaging with the services on offer.

Initiatives such as *Sure Start* in England, *Head Start* in the USA and *Flying Start* in Wales were set up to take a more proactive approach with vulnerable families and reduce poverty and social exclusion. They seek to offer a range of services including early education, child- and health-care and family support. The services are designed to meet local need and can include home-visiting and outreach work; play, learning and childcare facilities; and health services, as described above. They have been developed to enhance the life chances of *all* young children and families in areas of high deprivation and therefore seek to reduce the stigmatization often associated with services targeted at specific groups such as those vulnerable to neglecting their children.

A national evaluation of *Sure Start* was completed covering more than 9,000 families who received these services, and comparisons were made with children and families from similarly disadvantaged areas who had not received these services (Belsky and Melhuish, 2008). The evaluation highlights the advantages of providing integrated, organized and effective locally based services. The findings from the evaluation are positive and relate to the whole resident population, not different subgroups. Some of the benefits included parents showing less negative parenting and providing a better home learning environment. The families also used more child- and family-related services. With regard to the children, according to the parents, the three-year-olds in the area had better social development, with higher levels of positive social behaviour and independence/self-regulation. The evaluators also noted the importance of recognizing the particular needs of families from minority ethnic groups, which were similar to those described above in relation to children's centres.

Reynolds *et al.* (2010), in their systematic review of interventions to prevent child maltreatment, concluded that the American child–parent centres, such as *Head Start*, showed strong evidence of long-term maltreatment prevention. They believe that the combination of provision of family services together with child educational enrichment is likely to prevent later maltreatment.

Despite the benefits of these services for children at risk of neglect, Coe *et al.* (2008) found that families experiencing social isolation and other pressures may have difficulty proactively accessing these centres. In their English study of *Sure Start* they found that some parents did not understand what services were on offer, or had misconceptions about these services and did not think they would benefit their particular family. Coe *et al.* argue that in order to engage with 'hard-to-reach' families it is important to provide them with information that really demonstrates the advantages of engagement for their family. Moreover, they believe it is important to contact and engage with parents early, before misconceptions can arise.

Addressing the socio-economic factors that affect good enough parenting

As has been discussed in earlier chapters, one of the factors that may contribute to neglectful parenting is social isolation. Childcare centres can go a long way towards reducing this isolation. However, Ipsos MORI (2011), in their evaluation of *Flying Start* in Wales, found that parents who lack adequate support networks felt they received insufficient support from their children's centre and local parenting services. Small (2009, cited by Fisher and Gruescu, 2011) completed a study of ways in which vulnerable mothers in New York use childcare centres. He concluded that participation by mothers can assist the formation of friendship networks and reduced isolation, which in turn appeared to reduce material and mental hardship. He found the childcare centres that were able to offer the appropriate support:

- created conditions for carers to interact and form connections 'by chance', through normal activity – for example, encouraging parents to stay and chat when collecting and dropping off children
- actively organized for carers to look after each other through, for example, buddying new and older parents
- gave parents or carers responsibilities, such as fund raising and organizing trips, which provided them with a legitimate reason for engaging with other service users
- connected users to external resources, such as health services and financial advice.

As identified above, vulnerable, minority ethnic families may find it particularly challenging to access community resources, such as children's centres, for support. This can in turn lead to social isolation. Barn *et al.* (2006) identified some factors that workers may find useful when providing support for parenting to reduce social isolation and improve take-up of population-based and community services. These include:

- Recognizing that minority ethnic family life is complex, and consideration should be given to the impact of migration, ethnicity, socio-economic factors, language, multiculturalism and racism.
- Appreciating that the nature of contact may be perceived differently amongst various ethnic groups. For example, amongst the participants in the study by Barn *et al.*, black minority ethnic families reported more contact with extended families than white families but less contact with friends. What was also noted, however, was that migration may have resulted in the fragmentation of those wider family networks and an increased sense of isolation.
- Being aware of subjects that were considered appropriate for exploration outside the family. For example, some groups were prepared to discuss housing problems but less likely to discuss children's behavioural problems outside the family.

- Understanding minority group parents have additional parenting tasks, such as promoting positive messages to their children about difference, diversity and a sense of belonging. Therefore, resources to support this may be important.

Living in poverty

Stokes and Schmidt (2011) note that in Canada, the USA and the UK children who are living in poverty are over-represented in the child protection system and, as indicated in Chapter 2, children living in poverty are particularly vulnerable to neglect. It is not the poverty as such; rather, it is poor housing conditions, fewer community resources, and parenting stress, such as spiralling debt, that affect a parent's ability to meet the needs of their child and make parenting so much more challenging, leading in some cases, but by no means all, to neglect (Moraes *et al.*, 2005; Jonson-Reid *et al.*, 2009). Whilst not always leading to child maltreatment, poverty (as discussed in Chapter 2) is associated with reduced life chances.

As many developed countries enter a period of austerity, there is likely to be an increase in the number of families living in poverty and therefore the number of parents experiencing the stresses of meeting the needs of children with a very limited income. Barnardo's (2009), in a study of families in poverty in the UK, found that parents recognized that work was the most effective route out of poverty. The problem is that whilst governments, such as those in the USA and UK, have introduced several policies to 'make work pay', the level of earnings for these parents means they are still in poverty. Barnardo's notes, for example, that more than half of children in poverty have a parent in paid work. Moreover, 32 per cent of children in lone parent households, where the parent is working either full-time or part-time, are still living in poverty. The Joseph Rowntree Foundation (2010b) argue that the challenges that need to be addressed by governments to reduce poverty are: in-work poverty, the number of young adults with few or no qualifications, young adult unemployment, health inequalities, low-income households and lack of access to essential services.

Field (2010, p. 6), in his report on preventing poor children becoming poor adults, argues that extensive public spending as the sole means for tackling poverty is inadequate because income is not necessarily the exclusive reason for generations remaining in poverty. He emphasizes the importance of a shift in focus 'towards providing high quality integrated services aimed at supporting parents and improving the abilities of the poorest children during the period when it is most effective to do so', that is, the early years. This approach has been piloted in Wales through a scheme called the *Families First Pioneers*, which seeks to support families and children living in poverty. The programmes are designed to provide a 'team around the family' by offering an integrated range of services to prevent issues associated with poverty from escalating. Services provided include welfare rights advice; community conferencing, which brings families and communities together to identify and address social issues; *Flying Start*, the Welsh equivalent of *Sure Start*; and the development of family information services that enable families to access support regarding parenting, childcare, education and training. Early indicators are that this approach shows promise (Mason, 2011).

There is one group where the impact of poverty can be particularly severe and make children particularly vulnerable to neglect – that is, families with a disabled child. Parents of these children have a significant number of additional costs, such as heating, increased laundry costs, travel, specific dietary requirements, and so on. The Children's Society (2011) estimates that around 320,000 of the 800,000 disabled children in the UK are living in poverty. When there is a disabled adult in the house the level of poverty encountered is even higher, with 155,000 of the 320,000 disabled children identified above living with a disabled adult. The Children's Society concludes that there are two reasons for families that include children with disabilities being more likely to live in poverty than other families. First, the additional childcare requirements of a disabled child mean that families are less flexible about work location and hours. Second, earnings are likely to be low because of the ability of parents to invest in training alongside the demands of caring for a disabled child, and also the carers may be less able to take on full-time work. Bearing in mind the stresses of meeting the needs of a disabled child, together with managing on a low income, it is not surprising that some disabled children are vulnerable to neglect (Sullivan and Knutson, 2000).

Conclusion

Effective preventative services:

> are usually forged from a combination of good science and good art, where science refers to a systematic rigorous procedure for producing outcomes and evaluating them, and art is defined as the thoughtful and sensitive use of knowledge and skills in real-world contexts. (Sanson *et al.*, 2011, p. 86)

The quote above highlights the essential ingredients for an effective population-based approach. In this chapter consideration has been given to population-based services which can be useful in preventing the circumstances arising that lead to neglect, particularly amongst vulnerable groups of parents. Whilst these services are universally available to all, what is evident is that parents vulnerable to neglecting their children are less likely than other parents to access these services of their own volition. If these families are to benefit from population-based services, a number of factors need to be taken into account by both service providers and practitioners to encourage parents engage with and make use of these services:

- Many of these parents have low levels of self-esteem and confidence, and expecting them to approach a service without any support is not realistic.
- The parents fear stigmatization from staff and other parents because they are, for example, young mothers, living in poverty, from a minority ethnic group, and therefore need services that do not isolate or further stigmatize them.
- Many of the services on offer use methods for working with parents that do not meet the needs of these parents. This is evident in antenatal classes. Service providers should therefore look towards more innovative approaches, such as making use of communication technology, that are considered more relevant and engaging.
- Social isolation is a common issue for parents vulnerable to neglecting their children. Services that attempt to address this by, for example, providing a local resource in a non-stigmatizing setting that is within 'buggy-pushing' distance of the family home appear to be effective.
- There are few universal services available that specifically target fathers (discussed in more detail in Chapter 9). If men are to be actively involved in caring for their children and share caring responsibilities then services should be available for both fathers-to-be and fathers of young children that are attractive to fathers and encourage quality parenting.
- The lives of many of these parents are already very complex, with parenting issues, poverty and poor housing adding to the stresses associated with parenting. An integrated approach that recognizes these stresses and provides population-based services that aim to reduce the impact of negative socio-economic factors on parenting could be particularly beneficial.

Chapter 9

Addressing Emerging Concerns about Neglect in Under-Fives through Early Help

One great merit of Early Intervention is that it can help so many families under stress fulfil their mission of giving children a secure and loving space in which to grow up. It can keep families together and save many children from the trauma of break-up and removal. When all is said and done, enabling every child to develop social and emotional capability is nothing less than what most parents routinely do for their own children. (Allen, 2011)

Introduction

As Allen (2011) makes explicit in the quote above, identifying and addressing concerns about poor parenting early in the life of the problem or when children are young can have considerable long-term benefits for the child and family. In addition, it is more cost effective for governments than spending money on the more intensive services necessary if the concerns become more serious (Moran, 2010; Easton and Gee, 2012). In terms of the 'river of child neglect' analogy (Daniel *et al.*, 2011, p. 150), this means identifying the children who have fallen in the river and can be helped out whilst still in shallow waters. The services offered to address emerging concerns are those described in Chapter 7 as level 2 services for children with needs over and above those that can be met through universal services and who require additional family support or early help.

There are key features that practitioners should take into account when identifying appropriate services at this level. First, interventions are likely to be effective if practitioners not only focus on areas of concern but also identify and enhance protective factors, sources of strength and family resilience. Second, early intervention does not necessarily equate to early years, and these services should be considered whenever there are emerging concerns during childhood and adolescence about parents or carers failing to meet the needs of the child. Third, the services themselves can be delivered as part of a package in combination with universal services.

Moreover, they should not be discounted if the child and their family have more complex needs and are receiving level 3 and 4 services: emerging concerns about a parental failure to meet a particular developmental need of the child may occur at any point in the child's journey through the child protection system.

In this chapter consideration will be given to early help interventions designed to address emerging concerns about neglect in preschool-age children. In Chapter 12 I focus more specifically on early help services for older children and young people. Whilst concerns regarding possible neglect may begin to appear later in childhood, addressing emerging concerns in early life is essential as the first few years are crucial in terms of positive brain and emotional development (Perry, 2002). Allen (2011) argues that families with multiple needs who have experienced intergenerational issues regarding inadequate parenting are those who most need early help before the child is three years of age – in other words, the potentially neglectful families that are showing signs of struggling to meet the needs of their child.

Scott (2010) subdivides early intervention provision into:

- home-visiting services, which, as the name suggests, refers to support provided in the family home
- centre-supported services that usually involve the family attending a programme or receiving a service primarily within an agency setting
- two-generation services that provide a combination of support and provision for both the child and the parent.

The three different types of service are considered below.

Home-visiting services

Home-visiting, as the name suggests, typically involves a trained professional or volunteer working with a vulnerable family within their home. The family is usually offered parenting advice, advice about child health and development and general support. Asawa *et al.* (2008) believe that home-visiting programmes eliminate the barriers to accessing services, such as lack of transport, by bringing the services to the home. Moreover, observing the family in the home enables workers to identify and work with safety issues and parenting capacity within a natural environment. English (1999) takes a similar view, arguing that home-visiting programmes offer good parenting role models, and, as neglect is associated with inadequate parenting, it can be a useful intervention for lower-risk non-chronic neglect.

Home-visiting programmes and neglect

Box 9.1: *Three home-visitation programmes that show promise in addressing concerns about neglect*

The Family Nurse Partnership (FNP)

This programme, originally developed by David Olds (2006), is designed to build on universal services by providing additional support to first-time mothers who have been identified as young and vulnerable. The aim is to improve pregnancy outcomes, child health and development, and economic family self-sufficiency. Professionals using the programme are expected to adhere to a manual divided into three phases: pregnancy, infancy (0–12 months) and toddlerhood (13–24 months). The curriculum is informed by theories of attachment, self-efficacy and ecology, and draws, for its delivery, on motivational interviewing and strengths-based approaches. The three main activities that are the focus of the curriculum are: educating parents regarding infant and foetal development; getting family and friends involved in supporting the mother; and connecting the family to other services (Reynolds *et al.*, 2009). All of these curriculum elements should address emerging concerns regarding neglect. While there is a detailed curriculum, it is expected that the specially trained family nurses will use the materials flexibly, taking account of particular client needs, such as culture and faith. Visits are undertaken by a family nurse who, if working full time, has a maximum of 25 cases. The nurse visits weekly or fortnightly and, during each visit, will use curriculum materials and complete standardized records providing information about the visit, details of the participants and their progress. The family nurses receive frequent supervision. As they tend to work in teams of four to six, supervision includes both individual and group sessions.

Early Start

This is a home-visiting service that differs from the *FNP* in respect of programme philosophy, client recruitment and service delivery. It aims to improve child health, reduce the risk of child abuse, improve parenting skills, promote stable relationships between the partners and encourage socio-economic and material wellbeing. The programme draws on a social learning model rather than a psychosocial approach, focuses on families that are deemed to have two or more risk factors in terms of parent and family functioning, plus concerns about the carer's ability to meet the needs of the child. The programme is run by nurses or social workers who have received a five-week training programme, with the services tailored to meet the needs of the family. The worker sees the family over 50 times per year for between 60 and 90 minutes per visit, with services provided for up to five years.

Family Connections

This American, home-based programme is multifaceted and is designed specifically to reduce the risk factors associated with child neglect, increase the protective factors and improve the functioning of the parents and child or children. It draws on an ecological framework and therefore seeks to address issues related to the child, carer, family system and environment. Nine key practice principles underpin the programme: community outreach; individual family assessment; tailor-made interventions; forming a helping alliance; empowerment; a strengths perspective; cultural competence; developmental appropriateness; and outcome-driven plans. The programme has a number of core elements, including: emergency assistance; home-visiting with interventions that reflect the core principles; multifamily supportive and recreational activities; and advocacy and service coordination. The programme is delivered by social work and graduate students providing a service to the community. They are closely supervised by professionals through weekly supervision and clinical seminars, and follow a very detailed manual. Some families receive the service for three months and others for nine months, with an expectation of an hour's contact a week (DePanfilis *et al.*, 2008).

MacMillan *et al.* (2009) question the extent to which home-visiting programmes can actually address emerging concerns about child maltreatment and conclude that most of these programmes have not been shown to reduce physical abuse and neglect when assessed against the gold standard: randomized control trials (RCTs). They found, however, that the *Family Nurse Partnership* (FNP), originally developed in the USA, and the *Early Start* programme used in New Zealand are the two programmes that can have significant benefits in preventing abuse and neglect. These programmes are described in Box 9.1. What both *Early Start* and the *FNP* have in common is that they were originally developed as research programmes rather than for service provision, they use highly qualified workers, and fidelity to the programme is considered essential (MacMillan *et al.*, 2009).

The *FNP* has been subject to a rigorous and extensive number of evaluations, which indicate that the intervention can address emerging concerns about neglect and other forms of maltreatment. Reynolds *et al.* (2009), for example, noted preventative effects in relation to child maltreatment. In the USA three RCTs found benefits for both mothers and their children from participation, particularly for the most vulnerable families (Olds, 2006). These American trials found that the *FNP* contributed to a significant reduction in child abuse and neglect reports, fewer child injuries, improved maternal antenatal health, longer intervals between subsequent births, more father involvement, more maternal employment, less reliance on welfare support and better child school readiness. In addition, a 15-year follow-up found substantial long-term effects, with a reduction in reported child abuse and fewer behaviour problems (Olds *et al.*, 1999). Barnes *et al.* (2011) completed an evaluation of the *FNP* in England. Whilst there was no clear evidence from this evaluation that the *FNP* reduced maltreatment, it did appear to address many of the antecedents associated with neglect. For example, they found that rates of breastfeeding were higher amongst those who participated than amongst a comparable national sample (as discussed in Chapter 7, this can encourage bonding between mother and baby), and many are using reliable methods of contraception, with just one third becoming pregnant again during the two years following the first child's birth. More than a quarter of the mothers took part in some education following the birth of their child; half of those had not been in education at the start of the programme. The mothers tended to describe themselves and their children positively and were positive about their parenting capacity. They reported a high level of warmth in their parenting and a low level of harsh discipline. They also appeared to gain a sense of self-efficacy. Almost half the mothers had visited a children's centre since completing the *FNP*, mainly for mother and toddler play sessions, childcare or to see their health visitor.

Barnes *et al.* (2011) did find, however, that only half the mothers remained enrolled throughout the entire programme period, from early pregnancy to 24 months. Attrition rates were high during pregnancy, and whilst some fathers were involved, they tended to dip in and out of the programme. A small proportion of parents (8 per cent), however, reported their children having marked emotional or behavioural problems. More child behaviour problems were associated with more reported parental stress, less parenting warmth and a lower level of mastery.

The evaluation of the *Early Start* programme, described in Box 9.1, indicates that children whose parents were involved in the programme had significantly lower attendance at hospital for childhood injuries than the control group and fewer hospitalizations for severe abuse and neglect. There were, however, similar rates of referral to statutory childcare agencies, but this could have been because these families were under close surveillance (Fergusson *et al.*, 2005).

The *Family Connections* programme is a prevention programme designed specifically to address concerns about neglect. Whilst this programme, which is also described in Box 9.1, has, as yet, not been subject to the same rigorous reviews as the *FNP*, it shows promise. In an American evaluation of *Family Connections*, DePanfilis *et al.* (2008) found that, irrespective of the duration of the programme, there were positive changes in protective factors, such as parenting attitudes; reduced risk factors, such as parental depression; and improved child safety and behaviour. The three-month intervention was more cost effective than the nine-month intervention in relation to positive changes to risk, protective factors and child safety. However, the nine-month intervention was more cost effective in relation to *sustaining* improvements to the child's behaviour six months after the service ceased. This is not surprising if you take into account, as discussed in Chapters 3 and 5, the importance of not only changing parental behaviours but also ensuring parents are supported so that the changes become routinized. Lindsey *et al.* (2010) found that this programme was also effective in preventing behavioural problems amongst African American urban children at risk of neglect.

Other home-visiting programmes and the use of volunteers

Whilst only specific home-visiting programmes have been found to have an impact on reducing abuse and neglect, this does not necessarily mean that other forms of home-visiting should be eschewed. Any intervention that assists parents to become more attuned to the needs of the child, reduces isolation, provides support and helps parents develop parenting skills should go some way towards reducing the circumstances in which a carer fails to meet the needs of their child (Asawa *et al.*, 2008).

Munro (2011a) has indicated that volunteers can provide models of good parenting and can therefore support and assist families develop their parenting skills. A number of home-visiting programmes are delivered primarily by volunteers. In Ireland, the *Community Mothers* programme is a scheme dependent on experienced volunteer mothers who are able to reflect the ethos of the community they intend to visit. They undergo four weeks' training and are supported by a family development nurse. They not only support the parents in the immediate post-birth period but carry on with a monthly visit to both fathers and mothers for the first 24 months of the child's life. This programme is available in disadvantaged neighbourhoods in Dublin and is aimed at developing parenting skills and improving parents' confidence and self-esteem (C4EO, 2010a). Evaluations indicate that children are more likely to have received their immunizations and to have been exposed to more cognitive stimulation, such as games and nursery rhymes.

Moreover, children whose parents were involved in the programme have better outcomes at eight years of age than similar children in the community: they are likely to have better nutritional intake, to be reading books and to be visiting the dentist regularly. Moreover, the children were found to have had fewer hospital admissions for accidents or illness. The mothers were also more likely to feel positive about parenting this child and subsequent children (Johnson *et al.*, 2000; Hosking and Walsh, 2010).

Home Start works in a similar way to *Community Mothers* but operates in the UK. The project aims to provide support and practical assistance to families with children under five, many of whom are families where there are emerging or actual concerns about the quality of parenting. The volunteer works with a family using a strengths-based approach to encourage parenting capabilities and engagement with community services, and to provide reassurance. In a study by Barlow (2006) mothers were found to be enthusiastic about the service and experienced less parenting stress, exhibited fewer depressive symptoms and demonstrated increased levels of self-esteem alongside improvements in the child's development. Nevertheless, when followed up after the service ceased, they showed similar levels of improvement to mothers in similar circumstances who had not received this service. Furthermore, studies of similar volunteer schemes in the USA, such as Hawaii's *Healthy Start* programme and *Healthy Families*, have not been shown to have an impact on reducing reports regarding child protection concerns (MacMillan *et al.*, 2009). This would seem to reinforce the point that services need to last long enough to ensure that changes to parental behaviours are sufficiently routinized so that the parents can maintain those changes and also adapt these behaviours to accommodate the changing needs of the child.

Centre supported services

The second type of early intervention for addressing emerging concerns about neglect is centre-support services, such as group-based parenting programmes. These are often delivered in the children and family centres described in Chapter 8.

Parent-training programmes

Most centre-based parenting education or training programmes seek to help parents interact more effectively with their children; be realistic about what they can expect from the child; learn to be empathetic and nurture the child; and learn to provide appropriate boundaries and guidance. Some programmes may go beyond this to address parenting issues, such as social isolation and poor self-image (Barth, 2009). Most of the programmes are underpinned by a cognitive-behavioural approach, which is designed to assist parents to 'identify, confront and change their thinking and develop better child-management skills' (Barlow and McMillan, 2010, p. 61). They are usually 'manualized', with clearly defined interventions designed to address specific problems through following a set curriculum or core programme, and fidelity to the programme is considered essential. In order to achieve this, programmes have to be delivered by trained and supervised group leaders. Programmes can be adapted, however, to recognize the needs of particular groups, but what is stressed is that adaptations should not affect the core components of the programme.

Barth (2009), drawing on studies of parenting programmes, concludes that these programmes are effective if:

- parents are actively involved and, as with the home-visiting programmes, prepared to change
- programmes have multiple clinical and service applications
- benchmarks exist for assessing the quality of care
- simplified therapy training techniques are used that focus on key techniques
- a modular, incremental programme is used that takes into account individual needs
- there is a clearly articulated theoretical base to the programme
- the programme targets a specified group
- explicit strategies for recruitment, engagement and retention exist
- the programme is of long duration with follow-up and booster sessions
- programme integrity is maintained.

There has been little research into the cultural sensitivity and adaptation of programmes to meet the needs of families from minority ethnic groups. Drawing on a study of family-based interventions, however, Kumpfer *et al.* (2002) warn that culturally adapting programmes by reducing dosage and critical elements may increase retention but may reduce positive outcomes. There also appears to be little consideration given to programmes that meet the needs of fathers (this is considered in more detail later in the chapter).

Parenting programmes that have many of the factors identified by Barth are the *Triple P – Positive Parenting Program*, *The Incredible Years* or *Webster-Stratton Programme*, and the *Parents Plus Early Years* (PPEY). A summary of these three programmes, as they relate to early intervention, is provided in Box 9.2. The modules that focus on meeting the needs of more complex neglectful families are considered in Chapter 10 and the ones focused on meeting the needs of school age children in Chapter 12.

Box 9.2: *Three centre-based parenting programmes that can assist in addressing emerging concerns about neglectful parental behaviours*

Triple P – Positive Parenting Programme (see also Chapter 10)

The *Triple P* programme was developed by Matthew Sanders in Australia over 25 years ago (Sanders *et al.*, 2000). The aim is to improve parental capacity and prevent poor parenting practices developing. It is based on a social learning approach with different levels of intervention geared for different groups of parents and for children at five developmental stages: infants, toddlers, preschoolers, primary school age, and teenagers. It seeks to develop self-regulation skills in parents, enabling them to respond in an appropriate manner to their child. The programme is underpinned by five principles: teaching positive parenting; ensuring a safe and engaging environment for the child; creating a positive learning environment; using assertive discipline; and taking care of oneself as a parent. In total there are five intervention levels, varying in intensity:

- *Level 1: Universal Triple P* This is targeted at promoting positive parenting amongst all parents, for example through mass distribution of leaflets to family households, web-based information and using TV, radio and newspaper media to disseminate information.
- *Level 2: Selected Triple P* At this level the focus is on a specific topic, such as bed-wetting. Parents receive one or two short, individual consultations or are invited to attend larger parenting seminars.
- *Level 3: Primary Care Triple P* This is directed at parents concerned about their child's behaviour or development. The intervention consists of four consultations lasting about 80 minutes that include active parenting skills training and the provision of parenting tip sheets, enabling them to learn how to manage their child's behaviour.
- *Level 4: Standard and Group Triple P* Parents at this level receive ten 90-minute sessions, which may take place on an individual basis and would include skills development, clinic observation and home visits. Alternatively, the programme might be delivered to a group. In this case the parents receive five two-hour group sessions designed around observation, discussion, practice and feedback. In addition, parents receive three 15–20 minute follow-up sessions by telephone. This level is designed for parents of children with more severe behaviour problems, such as aggression or conduct disorder.
- *Level 5: Enhanced Triple P* This is an expanded version of level 4, with optional modules including partner communication, mood

management and stress coping skills. It is designed for parents who not only have children with behavioural issues but also have problems themselves or within the family. The parents attend approximately 12 one-hour individual sessions that are tailor-made to their needs.

Whilst *Triple P* at the lower levels is very much about prevention, the third, fourth and fifth levels are designed to address emerging concerns and involve parent and child education in conjunction with opportunities to put the course principles into practice. There are a number of additional programmes that have developed from the original *Triple P*. These include *Teen Triple*, and *Stepping Stone Triple* for parents with a disabled child.

The Incredible Years (for further detail related to school-age children see Chapter 12)

Originally developed by Carolyn Webster-Stratton in the USA over 30 years ago, *The Incredible Years* Parent, Child and Teacher programmes have been used widely and evaluated rigorously, in Canada, Norway, England, Wales, Jamaica and New Zealand. The various programmes are designed to address issues associated with children who have conduct disorders or behaviour management problems. The programme uses a 'logic model', which is based on the view that giving parents the skills to manage children's behaviour will reduce parental stress and lead to improvements in behavioural and emotional problems. Through the visual 'parenting pyramid' parenting skills and strategies are linked to potential and specific benefits for the child, enabling parents to understand how their behaviour impacts on their child. The core programme explores these skills and strategies.

Parents Plus Early Years (PPEY)

This programme was developed in Ireland and is designed to address parental concerns about a child's behaviour, including emotional problems and their general development. The programme is designed for children between the ages of one and six years, with other programmes developed for older children using the same principles. At this level *PPEY* is normally delivered as a group-based centre programme with groups of up to 12 parents attending seven weekly sessions. Each session lasts between two and three hours. In addition, parents have five individual sessions. The programme runs for 12 weeks in total. *PPEY* uses a strengths-based approach and draws on theories of child development as well as attachment theory, family systems theory, social learning and cognitive-behavioural approaches.

The aim of the programme is to improve the parents' knowledge of positive parenting techniques, including discipline and child-centred play, and to improve the relationships between the children, their family and friends. They are assisted in reflecting on their current negative behaviours and their consequences, and given alternative strategies for interacting with their child. The parents are taught one positive parenting strategy and one positive discipline strategy each week. They then practise the strategies with their child using the individual sessions. Each strategy is illustrated using video examples of parents demonstrating correct and incorrect behaviours. The programme is manualized, and fidelity to the programme is expected. There is also an expectation that practitioners delivering the programme are trained in the use of the detailed curriculum and video-based feedback, and receive supervision.

MacMillan *et al.* (2009) found that although several parent-training programmes stated that one of their intentions was to prevent child maltreatment, they could not find any clinical trials that assessed actual outcomes in terms of levels of maltreatment. However, they did find, compared to families with similar issues who received 'services-as-usual', that there were positive effects of *Triple P* programmes on rates of substantiated maltreatment, out-of-home placements and child maltreatment injuries. Asawa *et al.* (2008) also found that *Triple P* can reduce the potential for abuse and neglect by improving parenting behaviour and attitudes. A number of studies have shown this programme to be effective as an intervention to improve parenting, most specifically in relation to improving children's behaviour, parent–child interaction and reducing parental conflicts (Hosking and Walsh, 2010). It is one of the programmes that is highly recommended by Allen in his English review into early interventions (Allen, 2011). However, it is important to note, as pointed out by McConnell *et al.* (2011a), that whilst there is compelling evidence to support the efficacy of *Triple P*, most studies have focused on the higher levels and few studies have considered the efficacy of levels 2 and 3. Moreover, a significant number of the studies have been undertaken by those who developed the programme.

Emotional and social dysfunction is often associated with neglect, resulting in parents feeling frustrated, angry or helpless that they cannot manage their children's behaviour. *The Incredible Years* programme can potentially reduce or prevent further problems developing (Gardner, 2008). The programme is also important in relation to addressing emerging concerns regarding neglectful parenting, as lack of or inconsistent parenting skills contribute to the establishment of conduct problems amongst children (Hildyard and Wolfe, 2002).

An interesting application of *The Incredible Years* programme is taking place in Wales. The programme is being integrated into mainstream early years' services provided by the *Flying Start* centres described in Chapter 8. An evaluation was completed of the 153 parents with children between the ages of three and five, considered at risk of significant behaviour problems, who participated in the experimental programme. The researchers found the use of the programme had positive benefits, with parents reporting that the problems they were experiencing with their children were less severe, and that they themselves felt under less stress and were less depressed. The evaluation focused on the behaviour of the target child that had led to inclusion in the programme and found they displayed significantly reduced antisocial behaviour compared with those placed on a comparison waiting list. Moreover, the researchers found that behaviour amongst the closest aged siblings in the family had also improved (Hutchings *et al.*, 2007). Webster-Stratton and Reid (2006) have reported a similar positive use of *The Incredible Years* programme with *Head Start*, the American equivalent of *Sure Start*. Moreover, they noted that parents, irrespective of ethnic group, were much more positive, nurturing and engaged with their children, and their disciplinary approaches were less harsh and critical. The *Sure Start* experience appears to have been enhanced by a programme that enabled staff to assist parents in developing skills and, by following a particular model, the staff were able to demonstrate a consistent response to the child and parents' behaviour.

The *Parents Plus Early Years* (PPEY) programme was developed in Ireland to address emerging concerns about a young child's behavioural and developmental difficulties, including ADHD, presented to practitioners in community mental health settings. This programme combines both group and individual sessions. There is promising evidence of its effectiveness, with studies indicating significant improvement in the children's behaviour as well as reductions in parental stress in comparison with the services-as-usual group of children. Moreover, the parents were able to maintain the positive parenting practices in the medium term (Sharry *et al.*, 2005; Griffin *et al.*, 2010; Kilroy *et al.*, 2010).

Ipsos MORI (2011), in a study of parenting programmes offered in *Flying Start* centres in Wales, explored the reasons why parents did not take up places on the programmes and engage in the programmes. These included practical reasons, such as being too busy or the course running at unsuitable times; attitudinal reasons, such as the parent feeling the content was not relevant or necessary; finally, not having the confidence to attend as they were too shy or would not know anyone there. Patel *et al.* (2011) challenge the assumption that members of ethnic minority groups do not attend and engage with parenting programmes because of cultural sensitivities. In their study, completed in England, they found that mothers from black minority ethnic groups were often very keen and interested in attending the parenting groups on offer but did not actually attend for a number of reasons. These included time demands, the location, and the fear of having to disclose personal information. What both these studies highlight is that it is not sufficient to offer a parenting group programme without providing support and facilitating parental engagement within these groups.

Two-generation interventions

The home-visiting and parenting programmes described above tend to focus on developing general parenting knowledge and skills. These types of programmes may not be appropriate to address emerging concerns regarding the mother failing to bond and become attuned to the needs of the child, and the child, as a consequence, failing to form a secure attachment to their caregiver. When these concerns appear, consideration needs to be given to early interventions that address the needs of both parent and child. This is particularly important when addressing emerging concerns of neglect parenting. For example, Hildyard and Wolfe (2007), as discussed in Chapter 2, note that neglectful mothers are more likely to have problems in information processing concerns about their child's emotions and behaviours. They advocate interventions that aim at improving the parents' ability to recognize and respond to the child's emotions. The majority of interventions that fall into this category, with regard to the infant or pre-school child, seek to achieve this by focusing on improving the interactions between the child and their carer. Law *et al.* (2009) conclude that there is a great deal of evidence to support the use of parenting groups as an intervention to assist in improving interactions between parents and young children who are already exhibiting emotional and behavioural problems. The programmes described in Box 9.3 and discussed below all include an element of group work.

Box 9.3: *Three two-generation interventions that may be useful in addressing concerns about parent–child relationship difficulties*

Mellow Parenting

This is delivered in specialist clinical settings by a team that draw on child psychiatry, psychology and social work. The programme is designed for families of children under five who are already experiencing relationship problems with their children and also have wider family difficulties, such as mental illness, domestic violence or social isolation. The 14-week course is delivered through a mix of group work, video feedback sessions and workshops. The parent, usually the mother, attends a day a week and the child attends a children's group in the morning, with parent and child coming together in the afternoon for specifically designed activities. As the programme is designed for parents who themselves have experienced poor parenting, it lends itself to supporting parents who may fail to meet the needs of their children because of their own experiences of maltreatment. The aim of the programme is to help these parents find better ways of relating to their children.

Circle of Security

This programme is both educational and psychotherapeutic and is based on attachment theory. Parents watch edited videotapes of their inter-actions with their children in order to improve attachment–caregiving interactions and develop mind-mindedness. This describes the ability of parents to interact with and respond to their children as individuals with minds of their own. The 20-week programme is for parents whose children are at high risk of a disorganized or insecure attachment. The parents themselves tend to have histories of poor attachments to their own parents, and the programme is designed to increase sensitivity and appropriate handling on the part of the parents. This includes a weekly mix of education and video reviews, with a focus on analysing what has been happening and why children respond as they do to particular parenting behaviours (Hosking and Walsh, 2010). The parents are intro-duced to the idea of providing a 'secure base' and a 'haven of safety' from which children can explore and return at times of anxiety and need; that is when their attachment system is activated. The aim is to help parents become aware not only of the child's attachment signals but also to be appropriately responsive to those signals. The parents are assisted to recognize how their own anxieties and attachment pattern affect the child and how insecure children miscue their feelings and needs.

Video Interactive Guidance (VIG)

VIG aims to enhance communication between the parent and child. It is founded on a strengths-based approach, attempting to empower the parent and promote and sustain positive change. *VIG* has been used widely in Scotland and the Netherlands, and is receiving increased atten-tion in England (Gardner, 2008). This approach is used when parents are already experiencing problems interacting with their child. The parent, whilst undertaking an activity chosen by the parent with their child in their home, is filmed by a trained worker. The videoing lasts for about 10 to15 minutes. The worker then selects a two- to three-minute section of the video where the parent is responding appropriately to the child. The worker then asks the parent to comment on what they have done well and uses this to develop their ability and skills. The purpose of *VIG* is to develop the parent's parenting capacity, sense of self-control and self-worth, and to assist them in developing a range of appropriate and sensitive responses to their child. For example, they learn to be atten-tive – encouraging, guiding and directing the child to increase the child's sense of security.

An evaluation for the Department of Health in England has shown that *Mellow Parenting* improves: mother–child interaction; mothers' wellbeing, effectiveness and confidence in parenting; the child's behaviour problems; and language and non-verbal abilities. These changes were sustained over an 18-month follow-up. The programme has been replicated successfully in many areas. A seven-year follow-up has shown a dilution of the effects on language and development but a sustained improvement in the children's behaviour as rated by their teachers (Puckering *et al.*, 1999). Different var-iations of *Mellow Parenting* have since been developed to meet specific needs. These include *Mellow Dads*, *Mellow Babies*, *Mellow Bumps* and *Mellow Grandparents*.

Moving on to the *Circle of Security* – despite its popularity, Hoffman *et al.* (2006) conclude that there is limited evidence that the quality of the child's attachment to their primary carer improved immediately following programme completion. The longer-term effects, however, are not clear.

Referring to *Video Interactive Guidance* (VIG), Gardner (2008) notes that young parents often find use of video more comfortable and manage-able than lengthy discussions, and the method offers a concrete route to solving the difficulties they are experiencing interacting with their child. She reports that this method has been used in a range of cases and has been particularly successful in cases of physical neglect both as an early inter-vention through to addressing more significant concerns.

Barth (2009) noted that whilst these types of programmes appear to have a significant positive effect on parenting behaviour, they have a more modest effect on the child's behaviour. Egeland and Bosquet (2002, cited in Siraj-Blatchard and Siraj-Blatchford, 2009) highlight a number of fac-tors that should be considered when planning the type of two-generation interventions described above. These include:

- going beyond the parent–child relationship to address other problems encountered by the family
- considering the mother's relationship with her partner and other family members

- beginning interventions as early as possible
- having a programme of sufficient length and intensity.

Early help and fathers

Dufour *et al.* (2008, p. 153) explored the influence of father figures in cases of neglect and concluded that 'it would appear crucial to consider fathers when intervening in cases of neglect, right from the time the situation is initially assessed'.

However, as discussed in Chapter 2, the focus in cases of neglect is primarily on mothers, although there are long-term benefits for the resilience and emotional wellbeing of children in having a quality relationship with a father (Hernandez-Martinez *et al.*, 2011). Not only is it important, therefore, to ensure attention is given to the roles, responsibilities and influences of fathers, it is also essential that they are motivated and have opportunities to both develop parenting knowledge and skills and develop a quality parent–child relationship. The contribution of fathers is particularly important if the mother has parenting issues, such as depression or anxiety. In this section consideration is given to what is known about actively engaging with fathers in the early years.

New fathers and early intervention

Lee *et al.* (2009) conclude, from an overview of the literature, that fathers tend to be excluded from family prevention services, particularly if they are not living in the same household as the mother. The reasons given for this marginalization include: cultural expectations regarding fathering; the father's role within the family; and workers' fears and uncertainties as to how to engage with fathers. Page *et al.* (2008) recognized these issues and found that a predominantly female workforce is also more likely to have problems identifying the needs of young and non-resident fathers. Yet the inclusion of fathers in parent training programmes has been found to result in more positive changes in parenting practices as well as in the behaviour of the child. This could be, however, because the more motivated fathers attended the training.

If fathers who are vulnerable to neglecting their children are to take a more central role in parenting then it is important to consider what they require if they are to engage in early preventative services. An interesting study was completed by Tyrer *et al.* (2005) of a particularly vulnerable group in relation to neglectful parenting: fathers in and leaving care. They found that if the fathers' needs were to be met, they required services that addressed three specific issues. First, social exclusion and limited opportunities to meet the needs of their family – that is, isolation experienced by these young fathers from their own childhood families, combined with lack of financial security, low educational achievement and poor work prospects. Second, trust – in view of their past experiences of both family life and service provision, they found it hard trusting both their partners and professionals, and therefore found long-lasting relationships with a trusted worker extremely valuable. Finally, they perceived services to be bureaucratic and 'a hassle' (p. 1119), more specifically they described them as inflexible, prioritizing issues other than fatherhood, with accessible information lacking and limited targeted service provision. Lewis and Lamb (2007) completed a review of the recent research on fatherhood. Their findings, in terms of what is required to engage with fathers, very much reflects the findings of Tyrer *et al.* (2005). They reinforce the importance of services being father friendly but highlight how this is often done in a clumsy manner, such as presuming that by providing sports activities fathers will engage. In the same way that mothers need to feel service providers recognize their particular needs, so do fathers. It is therefore important that fathers are made to feel welcome and comfortable, workers make an effort to engage with fathers, there is a clear presence of male workers with the centre not feeling feminized, and that parenting programmes include materials that are relevant to fathers. Furthermore, Tyrer *et al.* (2005) conclude that workers tend to stereotype and make presumptions about the role of fathers, for example presuming that men, such as those in prison or teenage fathers, want to take a minimal part in fathering when, in fact, the research indicates that this is not the case and fathers, irrespective of their own issues, usually want to be involved. The only exception, according to Lewis and Lamb, is in cases of violence by men against the mothers.

The Fatherhood Institute (2009) explored what works in terms of parenting programmes for fathers and concluded that single-sex groups are more acceptable to most fathers and should address fathers' issues such as gender roles, masculinity and caring, the part they can play in child development, and particular challenges, such as parenting across households, being a stepfather and the parenting alliance. They argue that engaging fathers is a process that begins early on, when the message that should be given to fathers, by midwives and health visitors, is that they are important and are expected to engage in child rearing, with the benefit of fathers' attendance to their child's needs being repeatedly emphasized. What is also important is that the programme is run at times and in a location that is acceptable to fathers and that non-attendance is followed up.

Early help: what works?

A number of common themes have been identified by researchers that practitioners, service commissioners and providers may wish to take into account when identifying the types of services that are likely to address emerging concerns about neglectful behaviours on the part of parents with young children. These are:

- It is important to recognize that quick fixes are not always the answer to sustained improvements in parenting. Programmes should therefore be of sufficient duration to enable positive changes in parenting to become established and routinized. It is also important that parents are supported for sufficient duration to ensure that they can maintain these behaviours during times of stress (Moran *et al.*, 2004; Siraj-Blatford and Siraj-Blatford, 2009; Reynolds *et al.*, 2009; Scott, 2010; Sharp and Filmer-Sankey, 2010).
- Programme fidelity is important in such programmes as the *FNP* and *Triple P – Positive Parenting Program*, yet some flexibility is also important so that material can be adapted for different contexts, cultures and faiths (Mitchell, 2011; Self-Brown *et al.*, 2011; Easton and Gee, 2012).
- Working in partnership with families, minority ethnic groups and communities in the design and development of interventions ensures that local needs and issues are taken into account and service users have a sense of ownership of the service (Moran *et al.*, 2004; Law *et al.*, 2009; Scott, 2010; Mitchell, 2011; Self-Brown *et al.*, 2011; Easton and Gee, 2012).
- Taking a holistic approach, including identifying and targeting multiple risks, means that issues regarding parenting are understood within a broader context that takes account of the influence of socio-economic factors (Barth, 2009; Siraj-Blatford and Siraj-Blatford, 2009; Long *et al.*, 2010; Sharp and Filmer-Sankey, 2010).
- Having a strong theoretical base, including a theoretical understanding of models of change, ensures that interventions draw on best evidence and a consistent approach is adopted (Moran *et al.*, 2004; Barth, 2009; Reynolds *et al.*, 2009; Scott, 2010; Sharp and Filmer-Sankey, 2010).
- For the high-quality delivery of the programme, staff have to be well trained. Practitioners also require the knowledge and skills not only to implement the identified intervention but also to identify need and support families in accessing and engaging with services (Olds, 2006; Barth, 2009; Easton and Gee, 2012).
- Effective and committed leadership recognizes the importance of a favourable organizational or community context, cultural competence, funding, client incentives and manageable caseloads (Moran *et al.*, 2004; Reynolds *et al.*, 2009; Siraj-Blatford and Siraj-Blatford, 2009; Long *et al.*, 2010; Scott, 2010; Sharp and Filmer-Sankey, 2010).
- Being mindful that many services have a poor image amongst the most hard-to-reach groups, services are designed to meet their needs without families feeling labelled as 'problem families' (Moran *et al.*, 2004; Sharp

and Filmer-Sankey, 2010). Moreover, families should be signposted and supported to access additional, appropriate services once they have completed programmes (Easton and Gee, 2012).

- Programmes should focus not just on problems but also on strengths, and provide participants with useful, practical tips to promote positive parenting (Barth, 2009).
- Programme providers should be aware that engagement with programmes is dependent on the carer's perception of the service, their objective and subjective views of the programme experience and their readiness to change (McCurdy and Daro, 2001; Damashek *et al.*, 2011; Ipsos MORI, 2011).
- Recognizing the need to establish a positive 'working alliance' (Platt, 2012, p. 141) between workers and family members is crucial (Girvin *et al.*, 2011). The workforce should be sufficiently stable to enable long-term positive working relationships to be developed with service users (Olds, 2006).

Conclusion

> The most striking message is that early intervention clearly works – when it is an appropriate intervention, applied well, following timely identification of a problem; and the earlier the better to secure maximum impact and greatest long term sustainability (both as early in the child's life as possible and/or as soon as possible after a difficulty becomes apparent). (C4EO, 2010a, p. 34)

There are a range of early help interventions that can be used to address emerging concerns about neglect. However, as summarized in the quote above, certain conditions are necessary if these early interventions are to be effective. What is particularly important, however, is that practitioners avoid putting square pegs into round holes. Moreover, they should ensure that the parent will engage with the service and that the intervention will address the identified need. When considering the appropriateness of an early intervention service for a particular parent, practitioners should ask themselves the following questions (a case example is included for clarification):

- What is the presenting issue?
  Nursery concerned as lone mother is not disciplining her three-year-old.
- In what way is this issue impacting on the parent's ability to meet the needs of the child?
  The child is failing to develop a sense of appropriate behaviour, for example biting, swearing and screaming when not getting his way;

undertaking activities which are putting him at risk, such as climbing on window sills on the first floor of the house.

- In order to address the presenting concern and ensure the needs of the child are met currently and in the future, what aspects of parenting capacity need to be addressed?
  The parent needs to be able to provide appropriate guidance and boundaries, learn techniques for disciplining the child whilst maintaining a positive emotional relationship with the child.

- Is the presenting concern part of an established pattern of behaviour?
  The mother had problems disciplining her older child who is now five years old and described at school as 'unruly'.

- What do we know about the parent's past history that may be influencing her current behaviour and the type of intervention that she will find acceptable?
  The mother is the third in a family of four. She was brought up by her mother, who had alcohol issues; and her father spent considerable periods of her childhood in prison for offences associated with violence. All four children were taken into care when this mother was ten, because of neglect. She experienced seven foster placements, all of which broke down because of her 'disruptive' behaviour. She was eventually placed in a residential unit between the ages of 14 and 16 years. Her first child was born when she was 17 years and her second at 19 years. She is wary of accessing any child welfare service, fearing her boys will also be removed from her.

- Does the parent have the ability and motivation to address the concerns?
  In every other aspect this mother has both the ability and motivation to meet her boys' needs. The mother has told nursery staff that she does not know how to discipline her boys in a way that is both loving but firm. She indicated that her own mother just smacked or shouted at her or locked her in her room for wrongdoings, and this made her hate her mother. She is keen to learn techniques that will assist her.

- In light of the responses to the questions above, what resource/s are likely to meet the needs of this family? Is a home- or centre-based programme most appropriate?
  This mother has demonstrated some parental abilities and would benefit from an intervention that enabled her to recognize these strengths and reinforced her positive parenting abilities. The Incredible Years programme is available at the local children's centre and would provide her with an opportunity to address areas of concern whilst reinforcing what she does well. The programme would provide the mother with opportunities to learn appropriate techniques for managing her boys' behaviour in a non-stigmatizing setting. Undertaking this programme would assist

the mother appreciate that disciplining can be achieved within a loving relationship. Moreover, she has demonstrated, through her interactions with staff and other parents at the nursery, that she has the confidence to engage in a centre-based programme despite her concerns about accessing particular services.

Chapter 10

Chronic Neglect: Working with Complexity

Introduction

In the previous two chapters the focus has been on population-based services to prevent child neglect occurring and early help interventions to address emerging concerns. But what if these services fail to address concerns about neglect and the parents' behaviour is causing or is likely to cause significant harm to the child? This chapter seeks to answer this question with a particular focus on those situations which are particularly challenging to practitioners – cases of chronic neglect. For the purposes of this book, chronic neglect is defined as a persistent failure on the part of the parent to consistently meet the needs of the child or children in the family, despite the provision of services. There are a range of services that are available to meet the diverse needs of these families. They are usually referred to as 'family preservation services' and are designed to prevent further child maltreatment, improve family functioning and thereby avoid out-of-home placement of the children. In many nation states, as discussed in Chapter 6, these services are delivered as part of a child protection plan by statutory services.

Before beginning to consider the interventions, it is important to explore in more detail what we know about these families and their often complex needs.

Who are the chronic neglectful families?

Parents in chronic neglect cases are likely to be struggling with both child rearing and a number of parenting issues. The two are often inextricably linked, with various combinations of mental health problems, alcohol and substance misuse, domestic violence, economic hardship and social isolation playing a part in a significant number of cases (Chambers and Potter, 2009). Policy makers have begun to focus increasing attention on these families. Spratt (2011), however, argues that this interest is not altruistic. Rather, in a time of austerity, it is a desire to identify high-cost and low-productive populations and reduce these so that they do not becoming a

167

drain on an economy with an ageing population. The families described by the current Department for Education in England as falling into this category tend to be:

> very disadvantaged, larger families often with a lone parent with a range of risk factors associated with family functioning and health problems. They are likely to already be in contact with one or more local services as a result of concerns about the safety of the children in the family or their truancy or nuisance behaviour or as a result of adult family members having mental health, drug or alcohol dependency problems, serious debt or involvement in criminal or nuisance behaviour. (DfE, 2011, p. 1)

The Department for Education believe that in England this describes 2 per cent (n = 117,000) of all families. Poor parenting is the most commonly identified problem amongst this group, affecting 68 per cent of the families, with 46,000 of the children in this cohort displaying problems, such as truancy and challenging behaviour or having special educational needs. Over one third of the families are thought to have issues associated with mental health, substance and alcohol misuse (DfE, 2011).

Whilst the description above by no means describes all the families labelled as cases of 'chronic neglect', and indeed not all of these families will be neglecting their children, it certainly provides insight into the issues encountered and the needs of many of them. For example, Thoburn *et al.* (2009, p. 4) note that these characteristics are associated with families who are known to statutory agencies because of child protection concerns but are difficult to help and 'hard to change'. As these families do not engage easily with professionals it is not surprising that Spratt and Devaney (2009) found, in Northern Ireland, Australia and the USA, that families with characteristics that included concerns about child neglect, economic problems, domestic violence, single parenthood, drug and alcohol abuse and mental health issues were being referred to statutory child protection agencies on multiple occasions. And, in another study completed in Northern Ireland, children who were either the subject of repeat child protection registrations or remained on the register for long periods were usually members of these multiple problem families (Devaney, 2009). This would appear to be the position in relation to neglect in most developed countries (Firth, 1999).

What works when intervening in cases of chronic neglect?

If these families are difficult to help and hard to change, where does one begin intervening in their lives to promote better outcomes for children in the family?

Multifaceted interventions designed to address complex needs

As anyone who has worked with chronic neglect will know, finding targeted and specialist interventions that work at this level is not easy. Davies
and Ward (2012), reflecting on the findings of the research studies commissioned by the Department for Education in England, note that many
of these families do not respond to routine services such as casework.
Furthermore, high rates of re-abuse and poor outcomes are often found
when very specific interventions are used. This view is supported by Barlow
and Scott (2010) who, in a review of what works with these complex families, concludes that no one service or approach has been found to be effective in protecting children from the risk of significant harm. This is almost
inevitable if one takes into account the multiple problems these families
are encountering. Therefore, effective multifaceted intervention packages
should be constructed, drawing on a comprehensive assessment that clearly
indicates how the interventions will address the identified needs of the child
and other family members. Frameworks, such as the *Framework for the
Assessment of Children in Need and Their Families*, discussed in Chapter
4, together with relevant scales and questionnaires, should assist practitioners in gathering this information (Cox and Bentovim, 2000; DH *et al.*,
2000). A comprehensive assessment that identifies, specifically, the very
varied needs of the parents and their children is essential if these needs are
to be met. A multifaceted package is as good as the services that make up
the package and the way in which the services are delivered. What appears
to be crucially important, when developing an intensive support package, is
to ensure that there is a match between the needs of the family and the services provided. The more specific practitioners can be as to cause and effect
and desired outcome, the more likely it is that practitioners can identify the
most appropriate service and work with the family to secure meaningful
engagement with the intervention package.

Services of sufficient depth and duration

As discussed in the chapters on planning, a short-term intervention is
of itself unlikely to address the entrenched, and often intergenerational,
problems associated with chronic neglect (Stevenson, 2005; Spratt and
Devaney, 2009). This point is reinforced in the findings of an evaluation
of an American intensive in-home treatment programme to prevent out-of-
home placement (Tyuse *et al.*, 2010). The programme was based on a crisis
intervention model. It provided intensive counselling services for six weeks,
with interventions lasting from eight to ten hours a week. At the end of the
intervention, whilst there were improvements in family functioning and
child wellbeing, some of the significant issues that contributed to family

stresses, such as employment, financial management, community safety and relationship difficulties, had not been addressed and therefore continued to impact on family life. What is also of note is that, first, some programmes are most effective within the first few months and then have an increasingly diminishing impact; second, parents can become over-dependent on services and fail to take responsibility for their child, and finally, the cost of long-term provision is significant and can be a difficult commitment for managers to make (Davies and Ward, 2012). As is evident when one considers the pathway to change discussed in Chapter 4, in order to sustain and consolidate any changes resulting from intensive family interventions, ongoing support is essential. Practitioners should therefore be mindful of the range of population-based and early support services which can have a significant part to play in supporting families to maintain change once the specialist services are no longer considered necessary.

Effective worker–client relationship

Barlow and Scott (2010) highlight that a dependable and professional relationship is crucial to the effectiveness of interventions; and the evidence indicates that practitioners working with these families need to be highly skilled and experienced in terms of relationship-based practice. They also need to be able to empathize with the parents whilst at the same time keeping a focus on the needs of the child. The importance of establishing and maintaining a quality relationship between workers and neglecting parents and children has been discussed in Chapter 6. Nevertheless, it is worth emphasizing, as highlighted by Lloyd *et al.* (2011) and York Consulting (2011), the importance of having a persistent, skilled and assertive key worker who works intensively with the family with complex needs, and not only provides case leadership but acts as the 'lynchpin' to the multidisciplinary team delivering the intervention package. This critical role usually falls to the social worker. If one considers the aetiology of neglect then it is not surprising that the relationship between key worker and the family can be crucial in influencing outcomes in cases of chronic neglect. Barlow and Scott (2010, p. 62) conclude that parents who have experienced insecure attachments in their own childhood require an 'emotionally corrective relationship'. Drawing on the work of Luther *et al.* (2007), they go on to argue that this should include:

- a supportive therapeutic approach that is based on acceptance, empathy, genuineness and trust, which are used to establish a partnership between the worker and parent to identify and meet some of the parent's unmet needs

- a focus in the intervention on interpersonal and relational issues so that the parents can consider their parenting in the light of their own experiences of being parented.

In this chapter, interventions that draw on 'what works' are considered in more detail.

Parenting programmes

In Chapter 9, consideration was given to parenting programmes designed to address emerging concerns about neglect, but intensive versions of some of these programmes – *The Incredible Years* and the *Triple P* – are also available to address neglect when parenting is causing or is likely to cause significant harm to a child. Thoburn *et al.* (2009) conclude that these particular programmes show promise for addressing neglecting and abusive parenting, particularly when 'parent-focused interventions are based on clear models geared to strengthening the parent child interactions and reducing child conduct problems' (p. 12).

However, whilst these programmes have been found to improve parental psychosocial functioning and address child behaviour concerns, there is very little evidence, as discussed below, that on their own they are effective in relation to addressing child maltreatment. Thus, the limits of these programmes need to be recognized when putting together an intervention package.

Box 10.1: *Parenting programmes for use in cases of chronic neglect*

Triple P

Standard Triple P (level 4) is a ten-session programme, with sessions lasting between 40 and 60 minutes, which is delivered individually within the family home or at a centre. The sessions cover causes of children's behaviour problems, strategies for encouraging both children's development and managing misbehaviour, identifying high-risk situations and developing planned activities and routines. The sessions provide opportunities for skill development through modelling, rehearsal, self-evaluation and homework tasks. Parents are observed interacting with their child and implementing parenting skills, and are subsequently encouraged to self-evaluate their progress towards meeting their goals, which can be selected to address particular concerns.

Group Triple P is an eight-session group programme for 10–12 parents. It consists of four two-hour group sessions, which provide opportunities for parents to learn through observation, discussion, practice and feedback. DVD segments are used to demonstrate positive parenting skills, which are then practised in small groups, with parents receiving feedback. Parents are expected to complete tasks between sessions to consolidate their learning. Following the group sessions, three 15- to 30-minute follow-up telephone sessions provide additional support to parents as they put into practice what they have learned in the group sessions. A final group session completes the programme. There is a particular group programme that focuses on parenting teenagers.

Enhanced Triple P (level 5) extends the focus of level 4 to include home-based skills training, mood management and stress coping skills for parents, and marital communication skills as required. The first session evaluates the progress parents have made, and plans for further sessions that draw on the following themes: practice, coping skills and partner support. Each theme is explored in a maximum of three sessions lasting up to 90 minutes each (with the exception of practice sessions, which should last 40 minutes each). The actual content is designed with the needs of the family in mind. Parents develop their knowledge and skills through observation, discussion, practice and feedback. Between sessions, parents are once again expected to complete tasks to consolidate their learning. A final evaluation session is held.

Pathways Triple P is a four-session intervention specifically designed for parents at risk of maltreating their children. It is used in combination with either *Group* or *Standard Triple P. Pathways Triple P* aims to help parents understand and develop effective strategies to manage their emotions, control their anger and review ways in which they interpret their child's or children's behaviour. Active skills training techniques are used that are designed to assist parents acquire new skills in managing their own emotions and behaviours along with those of their children. (For more information on *Triple P*, see www.triplep.net)

Enhanced Incredible Years

The programme is designed for parents who have to manage behavioural problems amongst their children – problems that are often caused by their lack of parenting skills and bonding issues. In addition to *The Incredible Years* core content, described in Chapter 7, content centres on: strengthening parent–child relationships and bonding; parents' interpersonal skills and supportive networks; and promoting routines, effective limit setting, non-punitive discipline and problem solving. In order to cover the additional material, the programme consists of between 18 and 20 sessions rather than the usual 12 sessions of the core programme. Furthermore, the enhanced programme includes a minimum of four home visits, which follow a prescribed curriculum.

SafeCare

Parents are 'trained' using a seven-step format that is prescribed. It is designed to identify desired behaviours, model desired behaviours, practise the behaviours with positive and constructive feedback provided by the trainer, review performance and set revised goals each week, with the aim of generalizing skills from the specific to more general parenting. *SafeCare* has been derived from *Project 12-Ways*. As its name suggests, this offers parents 12 different components, including parent training, money management, home-safety training, parent–child training and behaviour management. The programme was designed to ameliorate the social and ecological factors that appear to contribute to child neglect (National Center for Injury Prevention and Control, 2004). However, implementation of the programme highlighted that parents did not necessarily have needs in all 12 areas and paraprofessionals did not have the required skills to deliver the programme effectively in all areas. Because of this, another programme was developed – *SafeCare*, which is based on addressing the three most common parental behaviours associated with neglect: home safety and organisation; child health and nutrition; and child behaviour management. The programme draws on behavioural theory, taking the stance that a skills deficit contributes to child neglect. The recommendation is that the programme focuses on addressing this skills deficit but it should be delivered as part of a package that addresses the other issues.

Triple P

The different levels of *Triple P* were described in Chapter 9, and in that chapter the focus was on the first three levels. The fourth and fifth levels of *Triple P*, described in Box 10.1, are more suitable for families where neglect is persistent and ongoing. Whilst these programmes at levels 4 and 5 have been found to improve parental psychosocial functioning and address child behaviour concerns, does *Pathways Triple P* reduce the risk of child maltreatment? Sanders *et al.* (2004) attempted to answer this question and ran a pilot evaluation comparing the *Enhanced* programme to the *Standard* one. All the families participating in the study had been the subject of at least one referral to a statutory child protection agency or there were concerns about their use of anger. The *Enhanced* programme outperformed the *Standard* training in two areas: first, in terms of the parents' expectations of their children, the parents who participated in the *Enhanced* programme had significantly reduced unrealistic expectations of their child; second, these parents showed fewer negative interpretations of the behaviour of their child. In relation to anger management, a key component of the *Enhanced* programme, there were no marked reductions in the expression of anger by parents who completed level 4. This was a small-scale study, however, and was undertaken by researchers who had been involved in the development of *Triple P*. At the time of writing a much larger evaluation of this more specialized programme is about to commence in the USA. The aim of this randomized control trial is to examine the effectiveness of the programme with families who have a history of abusing and neglecting their children (Triple P, 2011).

Enhanced Incredible Years

Webster-Stratton and Reid (2010) have recently developed an *Enhanced* version of the *The Incredible Years* programme for families involved in the American child welfare system – that is, families where there are concerns about abuse and neglect and the children are either at risk of being removed or the courts have mandated parents to attend a parenting programme. A number of pilots have been undertaken and the revised programme shows promise, with positive changes to perceptions of children, parent–child interactions and parenting practices. What is of note is that whilst fathers' attitudes and approaches changed positively, the most comprehensive changes took place amongst the mothers. Webster-Stratton and Reid (2010) also found that parenting satisfaction with the programme was high.

SafeCare

SafeCare, as described in Box 10.1, is another American manualized programme designed for use with multiple-problem families who, as with the *Enhanced Incredible Years*, are involved in the child welfare system, or at risk of becoming involved, because of concerns about maltreatment. At the time of writing, it is being trialled in parts of the UK. A specific aim of the programme is to reduce child maltreatment. This programme is particularly valuable for neglectful families as it focuses on behaviours constituting neglect of young children. Unlike the programmes above, it is designed as a home-based service that can be delivered by paraprofessional staff, such as family support workers. The programme has been found to break the intergenerational cycle of neglect (Wiehe, 1996). Whilst evaluation is in the early stages, this programme would seem to reduce recidivism in relation to neglect: follow-ups of parents who completed *SafeCare* 24 months after completion of the programme indicated that recidivism was at 15 per cent compared to 44 per cent for parents who had received just family preservation services (Hecht *et al.*, 2008).

As with other parenting programmes, Hecht *et al.* (2008) emphasize the importance of programme fidelity by trained staff. They found that the quality of training was significantly improved if staff were trained in small, intact practitioner teams of between three and five; the focus is on clear and specific skills, broken into manageable segments, and is followed by intermittent live modelling and *in situ* direct observation. They also emphasize the importance of strong organizational leadership, recognizing both the financial and structural commitment required to make the programme effective.

Multisystemic Therapy (MST)

The focus of many of the interventions discussed thus far has been on improving parenting capacity in relation to meeting the needs of younger children. *Multisystemic Therapy (MST)* is a programme that, whilst used to reduce neglect and abuse, is currently more commonly used in relation to reducing offending or addressing violent and challenging behaviours amongst young people (Moran, 2010). The interventions are tailor-made to address the specific needs of the young person and include: skills training, parenting training, strategies to reduce engagement with peers who have a negative influence on the young person; and interventions to improve engagement and performance at school. It is explored further from the perspective of meeting the needs of young people in Chapters 12 and 13.

Macdonald (2005, p. 284) notes that 'MST comprises a pragmatic amalgam of intervention strategies, including interventions based on strategic family therapy, structural family therapy and cognitive-behavioural therapy.' It draws on ecological and family systems theories as well as research into the causes and correlates of antisocial behaviour in young people. This means it is multifaceted and well placed to address not only psychosocial issues within the neglectful family but also wider issues affecting the family's functioning. The programme is once again manualized, but professional therapists working with social workers and psychiatrists can draw on a range of evidence-based methods to identify and address the particular needs of a family. Services are offered to the whole family over a limited period of time, usually four to six months. The programme is intensive and the team is available, at any time of day or night, to the family throughout their involvement in the programme, which usually lasts six to nine months. Therapists complete an assessment focusing on child development, family interactions, and engagement of family members in social systems outside of the family. They work with the family to identify goals and then tasks that are completed by different family members to achieve these goals. These tasks may involve engaging with other professionals or members of the community. Progress is monitored, possibly on a daily basis, within the home environment.

Littell (2005, p. 445), in a challenging review of *MST*, concludes that there are inconsistencies in the results of controlled studies of the effects of *MST*. Moreover, she notes variations in implementation of the research methods and interpretations of findings from previous reviews. Bearing in mind the nature of the studies, Littell argues that evidence as to the effectiveness of *MST* is inconclusive. DePanfilis (2006b), however, believes that despite the concerns expressed by Littell, *MST* suggests promise, arguing that this is in part due to the therapist's ability to select from a range of evidence-based strategies that can be tailored to the needs of the particular family. This is supported by a more recent randomized effectiveness trial, completed in the USA by Swenson *et al.* (2010), of families with adolescents where the parents had physically abused their children. They conclude that an *MST* programme designed to address issues of physical abuse and neglect was more effective than standard services normally provided to these families. It was most effective in reducing mental health symptoms amongst young people, parent psychiatric distress, and parenting behaviours associated with maltreatment. *MST* also appeared to be more effective in improving the support networks available to the parents. But what was notable was that differences in service provision in relation to re-abuse was statistically insignificant, although the adolescents whose families had been through the *MST* programme were less likely to be placed out-of-home and, when they were, they did not experience as many placement changes.

Intensive family support

While programme design and specific interventions differ, most of the intensive family support programmes – such as *Homebuilders* in the USA (discussed in detail in Chapter 11), which has influenced the development of programmes in the UK – have a number of common features (Nelson *et al.*, 2009):

- Workers have caseloads of two to six families and work intensively with families for a time-limited period.

- Workers are expected to establish a supportive, empowering relationship with the family. The parents retain parental responsibility.
- There is a system of back-up for the primary worker.
- Workers are available 24 hours a day for emergencies.
- A diverse range of services are used flexibly to meet the family's needs.
- Much work takes place in the home, allowing for skill development *in situ*.
- Family and community networks are used.

As has been described above, governments recently, particularly in the UK, have shown a keen interest in intensive family support programmes. This recent interest owes much to the successful social and economic outcomes obtained from the Scottish Action for Children *Dundee Families Project*. This project was set up in 1995 with the intention of both reducing antisocial behaviour and stabilizing the circumstances of families on the brink of eviction in Dundee, Scotland. Practitioners had caseloads of three families and worked with them intensively for around nine to 12 months, using a range of methods including, in some cases, a residential component. A small-scale project evaluation found that intensive family support, such as that provided by the Dundee project, can keep children out of care, prevent antisocial behaviour, raise the self-esteem of vulnerable parents and help overcome neglect, particularly in tackling neglect issues in the early stages (Dillane *et al.*, 2001; Action for Children, 2011).

This type of project really highlights the importance of a multidisciplinary, team-around-the-family approach. The success of the Dundee project has been attributed to agencies such as social services, housing, health, youth offending, police, education and schools working together to meet the needs of these families (Action for Children, 2011). Moreover, good management, stable staff, shared ownership by other agencies and a holistic approach are considered crucial to the success of the project (Dillane *et al.*, 2001). Action for Children have built on the successes of the Dundee project and developed other intensive family support projects across the UK, reporting positive results in terms of keeping children safe and out of care, reducing antisocial behaviour, and improving parenting capacity as well as the issues impacting on capacity.

Unfortunately, however, these projects are not the panacea for managing all chronic neglect cases. Dillane *et al.* (2001) noted that despite all these interventions, some families still had serious ongoing childcare problems. Their note of caution is reinforced by the findings of an American review of the evidence on these schemes (Nelson *et al.*, 2009). Although some of the studies reported promising results, Nelson *et al.* conclude that there is little known, as yet, about the services and programme content that work best for particular groups, such as racial and ethnic minorities and those involved in different forms of maltreatment or presenting with different parenting problems. Moreover, more research is required into the effectiveness of these services with different groups of children.

Despite the lack of evidence, the notion of intensive family intervention has been developed further by government policy in England, through *Family Pathfinder* programmes, which are also known as *Family Intervention Projects* (FIPs). (There is also a *Young Carer Pathfinders* programme, considered in Chapter 12.) The programme uses 'intensive, family-focused approaches to addressing the needs of families who face multiple and complex problems' (York Consulting, 2011, p. 1), including child protection concerns and many of the socio-economic problems encountered by neglecting families. The findings have been positive, with reductions recorded in terms of parenting issues, relationships between family members, child protection concerns, housing issues, school attendance and antisocial behaviour. Lloyd *et al.* (2011), in another English study of these types of interventions, 'cautiously conclude[d]' (p. 7), from a follow-up of 470 families 14 months after they exited the intervention, that these programmes are most effective in terms of sustaining a successful outcome in relation to family functioning, crime and antisocial behaviour.

Both Lloyd *et al.* and York Consulting identify a number of factors that contribute to the effectiveness of intensive family intervention programmes. These include:

- a phased, multidisciplinary approach that begins by addressing the underlying causes of family tensions and stress, moving on to addressing individual issues and finally socio-economic factors and parenting issues
- a persistent, skilled and assertive key worker who works intensively with the family and provides case leadership
- a team-around-the-family approach with key worker as 'lynchpin'
- a robust framework of support and supervision for staff
- an intensive and flexible family-focused response
- an ability to provide necessary services to meet need without encountering issues related to service demarcations and inflexible budgets
- clear support plans for families on exit to ensure positive outcomes are maintained
- engaging with families over a considerable period of time.

It is worth noting that Lloyd *et al.* (2011) found that only 3 per cent of the families in their study of 8,841 families involved in intensive family preservation services were black, 2 per cent were Asian and 7 per cent were classified as 'other or mixed race'. They also found that non-white families were less likely than others to address family functioning problems. Whilst many of the barriers discussed in Chapter 9 that affect the take-up of early help services by families from ethnic minority groups may also apply to families with complex needs, as yet there is little research evidence to substantiate this.

Conclusion

> There isn't one single intervention or agency that makes a difference for families with multiple needs. The teams-around-the-family concept is at the heart of all these interventions, as is a multidisciplinary plan, co-ordinated by a key worker. Those are the three essential ingredients, but sometimes we lose our focus on those proven things. (Davies, National Family Intervention Strategy Group, cited in Higgs, 2011, p. 1)

As is explicit in this quote, interventions to address chronic neglect have to be multifaceted in order to address the multiple problems that these families face in relation to the needs of their children, their own parenting needs and issues, as well as the socio-economic factors that are influencing their family functioning. In this chapter the importance of a team-around-the-family approach, combined with a meaningful relationship with a key worker, has been explored. What is also evident, from an exploration of the interventions for these complex families, is the importance of finding strategies that engage the parents positively in the interventions and then sustain their meaningful participation. Crucial to that engagement are workers establishing a meaningful 'working alliance' (Platt, 2012, p. 141) with the family members and ensuring that support and guidance is of sufficient duration to enable positive changes to behaviours to be sustained, even during times of stress and family crises.

Mullins *et al.* (2011) recognized the importance of these areas to family engagement in intensive service provision. Drawing on their work, a series of questions are presented below that are designed to ensure the best possible chance of engagement by the family in the relevant services. They are particularly useful for consideration at core group meetings or other meetings where interventions with a family are being evaluated.

Service delivery:

- Do parents understand why services are being provided and have they been involved in planning the timing and nature of the interventions?
- Are they aware of what outcomes professionals hope to achieve and what it would look like when the aims have been achieved?
- Are the parents clear about the consequences of not engaging meaningfully in the intervention for the child and family?
- Have parameters to non-acceptable behaviour, such as violence and aggression, been made clear?
- Do they understand the roles and responsibilities of the different professionals involved in delivering the package?
- Do the parents have confidence in the knowledge and skills of the practitioners who are working with them?
- Are the service providers accessible and reliable?

Service content:

- Do parents understand the relevance of the content?
- Is the content addressing their immediate needs and do they feel it is equipping them to cope with everyday life?
- Are the resources being used appropriately, bearing in mind ability, culture and ethnicity, and the specific needs of different family members?
- Do the parents feel that they are being seen as individuals rather than having a particular type of problem?
- Is there the potential for a parent/carer and/or child to feel ignored or marginalized as a result of the focus of the interventions?
- Is the content sufficiently flexible to address changing needs and circumstances?

Emotional support:

- Is sufficient emotional support, reassurance and encouragement provided to assist families to make changes?
- How is anxiety being managed and contained?
- What is the quality of the relationship between the parent/s and service providers?
- Do family members and practitioners communicate effectively, relate well and feel comfortable with each other?
- Are all the practitioners who are working with the family consistent in their expectations and approach?
- Do the parents feel workers understand and are supportive whilst remaining focused on the needs of the child or children?

Tangible support

- Is practical help provided to address material and financial needs?
- Are concrete solutions offered for issues associated with housing, fuel/energy, unemployment, benefits, food, clothing, and so on?

Chapter 11

Addressing Parenting Issues within Neglectful Families

A 'web of disadvantage'[1]

Child maltreatment, including neglect, is often accompanied by what is frequently described as the 'toxic three': domestic violence, mental health problems, alcohol and drugs misuse. This would seem to be the case irrespective of jurisdiction. Butchart *et al.* (2006) highlight, for example, the strong links between child abuse, neglect and alcohol misuse in countries as diverse as South Africa, Columbia, Latvia, Lithuania, Moldova, the USA, Germany and the UK. In Canada 34 per cent of child welfare investigations included reports of alcohol and drug use; in Western Australia alcohol or drug misuse were considered a contributory factor in 57 per cent of out-of-home care applications (Butchart *et al.*, 2006). In England and Wales, 2–3 per cent of children under 16 are living with one or both parents with a serious drug problem, whilst in Scotland it is believed to be between 4 and 6 per cent (Advisory Council on the Misuse of Drugs, 2003). Concerns about mental health issues were evident in between 10 and 42 per cent of child protection cases in the UK, Western Europe, Australia, Canada and the USA (Darlington *et al.*, 2005; Parrott *et al.*, 2008).

Moving on to consider the evidence regarding parenting issues and child neglect specifically, Forrester (2000) studied 50 families in England where professionals had concerns that the children were suffering or likely to suffer significant harm, and found substance misuse was strongly associated with neglect. Moreover, these were cases where the children were twice as likely to be subject to care proceedings. Antle *et al.* (2007) studied 2,350 families investigated for child neglect in Kentucky, USA and found that in 29 per cent of cases domestic violence was a factor. And children whose parents have a learning disability are over-represented in child protection cases. For example, in Canada these children make up 10 per cent of all child protection cases (McConnell *et al.*, 2011b). Similar percentages have been found in the UK (Cleaver and Nicholson, 2007) and Australia (Lamont and Bromfield, 2009), with neglect the most frequently cited form of maltreatment. It is challenging enough finding interventions that address both neglect and a particular parenting issue; it is much more complex when a number of issues coexist, as is frequently the case. For example, in a study completed in South Australia, Jeffreys *et al.* (2011) found that families engaged in the child protection system had multiple problems, including mental health issues complicated by substance misuse, problematic partner relationships, housing difficulties, poverty, lack of social supports and a history of abuse and childhood trauma. Similar findings were identified in the systematic review completed by Barlow and Schrader McMillan (2010). Both Forrester and Harwin (2011) and Cleaver *et al.* (2007) found that a high proportion of children referred to children's social care in England live with both domestic violence and substance misuse. Moreover, social isolation, prostitution, partner disharmony, and violence are also associated with drug misuse (Advisory Council on the Misuse of Drugs, 2003; Donohue, 2004; DePanfilis, 2006a; Cleaver *et al.*, 2007; Forrester and Harwin, 2011). Mental health problems also appear to be more prevalent amongst adults with a learning disability (Lamont and Bromfield, 2009). Brandon *et al.* (2010) conclude that these parenting issues, accompanied by a parenting background of neglect in childhood and other stresses, are a combination that is particularly lethal; Forrester and Harwin (2011, p. 32) describe this as a 'web of disadvantage'. The interconnectedness between the issues makes it difficult for practitioners both to establish exactly what impact the parenting issues are having on parenting, as opposed to other personal and socio-economic factors, and to know how to respond. In addition, it can be hard determining cause and effect (Dunn *et al.*, 2002).

The complexity of managing these cases might explain the inconsistent responses of professionals to the different issues. Forrester and Harwin (2011), in a study of ways in which professionals respond to cases of alcohol and substance misuse, found that illegal drug use, such as use of heroin and crack cocaine, was more likely to lead to a referral to statutory child protection services *before* the child had suffered harm, with many professionals being concerned about potential harm. This was not the case with alcohol use, with referrals being made when the child was older and had *already* suffered harm. Jeffreys *et al.* (2011) found that practitioners struggle to identify appropriate interventions in cases where a parent had a mental illness. This was because the nature of the need and the services required are likely to change, with periods of need being interspersed with periods of quality caregiving. Booth and Booth (1994, 1997) and Booth *et al.* (2004), referring to the UK, and McConnell *et al.* (2011b), drawing on Canadian research, argue that there is an over-representation of children undergoing care proceedings whose parents have a learning disability. Cleaver and Nicholson (2007), however, in a subsequent study of 76 children living with parents with a learning disability, found that social workers in children's services were actually committed to working in partnership with these families and indeed spent considerable time trying to engage them in both assessment and service planning. Tarlton *et al.* (2006), in a study of provision of services to families where the parents had a learning disability, concluded that staff often hold negative or stereotypical attitudes towards these parents and allow such attitudes to prejudice their assessments of individual cases. They also believe that in these situations practitioners may be overly risk averse and, as a consequence, set extremely high standards. The parents in turn may disengage from services as they feel workers have a negative view of them, and whatever they do the workers will want to remove the children.

Collaboration

The 'web of disadvantage' that surrounds many families means that coordinated, multifaceted, rather than individual, interventions are necessary. However, Chambers and Potter (2009), in an American study of 160 substantiated child neglect cases, conclude that few interventions focus on how to integrate child protection concerns with those addressing substance misuse. This would also appear to be the case in the UK, with Forrester and Harwin (2011) finding that in 71 per cent of the cases they studied there was no record of involvement from a substance misuse professional. There are a number of reasons why meaningful collaboration does not take place. First, practitioners are poorly prepared to work collaboratively with these complex cases (Cleaver and Nicholson, 2007; Cleaver *et al.*, 2011). This is in part due to a lack of understanding of roles, which was also noted in the Anytown neglect study (see Box 0.1 and Appendix), as discussed in Chapter 6. Slack and Webber (2008), for example, in an English study of mental health professionals, found that whilst mental health professionals considered supporting children important, they did not necessarily believe it was their role or responsibility to do so. They also found that mental health professionals, working in an in-patient setting, were far more likely than their colleagues in community settings to believe this was not their role. Hester (2011, p. 846), referring to domestic violence, puts it well, using the analogy of planets:

> On the 'child protection planet' the focus is on protecting children, not adults...although domestic violence is recognised, practice with families experiencing domestic violence is largely carried out within 'planetary' boundaries and links with the 'domestic violence planet' appear neither cohesive nor extensive.

Poor collaboration is exacerbated by issues of confidentiality, gaps in interagency processes, unrealistic expectations and professional knowledge (Darlington *et al.*, 2005). The situation is exacerbated by the lack of integrated services that focus on addressing the parenting issue or issues, the impact on parenting capacity and the needs of the child (Alcohol Concern and The Princess Royal Trust for Carers, 2008; Davies and Ward, 2012).

Meeting the additional needs of neglected children and young people affected by parenting issues

Multidisciplinary working does not mean just focusing on the parenting issue or issues and parenting capacity, it also means addressing the needs of the child. In an exploration of programmes specifically designed for children of parents who misuse drugs, Banwell *et al.* (2002) identified that whilst multiagency collaboration is important, practitioners should work flexibly, recognizing the need to gain the trust of the child, and at the same time providing an appropriate level of intervention. Through these interventions children should have a supportive multidisciplinary team who ensure a package is constructed that provides them with a stable home environment; develops their resilience so that despite these issues they have a positive sense of self; ensures that there is at least someone who can provide the necessary stabilizing influence; and that they have an alternative safe and supportive place to the family home if necessary (Templeton *et al.*, 2010; Cleaver *et al.*, 2011). In order to ensure the package meets the needs of the child, it is necessary to consider how the various parenting issues affect the child.

Effects of parenting issues on children and young people

Parenting issues can have a significant and profound impact on the child, compromising their health and development from conception to adulthood. It is not the issue per se which is the problem: it is the way it impacts on the child's lived experience. Children who are neglected as a result of parenting issues such as drug and alcohol use, domestic violence, learning disability and mental health issues are likely not to have had a positive start in life. Babies whose mothers used drugs and/or alcohol during pregnancy may be neurologically and physically damaged. They may also be born with HIV or hepatitis B or C virus. As infants and during the preschool years these children may form insecure attachments, experience emotional and behavioural problems with their cognitive development and have delayed language because of erratic behaviour, and lack of engagement and stimulation, from parents. As they become aware of their environment they may fail to develop a positive identity and sense of self-worth because their needs are not a priority for the parent. Moreover, they may demonstrate inappropriate behavioural responses learnt through, for example, witnessing domestic violence. All of this takes place against a likely backcloth of living in an impoverished environment, increasingly being expected to fend for themselves or taking on inappropriate responsibilities because of their parents' incapacity, having a poor diet, not having their basic health and physical care needs met and becoming isolated from other children (Alcohol Concern and The Princess Royal Trust for Carers, 2008; Cleaver *et al.*, 2011).

It is not surprising, therefore, that by the time these children are of school age they have a diverse range of needs. Cleaver and Nicholson (2007), in their studies of 40 children living with parental substance misuse and 43 with domestic violence, found that between the ages of five and nine years they had significant unmet needs. For example, 57 per cent of those living with parental substance misuse had unmet educational needs, and half the children affected by domestic violence and parental substance misuse had unmet needs in relation to both emotional and behavioural development, and family and social relationships. Donohue (2004) found that children exposed to substance misuse often fail to have their physical and educational needs met as a result of constant moves and inadequate living conditions. Cleaver and Nicholson (2007) found that children living with parental learning disability fared worst, with unmet needs identified for the majority in relation to all aspects of their health and wellbeing.

Addressing the needs of a neglected child where parenting issues are a concern

Gorin (2004) found that children living with a range of parenting issues worried about their parents, far more than was generally recognized by professionals. Moreover, they were often torn between loving their parents and the negative impact of their parents' behaviour on their lives. An important finding from Gorin's (2004) study was that the children said that being involved in finding solutions to the problem helped them cope. Accessing information through websites or helplines can be important for children experiencing domestic violence and other issues. Use of websites appears to empower children as they are able to control the level and degree of communication with professionals and volunteers, can remain anonymous and retain confidentiality (Waldman and Storey, 2004). For some, this is the first step towards seeking support. Children reported, for example, finding the NSPCC's *There4Me* website valuable and accessible as it provided information on many of the problems young people experience (Perry, 2002).

Interventions for neglected children acting as carers

Many children, as they grow up with these parenting issues, take on increasing caregiving responsibilities within the home, including intimate care and household tasks. They may also take responsibility for caring for their siblings when they witness the needs of their siblings not being met by their parents. For many young carers, projects can provide respite and can be a particularly beneficial form of support. An example of this is the English *Extended Family Pathfinder Programme*. These programmes focus on preventing the commencement of young caring in families affected by various parenting issues. Like the *Pathfinder* programmes described in Chapter 10, they take a multidisciplinary approach to identifying and meeting the needs of family members as well as extending the remit of existing young carers provision in order to identify those in need of early help. In addition, they raise awareness amongst adult and children's services of the needs of young carers. Early indications are that these programmes are contributing to identifying and meeting the needs of these children (Page *et al.*, 2008).

Making the most of school

McGee (2000), referring to children who experience domestic violence, notes that the children in her Scottish study found they experienced aggression and hostility in school, lacked concentration and often missed school because of fear of leaving their mother. Yet these children can benefit greatly from access to a positive school climate and sympathetic and vigilant teachers, in terms not only of their academic needs but also emotional and social support. Moreover, schools appear to be increasingly aware of the needs of these children and are finding ways of addressing them. Facilitating regular attendance at school and ensuring regular school medicals to monitor the child's health and development can be particularly beneficial. Practical help, such as assistance when children fall behind academically, and homework, after-school and breakfast clubs are also important, particularly for those children experiencing both neglect and parenting issues.

Raising awareness amongst school staff of the caring roles taken on by children is also important. Some of the *Extended Pathfinder Programmes* described above have a member of staff with a specific responsibility for liaising and developing work in schools. The staff also work with young children in school, enabling them to identify themselves as young carers (Page *et al.*, 2008).

Moving beyond the individual child, schools also need to ensure they have an effective anti-bullying policy within the school that takes account of the vulnerability of children living with a diverse range of parenting issues to being bullied and bullying (Cleaver *et al.*, 2011).

Creating a support network

Developing a social network outside the family; ensuring a caring and consistent adult is available who can respond to the cognitive and emotional needs of the child; enabling the child to join in out-of-school activities; and promoting peer acceptance and friendships can all be of great benefit to children living with parenting issues (Cleaver *et al.*, 2011). Creating a support network for neglected children, which draws on members of the community, is explored further in Chapter 12.

Many of these children who are living with parenting issues receive support from the extended family. This can literally be a lifesaver. Barnard (2007) found that parents emphasized the value of support from the extended family in terms of meeting the needs of their children. When this support was not available the children were more likely to be taken into the care of the local authority. Children too describe the importance of extended family as providing a safe haven, particularly when they are frightened by their parents' behaviour (Hester *et al.*, 2007; Stanley *et al.*, 2009).

Interventions for neglectful families affected by drug and alcohol misuse

DePanfilis (2006a) notes that parents who misuse substances are often hard to reach because they are fearful of the consequences of asking for help. Their fears are twofold: first, they may not wish, or are unable, to give up their addiction and may deny or minimize the problem, and second, they are concerned that the damage they may be causing to their children could result in the children being removed. Combine this with Moran's findings (2010), in her review of the evidence, that little is known as to how to intervene effectively in these cases, and the challenge for professionals is significant.

Studies do, however, provide some indication of what is needed. For example, Cleaver *et al.* (2007) conclude that families affected by substance misuse require services from practitioners who have the specialist skills to ensure that parenting is accurately assessed and plans are well targeted and realistic. Moreover, the services provided should address the needs of both the children and their parents. Cleaver *et al.* (2011, p. 91) have drawn on the literature to provide a useful list of the factors that can protect children and young people from the negative impact of parental alcohol and drug misuse. Paying attention to these factors when devising an intervention package may reduce the risk of harm to children. The factors include:

- having one parent with no problems with alcohol or drug use
- providing treatment to the parent with issues
- ensuring the parents have the capacity to meet the needs of the child
- the parents managing to maintain a cohesive relationship and presenting a united and caring front to the child

- involving other responsible adults in childcare and ensuring the child has someone responsible in whom they can confide
- maintaining family rituals and activities
- keeping drugs, needles and syringes out of reach
- ensuring the child is not present when drugs are taken and substance misuse does not occur in the home
- not exposing the child to contact with drug users and other criminal activity
- providing a stable home with adequate financial resources
- developing local community involvement.

As with so many other issues discussed in this chapter, the problems associated with neglect and alcohol or drug misuse will not be addressed through short-term interventions; rather, long-term, well-targeted support from a range of agencies is required. Some interventions that appear to show promise are discussed below.

Pre-birth and early years

Women who have been misusing substances before and during pregnancy may be anxious about the attitudes of health care and social services staff towards them, or they may be overwhelmed by the involvement of a diverse range of agencies (National Institute for Health and Clinical Excellence, 2010). It is important, therefore, that any package addresses their fears and guilt. It is also important to recognize that these mothers and their partners are likely to require additional support to help them both prepare for and then create a secure and safe environment for their baby. In addition, they will need assistance to develop coping strategies that prevent or reduce the effects of their substance misuse on the baby (Turning Point, 2006).

A number of projects attempt to provide this kind of service. For example, in Glasgow problem drug users receive antenatal care in specialist multidisciplinary clinics held in community health centres in areas of high drug use. The birth then takes place in a dedicated maternity ward with follow-up care provided in the same health centres (Advisory Council on the Misuse of Drugs, 2003). What has been found to be important is the continuity of care, with maternity services working closely with neonatal paediatric services so that the mother and child do not fall between different services, and the family are able to maintain any positive relationships that have already been developed with professionals.

Barlow and Schrader McMillan (2010) identified a small-scale Australian study by Suchman *et al.* (2008) that showed promising results in using attachment-based interventions to increase the capacity of substance misusing mothers to support their child's socio-emotional development. The intervention consisted of 12 weeks of individual therapy provided alongside standard outpatient substance misusing treatment programmes. The focus of these individual sessions is to increase the mother's capacity for sensitivity and responsiveness to the baby's cues by improving her maternal representational balance and capacity for reflective functioning. This is particularly important for substance misusing parents as babies born to these mothers may well have restricted growth and complex health and/or serious developmental problems from exposure to drugs and alcohol during early pregnancy. The parents therefore have to be prepared to manage these babies in a manner that meets the needs of the infant.

Another interesting but small-scale study, completed in France, has some promising results in relation to preventing future alcohol-related pregnancies as well as reducing child neglect. Dumaret *et al.* (2009) describe a family support service that is operated by professionals and volunteers to families living in extremely poor environments with transgenerational alcoholism, substance misuse and violence issues. The key concept is of continual accessible support, with families always meeting with the same members of staff. The families, mainly mothers and young children, come together once a week for the *Tuesday Group*. Fifteen families participate at each meeting, attending on a strictly voluntary basis. The meetings are held all year round, one afternoon a week for two hours. The emphasis is on preschool-age children and long-term involvement, with families usually remaining involved for around 30 months. Staff and volunteers identify individual needs and provide constructive support. Twenty-two families were observed for an average of seven years after their participation in the group ended. The findings indicate that most of the parents recovered a significant degree of social autonomy and had developed the capacity to care for their children. Alcohol misuse, violence and child neglect had also decreased significantly.

Home-visiting: Parents under Pressure (PUP)

Parents under Pressure (PUP) draws on a strengths-based approach to help parents who misuse substances develop a secure relationship with their child and be able to meet the needs of that child. The programme is delivered in the home over a 20-week period and is tailor-made to address the specific needs of the family, which are identified through a detailed assessment. During the assessment a plan is constructed with clearly identified priorities and goals, and the parents are given a family workbook to monitor their progress. The delivery of the programme modules are designed with this plan in mind and cover a range of topics, including child management and play, perceptions of self as parent, relationships and lifestyle.

The programme uses 'mindfulness' techniques. This requires the parents to focus on the present moment so that they do not feel overwhelmed by past negative thoughts, feelings of stress and anxiety. A final session is spent on closure, reflecting on the parents' achievements over the course of the programme (Harnett and Dawe, 2008).

The *PUP* programme originated in Australia, for methadone-maintained parents of children between the ages of two and eight years. The NSPCC in the UK is currently trialling this programme with 650 methadone-maintained and alcohol-dependent parents of children aged under two years. Alongside the delivery of *PUP* the parents receive treatment from drug and alcohol teams.

In a randomized control trial, parents who had completed *PUP*, as opposed to parents receiving treatment from a substance-misuse clinic or more traditional parenting programmes as described in Chapters 8 and 9, were found to have reduced factors associated with maltreatment, such as stress and less methadone use. Moreover, their children had fewer behavioural problems and in tests had improved prosocial scores (Harnett and Dawe, 2008; Burgess *et al.*, 2012).

Family intensive preservation services

Family intensive programmes, particularly designed for substance misusing parents and their children, have also been piloted in England and Wales. They often build on the *Homebuilders* programme, which originated in the USA in the 1970s. This programme has received much attention as early evaluations found it to be successful in reducing the number of out-of-home placements for children living with parents who misuse substances. However, questions have been raised regarding the nature of those evaluations, and more rigorous evaluations indicate that the programme may not be as effective as originally thought (Forrester and Harwin, 2011). Nevertheless, there is some value in considering the approach that informs *Homebuilders*. Unlike some of the interventions discussed in earlier chapters, this intervention does not draw on a specific therapeutic framework or model. Rather, it is based on key principles that should inform the approach taken by workers. These principles include: recognizing that children need families but that the child's safety is of paramount importance; and that crises bring opportunities for change, and interventions should therefore be intensive and flexible and focus on what will reduce family stresses. What is significant is that *Homebuilders* starts from the premise that the power to change lies within the family and that families do care about each other, with members doing their best under often difficult circumstances (Whittaker *et al.*, 1990).

Drawing on this approach, the Welsh Assembly Government funded a pilot programme called *Option 2* (Forrester *et al.*, 2008). This programme is designed for families where the parents have drug or alcohol problems, with the aim of reducing the need for public care and improving family functioning in order to safeguard the welfare of the children. The intervention lasts for four to six weeks but is intensive, with workers available to families 24 hours a day, seven days a week. The focus is on therapeutic and practical interventions underpinned by motivational interviewing and a solution-focused approach. An evaluation of families was undertaken approximately three and a half years after referral to the scheme and a comparison made with families with similar issues who had not received the service. Children whose families had received *Option 2* services were less likely to have been removed from home. Whilst this may seem encouraging, the team who completed the evaluation add a note of caution indicating that little was known about the quality of life for those children who remained at home. Moreover, they found that *Option 2* was much more effective with families with less severe problems and they therefore question whether the impact lasts as long with families with more entrenched problems. They also raise questions as to whether short intensive support is sufficient without adequate, intensive, longer-term follow-on support (Forrester *et al.*, 2008).

The family drug and alcohol court

Building on their success in the USA, family drug and alcohol courts have been piloted in England and Scotland since 2007. The focus for these courts are families where the local authority has made a decision to initiate care proceedings because of concerns that parental substance misuse is causing or is likely to cause significant harm to the child or children in the family. The family drug and alcohol court uses an alternative approach to that usually taken towards care proceedings, as discussed in Chapter 13. In these courts the cases are heard by a dedicated district judge who deals with the case throughout its life. A guardian is appointed straight away and legal representatives only attend the first two hearings, unless there are particular issues requiring their input. After that, the judge holds fortnightly reviews with the parents and members of a specialist multidisciplinary team of practitioners and volunteer mentors, who undertake assessments, develop a plan for intervention, work with the family and evaluate progress. This approach is far more timely, coordinated and integrated than in ordinary care proceedings. In addition, judicial continuity and regular court reviews without lawyers appear to result in less antagonism and more engagement from parents (Harwin *et al.*, 2011).

An evaluation of the family drug and alcohol court operating in London was completed by Harwin *et al.* (2011). They found that this approach shows promise, with more parents seen in these courts, as opposed to ordinary family courts, and more parents having controlled their substance misuse by the end of the proceedings and been reunited with their children. Moreover, they found that parents remained engaged with substance misuse services for a longer period of time. Harwin *et al.* go on to describe the elements of the scheme that they believe made this form of intervention successful. These are worth noting as they encapsulate many of the elements that the literature indicates makes for successful interventions in relation to working with parents who are misusing substances. They include:

- a problem-solving approach
- the combined expertise of a multidisciplinary team to tackle the diverse range of family problems, and a whole-family approach
- the speed of multidisciplinary assessment, and coordinated planning and treatment
- the extent and continuity of support to motivate parents
- a transparent process promoting honesty
- conveying a sense of hope that change is possible whilst remaining focused on the safety and needs of the child.

What appears to be significant is striking whilst the iron is hot, such as when there is real possibility that their children will be removed. At this point they are likely not only to contemplate change but are sufficiently motivated to actively engage in the change process discussed in Chapter 4. Moreover, support and services are available to not only assist with that change but also to ensure that it is maintained.

Residential interventions

Another type of intervention that shows some promise, although studies are usually small scale, are residential programmes. One such programme is a six-month family-based residential programme run at Phoenix House in Sheffield, England, for heroin addicts and their children. This was subject to a retrospective, small-scale, cohort study using clinical and residential records. The centre seeks to act as a detoxification unit whilst at the same time assisting parents to develop parenting skills. The researchers found that older parents who were not poly-drug users had significantly better outcomes, and there was evidence such programmes can keep families together (Ward *et al.*, 2012).

Addressing mental health issues: what works – parents' and workers' perspectives

Cleaver *et al.* (2011) drew on the literature to identify the conditions under which children are *less* likely to be affected by parental mental illness. These conditions are combined below with the parental factors that Jeffreys *et al.* (2011), in a study involving 28 parents with different mental health conditions together with a diverse group of professionals, conclude are most likely to lead to effective interventions. This combination provides practitioners with some guidance as to the factors that are likely to achieve better outcomes for children:

- As children are less likely to be affected by parental mental illness if it is mild and of short duration, parents should be encouraged to seek help at an early stage.
- Motivation, acceptance of responsibility, engaging with interventions and treatment compliance by the parent underpin effective interventions.
- Creating a stress-free environment, and protecting the child from family discord, conflict and disorganization in the home improve the child's experience.
- Providing high-quality support to the child and parent/family member who is not affected by mental illness but is supporting the child and parent with mental health concerns helps meet the needs of the child.

Postnatal depression

Between 10 and 15 women in every hundred who have a baby are estimated to suffer mild postnatal depression. At its most extreme, postnatal depression is puerperal psychosis, which is associated with paranoia, delusional and unpredictable behaviour and requires urgent medical in-patient treatment. Mothers who experience postnatal depression, even if it is mild, are still suffering, experiencing symptoms such as feeling miserable, tearful and low; constant exhaustion with low energy levels; problems with sleeping and appetite; not being able to cope and consequently feeling guilty; being overwhelmingly anxious about the baby; and having difficulties bonding with the infant. One can see how a mother experiencing some of these symptoms may neglect her baby. And postnatal depression can be associated with lack of support, relationship difficulties, financial or housing worries and a family history of mental illness: factors also associated with child neglect (National Collaborating Centre for Mental Health, 2007). Furthermore, Edge (2011) concludes, from a study of 45 health and social care professionals in England and Wales, that perinatal mental illness amongst black and minority ethnic minority women is more likely to be under-detected and untreated than amongst the rest of this population of mothers.

There appears to be evidence that cognitive-behavioural interventions may be effective in these cases (Macdonald, 2005). However, despite the National Institute for Clinical Excellence (NICE) in the UK recommending psychological therapies to assist these mothers, doctors still tend to prescribe antidepressants (4Children, 2011). 4Children found that the needs of partners and the role they can play in supporting the mother and baby are often overlooked. They conclude that more effective interventions require:

- a proactive approach to identifying potential risk factors during pregnancy, with quick access to treatment following diagnosis
- professionals, particularly health visitors, to have the knowledge and skills not only to assess but also identify appropriate interventions – for example, training in the use of the Edinburgh Postnatal Depression Scale
- that GPs consider and have access to talking and psychological therapies, and recognize the importance of 'social prescribing', such as support groups and befriending schemes
- more information to be readily available for fathers
- priority to be given to strengthening family relationships and bonds as part of the intervention.

Domestic violence

Antle *et al.* (2007) studied 2,350 families investigated for child neglect in Kentucky, USA, and found that workers rated families at significantly greater risk when domestic violence was present alongside neglect. Moreover, the workers correlated more severe neglect and limited social support networks with the presence of domestic violence. Domestic violence is associated with neglect in two different ways. First, witnessing domestic violence can have negative effects on children's behavioural, emotional and psychological wellbeing (Hester *et al.*, 2007). Therefore, seeing domestic violence in the home is arguably a failure on the part of the parent to meet the needs of the child. Second, domestic violence can significantly impair the mother's (this is the focus as it is predominantly men who are the perpetrators of domestic violence) functioning, her health and wellbeing and her interactions with her children (English *et al.*, 2003; Stanley, 2011). Moreover, exposure to domestic violence can leave women feeling degraded, depressed and lacking in confidence, and therefore vulnerable to attracting another abusive partner (Davies and Ward, 2012).

Bearing in mind the impact that witnessing or hearing domestic violence can have on a child, it was timely that section 120 of the English Adoption and Children Act 2002, which applies in England and Wales, extended the legal definition of harm to include the impairment suffered from seeing or hearing the ill-treatment of another, especially in the home, even if the child or young person themselves has not been directly assaulted or abused. Witnessing or hearing domestic violence is also considered a form of maltreatment in a range of other countries, such as Scotland under the Scotland Act 1995, and in 22 states of the USA (Child Welfare Information Gateway, 2009).

Despite evidence that domestic violence can have a major impact on both parenting capacity and the wellbeing of children, we do not, as yet, have the evidence to know what makes for effective interventions to prevent or address emerging concerns regarding domestic violence (MacMillan *et al.*, 2009). What is apparent, however, is that any intervention in cases where both neglect and domestic violence are of concern should not only address the domestic violence and the neglect but also the combined effects of the two. Eckenrode *et al.* (2000) in the USA found, for example, that the presence of domestic violence limits the effects of the *Family Nurse Partnership*, described in Chapter 9, and that the treatment effect decreased as the level of violence increased. Moreover, Barnes *et al.* (2009), in England, found that despite many of the cases being referred to the programme because of concerns about domestic violence, there was no evidence to indicate that participants in the programme were experiencing less abuse from their partners. Barth (2009) also found this to be the case in relation to the *Triple P* parenting programme, and concludes that parenting training needs to run alongside interventions that address domestic violence. If this is the case, then a more holistic 'whole family' (Stanley, 2011, p. 92) or team-around-the-family approach would appear to be the most effective response to these complex cases. The programmes should include a focus on addressing both the domestic abuse and the impact of this on the failure to meet the needs of the child. In addition, individual support for the mother, refuge-based support and advocacy, counselling, group work and activities specifically designed for children who have experience of domestic violence are valuable (LGA *et al.*, 2006). What is crucial to any intervention is that the perpetrator does not become invisible or that the episodes of domestic violence are minimized through, for example, being referred to as 'marital conflict' (Hester, 2011).

Meeting the needs of victims of domestic violence from South Asian and African-Caribbean communities

Thiara and Gill (2012), in a small-scale UK study of domestic violence, separation and child contact involving 45 South Asian and African-Caribbean women and 19 children of similar background, concluded that many of these women had experienced high levels of severe abuse over long periods and that for many of the South Asian women the abuse was also perpetrated by family members. These women felt controlled and isolated and many lacked an understanding of how to obtain support and advice in the UK, fearing abduction or separation from their children. Mothering had often been undermined as part of the abuse and had negatively affected the mother–child relationship. They also found that some dominant stereotypes still influenced practice. For example, many professionals assumed that South Asian men, unlike African-Caribbean men, wanted to be part of their children's lives. They also tended to accept the view that South Asian women were the property of their fathers/families. In terms of interventions, Thiara and Gill (2012) identified what the respondents considered helpful. These included:

- services that offer advice, not only on leaving domestic violence but also guidance about child contact
- easy access to information, for example in GP practices or health centres, enabling women to get early help and support
- outreach support for women before, during and after separation, particularly with regard to addressing issues arising through child contact with perpetrators
- parenting support, tailored to the needs of women from minority ethnic groups to regain confidence regarding parenting skills
- accessible and safe, supervised contact centres sensitive to diverse needs
- perpetrator and parenting programmes targeted at South Asian and African-Caribbean men to address abusive behaviour and improve parenting skills.

Aggressive behaviour and mental health issues: a challenging combination

Mind (2009), in its report *Men and Mental Health: Get It off Your Chest*, draws on research from Europe to highlight that domestic violence and aggression by male perpetrators may be an indicator of mental health issues, such as depression or post-traumatic stress disorder (PTSD), and that it is important for practitioners to distinguish between premeditated violence and the behaviour of a man who is traumatized, anxious or depressed in order to ensure the man receives appropriate therapeutic treatment rather than perceiving the issue as a criminal act alone. Moreover, many of these men experience suicidal thoughts and may indeed attempt suicide (Akister, 2009). These issues are particularly important to consider at a time when there are a significant number of soldiers returning from war zones such as Iraq and Afghanistan, or asylum seekers and refugees who have been involved in wars and conflict.

FACT (Family Action for Choice Tomorrow) is a project in Birmingham that works with fathers who have mental health problems, such as PTSD, and perpetrate acts of domestic violence. It seeks to assist these men and support the rest of the family when the family have reached a crisis point, such as a referral to children's social care or court action due to mental health issues and domestic violence. The majority of fathers have been victims of war and violence, either as civilians in war zones or ex-servicemen, ex-policemen or members of the migrant community who feel displaced and isolated. A study has been undertaken of 41 of these complex-need families, who between them had 58 children. Some of the fathers were living with the family, others were separated or divorced and some were only permitted supervised contact of their children. The programme sought to change behaviour, improve parenting, increase understanding of child development and levels of self-esteem. This was achieved through one-to-one and group counselling, parenting programmes and training, horticultural therapy, men's drop-ins, family support and support for children. That many of the male workers, acting as mentors and role models, are fathers and originate from the same communities, understand the cultural and faith expectations and speak the first languages of the fathers undergoing the programme is considered key to its success. The project was evaluated through the use of clinical measures such as CORE (Clinical Outcomes Routine Evaluation), designed to measure wellbeing, psychological symptoms, functioning and risk to self and others; self-report; and reports from agencies. Study findings indicate 'that early intervention at the time of traumatic crisis enables the children to have a chance of some form of family reconciliation and of remaining in a safe family unit'. They also found that children's developmental progress had either improved after the interventions or returned to the level it was at before the issues with the father emerged (Akister, 2009, p. 4). FACT conclude that key to their success is: recognizing that domestic violence can be a symptom of a mental illness; working with the whole family to ensure an understanding by all family members of the negative behaviours and ways in which they can help each other; having a multi-skilled and intercultural team to assist families; and using male role models and male support workers. This enables the men to engage with services and appeared to be a stepping-stone towards accessing services and developing relationships with female professionals.

Parental learning disability and child neglect

Lamont and Bromfield (2009) undertook a literature review in an attempt to establish what we know about maltreatment and parents with a learning disability. They reviewed 25 studies from a range of developed countries that involved primary research, including qualitative, quantitative and mixed methods. Despite some methodological limitations, they found some common themes, the most significant being that it is not so much the intellectual limitations per se that should be considered as leading to neglect but other risk and protective factors that make the child vulnerable and affect parenting capacity. In other words, the system should not be driven by a focus on the parent-as-the-problem; rather, the focus should be more ecological (McConnell *et al.*, 2011b). Drawing on the studies Lamont and Bromfield (2009) reviewed, they provide a list of the factors that should be taken into account when considering appropriate interventions:

- *Parental relationships*: Parents with a learning disability appear to be more vulnerable than other parents to engaging with partners who are perpetrators of physical and sexual abuse and commit acts of domestic violence.
- *Social isolation*: Parents with a learning disability experience higher levels of social isolation than other parents, having fewer friends and supportive neighbours, and they are often dependent on their family for support. When support breaks down this can make them particularly vulnerable to engaging in relationships with inappropriate and potentially abusive partners.
- *Parental stress*: These parents often experience high stress levels, including stigmatization, unemployment, history of abuse, low socio-economic status and poverty.
- *Past histories of abuse*: Parents who have learning disabilities are more likely than other parents to have experienced abuse and neglect as children.
- *Health problems*: Physical and mental health problems are more common amongst these parents. What is of note is that mothers with a learning disability are twice as likely to have pre-term babies and a high rate of pre-eclampsia (a life threatening condition in pregnancy associated with hypertension and fluid retention).
- *Children's characteristics*: there is some evidence that the age of the child contributes to parental stress for mothers with a learning disability, with

mothers of school-age children reporting higher levels of stress than mothers of preschoolers. These parents may also struggle to cope with children who have complex medical and emotional needs.

Effective interventions: a family-centred rather than professional-centred approach

Wade *et al.* (2007) advocate a family-centred approach towards interventions with learning disabled adults that builds on strengths and reinforces positive parenting. Cleaver and Nicholson (2007) also support this approach. They found that involving parents, meaningfully, in assessments and plans is key to their satisfaction with the outcome of the assessment and, more importantly, their take-up of services. Bearing in mind the emphasis throughout this book on the 'working alliance' (Platt, 2012, p. 141), it is no surprise that the attitude of workers is crucial to the effectiveness of interventions. These parents need to feel that the worker accepts them, feels positive about their ability and is there to support them (Booth and Booth, 2004). This does not mean that other factors are unimportant. Wade *et al.* (2007), for example, found that practical details, such as having transport provided, and the manner in which the service is delivered, such as skill development in the home, were significant to engagement.

Parenting education programmes

The most effective parenting programmes for parents with learning disabilities appear to be those that take place within the home (McGaw *et al.*, 2002; Lamont and Bromfield, 2009). The Australian *Healthy Start* initiative (HealthyStart, 2009) identified some key elements for effective parenting education programmes designed to facilitate skill development amongst learning disabled parents. These include being:

- *Specific*: tailor-made to address the parent's particular needs. Visual aids work well provided they are meaningful to the particular family.
- *Situational*: learning 'on the job'. Teaching materials should be meaningful within the context of the parent's home and should be seen by the parent as useful and relevant to their daily life.
- *Structured and skill focused*: behavioural techniques work best with a focus on skills; and complex tasks should be broken down, with opportunities for modelling and feedback that encourage and reinforce good practice, promote maintenance and the generalization of skills. It is also important to recognize levels of concentration and tolerance for learning, and adapt the sessions accordingly.

- *Parent directed*: the programmes should be focused on what the family have identified as needs.
- *Contextually relevant*: the context, history, stresses, strengths and areas for development of each individual family should be recognized.
- *Long-term and regular*: support needs to be ongoing and consistent, taking into account that new skills will be required as the child or children develop. Regular and frequent sessions (once or twice a week) work best, with opportunities to practise between sessions.

Meeting wider support needs

Alongside structured interventions from agencies, Cleaver and Nicholson (2007) conclude that informal and formal support networks are important. If these are not in place, the families tend to stagger from one crisis to another. Moreover, supportive social networks can increase levels of confidence, self-esteem as well as assertiveness skills (McGaw *et al.*, 2002). One way of meeting these ongoing needs is through what Tarlton *et al.* (2006, p. vii) refer to as 'parenting with support'. This approach involves professionals who work with parents with learning disabilities acting as mediators, supporting parents and also educating professionals from other agencies, wider family, and community and voluntary agencies as to how best to work with the family to ensure the needs of the child are met and the parents feel supported. An example of this is a project in South Norfolk, England, where a multiagency consultation group has been established to provide support and advice to professionals working with families where a parent has a learning disability. The professional presents their case and receives advice from the group about how to progress developing support networks (DH and DfES, 2007).

The presence of a non-abusing partner in the house and support from the extended family can also be useful. Help with childcare and practical help in the home can help the parent to feel less isolated, provided this support is given in such a way that the parent feels they are in control (Tarlton *et al.*, 2006).

Advocacy

As parents with learning disabilities may struggle to access and negotiate services, such as health services, housing, and so on, an advocate may be of assistance in ensuring the parents access services necessary to ensure they meet the needs of the child. An advocate can help build confidence and self-esteem and can be particularly valuable when the parent has already had negative and difficult relationships with agencies, which may be the case in relation to child protection services. The services of an independent advocate are therefore worth considering if child protection interventions are being considered, whether the plan is to keep the child in the family or begin care proceedings (DH and DfES, 2007). Within the court setting the role of the advocate is to ensure that parents have a clear explanation of what is going on, know the different roles and responsibilities of those present in court and understand the implications of information shared and decisions made. If an advocate is to be effective in child protection cases, they should have a real understanding of both the adult and child protection systems, feel able to negotiate with all parties and challenge services (Tarlton *et al.*, 2006).

Conclusion

What is evident from this exploration of interventions into 'the toxic three' – alcohol and substance misuse, mental health issues and domestic violence – together with those for parents with learning disabilities, is that one cannot make generalizations. Each parent's parenting will be affected differently by the particular parenting issue or the combination of issues, the stresses they are experiencing and the context in which they are living, what Forrester and Harwin (2011, p. 32) refer to as the 'web of disadvantage'. This reinforces the importance of interventions being based on high-quality assessments that not only focus on the impact of the parenting issue on the parent's capacity to meet the needs of the child but also on the reasons why the parent is experiencing these issues. This last point becomes evident when one considers the conclusions drawn by Mind (2009) that domestic violence perpetrated by men may have mental health issues as its root cause. Likewise abuse, depression and isolation are all associated with engagement in substance misuse (Dunn *et al.*, 2002) and, as Brandon *et al.* (2010) found from a scrutiny of serious case reviews completed when children are seriously injured or die, it is the combination of parenting issues with the parents' own background of neglect that is particularly lethal.

What is also evident is that practitioners appear to hold stereotypical perceptions of the impact of these parenting issues on parenting. For example, professionals appear to be more concerned about the harm that drug misuse, rather than alcohol misuse, may cause in the future (Forrester and Harwin, 2011). Perceptions of roles and responsibilities in terms of engaging in interventions also play their part, with workers from children's services and those from adult services often orbiting around different planets (Hester, 2011).

The complexity of many of these families' situations, combined with the attitudes and approaches of workers from very disparate agencies, makes intervening in these cases challenging.

What is evident from all the interventions discussed above is that packages should be constructed that not only address the cause and effect of the parenting issue or issues but also the impact on the individual children in the family and other family members. In many situations children take on responsibilities that are not appropriate, becoming young carers. For other children education is affected, as is their ability to form social networks and engage in activities outside the home. It is crucial not to ignore how other family or community members, who do not have parenting issues, are able to support the child and protect them from the fall-out of these issues (Cleaver *et al.*, 2011). What is also important is that many of the parents feel disempowered, with low levels of self-esteem and poor levels of confidence, and they therefore need to feel motivated, not only to change their behaviour but also to sustain these changes. Times of crises provide windows for engaging with parents to bring about change, but this is only likely to be effective if professionals work in partnership with parents, recognizing their strengths and working with them to identify weaknesses and ways in which these can be addressed. That does not mean working at a pace that focuses primarily on the parents. Arguably, the greatest challenge of all is engaging with parents, recognizing the cause and impact of parenting issues on parenting capacity whilst at the same time remaining firmly focused on ensuring that the needs of the child are met in a timely manner.

Note

1. Forrester and Harwin (2011, p. 32).

Chapter 12

Meeting the Needs of Neglected Children and Young People

> The neurobiological tools for thoughtful choice are damaged as a result of adult thoughtlessness. Yet, we point the finger of blame and watch the child like a trapped circus animal fail to perform to our expectations. (Batmanghelidjh, 2006, p. 156)

Batmanghelidjh, in the quote above, summarises vividly and poignantly how, as the child grows up, the focus for professionals becomes their presenting negative behaviour rather than the cause of that behaviour. In the earlier chapters of this book I have considered interventions specifically designed to address emerging concerns regarding neglectful parenting of babies and preschoolers. In this chapter I concentrate on addressing the negative impact of neglect on school-age children and young people. For convenience I will continue to use the umbrella term 'children' to refer to this group. It is evident from statistics that many children of primary school age become or continue to be subject to neglect. Moreover, neglect remains the most common category of maltreatment for older children between 10 and 15 years of age, despite the effort of providers to address issues within early years interventions (Rees, 2011).

Tanner and Turney (2006) conclude, from their overview of effective interventions for children who have experienced neglect, that school-age children need direct work that will both promote resilience to the impact of the neglectful environment on the child's health and wellbeing and address the damaging effects of the neglect. Therefore, interventions for this group will be explored from two perspectives: consideration will be given, first, to interventions that promote resilience; and second, to interventions that address the effects of neglect on their physical health, their education, behaviour and psychosocial functioning.

Part 1: Promoting resilience amongst children vulnerable to neglect

Daniel et al. (1999, p. 129) comment that neglect 'erodes the key factors associated with resilience', such as secure attachments and self-esteem, and hinders a sense of self-efficacy. Why is it that then that not all young people who have abusive and neglectful experiences suffer the detrimental effect to their health and wellbeing one would anticipate? Rather, they achieve good outcomes. Why do some neglected children who have been ignored, bullied, uncared for and forgotten manage to reach their developmental milestones and go on to become well-functioning adults? As yet there is no clear scientific answer to this question (Bentovim, 2010). Davidson *et al.* (2010), however, argue there may be factors positively promoting the child's resilience. And, according to Iwaniec (2006), the children that do well are those who have cognitive ability, an easy temperament, are able to form relationships, and develop emotional and practical coping skills. She goes on to argue that these children also have an ability to recognize that the maltreatment is not their fault. In addition to these dispositional factors, the resilient neglected child is likely to have a supportive environment. Thus, in terms of interventions to promote resilience, a supportive network is valuable.

Establishing a supportive environment for the neglected child

Gilligan (2010, p. 178) notes that 'connectedness within a web of relationships based on norms of trust, reciprocity and mutual identification' can protect children from the impact of traumatic and stressful events, such as living with neglect. Moreover, this web of relationships helps the child gain confidence to try new experiences, take on challenges and cope with adversity (Baxter and Print, 1999). The National Scientific Council on the Developing Child (2004, 2010) also emphasizes the importance, particularly for young children, of having a positive emotional connection to someone. If a parent is unable to provide this then peers, extended family, members of the community and teachers are all potential sources able to offer that important quality relationship and emotional connection. Vulnerable children themselves also recognize the importance of a supportive environment. In a study by Seaman *et al.* (2006), completed in a very disadvantaged community in Glasgow, children identified family, friends and neighbours as important individuals providing a trusted and protective network. And for many children in this study, school was a haven from risks. Ways in which these different members of the community can support children are considered below.

Wider family

One of the striking features of the Anytown neglect study (see Box 0.1 and Appendix) was the role played by members of the extended family in supporting children in cases of chronic neglect. Grandparents, and aunts and uncles, attempted to meet the needs the parents were unable to meet. This was particularly noticeable if the parents had parenting issues. The support included providing children with meals, accommodating them when the situation at home became intolerable or having them live with them for lengthy periods of time. Stevenson (2007) argues, however, that members of the extended family, who themselves may have been abusers or abused, may not always provide satisfactory care or, indeed, they may be actively dysfunctional. Moreover, because of erratic lifestyles, the support may not be sustained. This was evident in one case in the Anytown study when a volatile relationship between the grandparent and the parent meant support to the child from the grandparent was erratic and depended on the current relationship between the parent and grandparent. Nevertheless, that does not mean that extended family should be discounted. For example, an aunt may have proved to be resilient in similar circumstances to the child, or has remained on the periphery of the family and may be well placed to support the neglected child.

What was evident in the Anytown study was that the extended family was often able to support children of primary school age. However, as these children moved into adolescence and exhibited challenging behaviours, such as substance misuse or offending, and became increasingly challenging, aggressive and violent, the extended family found they were no longer able to manage without a considerable amount of support from professionals. Key to providing a safe environment for the child with the extended family, therefore, is to ensure support is provided to them to assist the family in meeting the needs of the neglected child.

Peer relationships

Friendships provide children with the opportunity to learn how to engage with others, how to share and how to behave in different social contexts. Moreover, they are a source of fun and comfort and give children a sense of belonging. Children who have been neglected are ill equipped to manage peer relationships and are therefore less likely than other children to reap the benefits of friendships. They have poor role models, and may lack experience in terms of how to engage and play with their peers; this, in turn, makes them particularly vulnerable to victimization. A lack confidence and self-esteem means they struggle forming friendships and are also vulnerable to bullying and aggression from peers (Hildyard and Wolfe, 2002; Scourfield, 2006; Maxwell *et al.*, 2012). As one of the respondents in a study by Frederick and Goddard (2010, p. 25) put it: 'School was a nightmare, no other way of putting it, school was just a nightmare...I'd catch the bus home. They'd spit on me and I used to just sit there and take it and take it and take it.'

Iwaniec (2006) lists some helpful strategies that can be used to equip a neglected child to manage peer relationships effectively. These include: understanding what the child expects of friendships; using role play, modelling and activities to increase the child's understanding of peer relationships and providing them with opportunities to develop the skills to manage these relationships appropriately; finding opportunities for the child to engage with other children through sharing a common interest; and working with parents to increase their knowledge and understanding of appropriate behaviour for children of the relevant age.

One of the issues commonly encountered by neglected children, as described in the quote above, is being subject to bullying and, in some cases, these children can go on and become bullies themselves (Hildyard and Wolfe, 2002). Rigby (2004) believes there are five factors that contribute to bullying. First, neglected children may be developmentally delayed and do not have the skills to manage interpersonal relationships in the same way as their peers. Second, individual differences make children vulnerable to bullying; for a neglected child their appearance is a common target for bullies. Third, socio-cultural differences, such as the dominant macho male, leads to some children acting as bullies whilst others become more vulnerable. Fourth, group and peer pressure with children expected to conform to the norm of the group may make children who cannot afford the latest trainers, electronic game, and so on, vulnerable. And finally, the rationale for restorative justice has an influence. For example, the child may not appreciate that bullying is wrong or takes the view: 'I've been bullied. Now it is my turn.' In order to address bullying, therefore, it is important that consideration is given to the cause.

There are two common approaches in the literature to addressing bullying. The first is a focus on the environment, with consideration being given to developing a school culture that does not tolerate bullying and has systems in place for recognition that make it easy for children to report incidents, confident that they will be addressed and the child kept safe. The second is to address bullying at an individual level by providing opportunities to develop life skills, promoting strengths and a sense of self-worth, and teaching children how to engage in effective social relationships. Many of the programmes described below seek to achieve this.

Community support

Moving from extended families and friendships to the community, there are a number of schemes designed to broaden the child's support network by giving them the opportunity to engage with and hopefully bond with an adult, or in some cases an older child. A good example of this approach is the Australian *Aunties and Uncles Family Project*. This project has been running for over 30 years in Sydney. The aim is to provide a network for children who do not have a supportive family network through community volunteers who act as 'aunties and uncles' to these children. The volunteers offer mentoring and are expected to spend up to one weekend a month with their allocated child. They seek to establish a friendship with the child and their family, and aim to develop self-esteem and confidence. They also provide a mentoring role by demonstrating to parents how to interact with their children. Families can self-refer or referrals can come from support services. An evaluation was completed of this project with 66 volunteers, 25 children and 18 parents participating. The children reported valuing the experience of a positive and significant relationship, receiving encouragement from the volunteers and doing 'fun' things. The parents also valued the scheme and the benefits it brings to their children. What was of note was the reported value of the experience for the volunteers' own wellbeing (Helm, 2011). A similar mentoring scheme for primary school age children with behavioural problems has been operating in Liverpool, England. An evaluation of this scheme found that reported behavioural problems reduced amongst the children who participated and social skills increased (Fisher and Gruescu, 2011).

Such projects require a careful matching between child and mentor, and also volunteers who are prepared to make a long-term commitment to that child. Moreover, they have been found to be effective if the mentor gets to know the family and works collaboratively with the parents (Turney, 2012). Ross *et al.* (2011) conclude, from a review of the international literature, that mentoring is most effective when:

- it is included in a suite of interventions
- weekly meetings of at least five hours' duration take place
- there is an emphasis on emotional support
- careful consideration is given to matching mentee and mentor
- support is provided to the mentor.

Youth support services can also play a significant part in supporting young people who have been neglected. A government inspection completed in England (Ofsted, 2010) found that the provision of targeted youth support services for young people at risk increased the options of support for these young people. In eight of the 11 areas they visited they noted a reduction in the number of first-time offenders, and five services had made inroads into reducing the numbers of young people who were not in education, employment and training. These services were not, however, as effective at engaging young people over the age of 16 as they were at engaging younger adolescents.

Schools

Iwaniec (2006) argues that the predictable routines of a school day provide security and stability. In addition, attainment in academic and extra-curricular activities, such as sport and membership of clubs, can build a sense of self-esteem and confidence. Moreover, children have, through schools, the opportunity to form friendships with peers. Experiencing a positive school environment can give the neglected child positive respite from poor home conditions. Yet if neglected children are to make the most of these opportunities, then teaching staff and other professionals need to recognize some of the barriers that these neglected and abused children encounter in making the most of school. The issue for many neglected children is that they can be lost within the large school population, particularly that of a secondary school. In a small-scale Australian study using in-depth interviews with 14 adults who had been abused and neglected as children, Frederick and Goddard (2010) found these adults could identify a number of barriers to their effective engagement in schools. These included:

- isolation, bullying and harassment by other pupils
- hygiene-related social problems and poor self-image
- lack of confidence stemming from feelings of rejection at home
- frequent moves as a result, for example, of out-of-home placements and family lifestyle that result in social difficulties in coping with new situations
- lack of professional assistance to manage these issues within the school.

Frederick and Goddard note, however, that working to address these barriers is expensive and time consuming, and they express concern that with a reduction in public sector spending, which is occurring in many nation states and affecting the employment of professionals such as educational psychologists, educational support assistants and school nurses, there is a lack of appropriate pupil welfare support in schools.

Part 2: Interventions to enhance the socio-emotional development of the neglected child

Neglect, as outlined in Chapter 3, can have a significant impact on the socio-emotional development of the child and the relationships formed beyond that with the primary carer. Part of the problem for these children is that past experiences mean that they do not have the emotional knowledge to discriminate expressions and understand emotional contexts, which makes it difficult for them to interpret the behaviour of others and respond appropriately (Bentovim *et al.*, 2009).

With this in mind, interventions that are likely to be most effective are those that develop emotional competence and social skills, what are referred to as *Social and Emotional Aspects of Learning Programmes (SEAL)*. These are increasingly being provided as a universal programme within primary schools, designed to create an ethos about attitudes and behaviour. Payton *et al.* (2008) completed a meta-analysis of 213 such programmes delivered in the USA to 270,034 school-age children. They concluded that *SEAL* programmes do have significant and positive effects on the targeted socio-emotional competences as well as on attitudes about self, others and school. Moreover, they also increased prosocial behaviours, reduced conduct and internalized problems, and improved academic performance. They found that the programmes can be delivered successfully by class teachers and incorporated into the school day. What is important, however, as with the parenting programmes discussed in Chapter 9, is that the programmes are well designed and delivered effectively. Interactive programmes involving role play, modelling and structured activities were found to be effective, and it would appear that delivering the programme through, for example, class-based sessions as opposed to a multi-component programmes, influenced outcomes. They conclude that effective programme delivery requires staff within schools to have information about various programmes, decide on the best fit for their needs, implement the programme as intended by the programme designers, and evaluate progress. Whilst this meta-analysis focused on American programmes, a number of *SEAL* programmes are in use in the UK, and the conclusions of Durlak *et al.* (2011) would appear to be as relevant. A selection of *SEAL* programmes that show promise are summarized in Box 12.1.

Developing socio-emotional skills: a parent–child approach

Whilst some of the programmes described above may have an element of parental engagement, *The Incredible Years* programme and the *Dinosaur School* are specifically designed to ensure that the child develops the necessary socio-emotional skills at the same time as the parent learns how to ensure their behaviour facilitates this development. This programme builds on that described in Chapter 9 but is for use where the children are of school age and exhibiting challenging behaviour. A small-scale Canadian study of 35 parents who were being monitored by child protection services because of their neglecting behaviours participated in a 16-week *Incredible Years Programme*. The programme focused on: developing harmonious parent–child relationships; learning and using effective child-rearing practices; improving problem-solving skills and developing communication strategies, both within the family but also with schools. The results indicated that this programme can potentially contribute to improving

Box 12.1: School-based psychosocial interventions for neglected children

Title of programme	Summary of programme content	Studies of effectiveness
SEAL: Social and Emotional Aspects of Learning	This comprehensive programme, which is used extensively in the UK, takes a whole-school approach to promoting social and emotional skills. The rationale is that these skills underpin effective learning, positive behaviour, regular attendance and emotional wellbeing. It is delivered in three waves, children thereby receiving input that reflects their needs. The first wave is designed to create an ethos in the school, which is intended to promote social and emotional skills. The framework is divided into seven themes to be covered within a school year: • New beginnings • Getting on and falling out • Say 'no' to bullying • Going for goals • Good to be me • Relationships • Changes	Evaluations indicate that *SEAL* in primary schools may have some positive impacts on outcomes for children in terms of waves one and two. Improved social skills and more effective relationships have been noted in schools using universal *SEAL* interventions. The small-group interventions led to increases in emotional literacy and social skills, with reductions in peer problems and increased self-regulation, as reported by both teachers and the pupils themselves. Caution has, however, been expressed by Allen (2011) who is concerned that there is variability in terms of the way in which *SEAL* is used, which influences outcomes. Dyson *et al.* (2010), in a review of successful interventions for children with additional needs, conclude that there are particular features of the *SEAL* programme that contribute to its effectiveness, which have been highlighted in the wider literature as fundamental to successful social and

Box 12.1 cont.

Title of programme	Summary of programme content	Studies of effectiveness
	Used as a whole-school, cross-curricular approach, *SEAL* aims to help children become successful learners, responsible citizens and confident individuals. The second wave consists of small-group interventions, which continue to focus on the above themes, for children identified as requiring additional support. Careful child selection, adhering to the programme and using effective group facilitators are important (Humphrey et al., 2008). The final wave is for children who have not benefited from the previous interventions and focuses on one-to-one sessions. Support for parents is offered alongside the targeted interventions and may involve specialist professionals, such as mental health workers.	emotional learning programmes. These features reflect the findings of Durlak et al. (2011). They include: • using a whole-school approach, developing an ethos and creating an environment that consistently promotes positive relationships between children and adults and between children themselves • taking a population-based approach and seeking to prevent problems arising • integrating carefully targeted interventions into more general approaches, for example reinforcing small-group learning in classroom activities • engaging with parents so they are aware and understand the ethos, and can reinforce this at home.
FRIENDS and Coping Cat	The programme is manualized and consists of ten sessions. It uses a range of behavioural, cognitive and physiological strategies to teach children how to identify and manage feelings of anxiety and	*FRIENDS* was originally developed in the USA but positive evaluations of the impact, in terms of outcomes for children, have been noted in both the USA and other countries – for example,

stress. Each child has their own workbook and each session focuses on a particular topic, such as coping with worries by developing problem-solving skills. More targeted than *FRIENDS* and designed for 8- to 13-year-olds, *Coping Cat* is a 16-session programme that focuses on recognizing anxious feelings, clarifying the feelings that accompany them, developing a coping plan and evaluating performance. This programme is more likely to be delivered by a trained therapist.

Shortt *et al.* (2001) in Australia and Ferguson (2011) in England. The programme evaluated by Ferguson was delivered during the school day by trained school nurses. Levels of anxiety and self-esteem were measured in the six-month period prior to the programme and were found to be stable. Three months after programme completion anxiety had significantly decreased and self-esteem increased, with children with the severest emotional problems appearing to benefit most. The programme was run in three schools amongst nine- to ten-year-olds. Two of the schools had a high population of children with existing emotional and behavioural problems. Whilst 106 children participated in the programmes, only 69 completed all the tests that enabled the researchers to measure changes. This study is clearly limited but findings chime with those of other more rigorous evaluations (Aubrey and Dahl, 2006). What is valuable about this programme is that it is non-stigmatizing, and by providing the programme to all children in a year group ensures that children who may not access more targeted services receive support. Moreover, there appear to be advantages in school nurses rather than teachers delivering the programme as this signalled to the children that

Box 12.1 cont.

Title of programme	Summary of programme content	Studies of effectiveness
		these sessions were different from other classes and there were not necessarily right or wrong answers to the various problems that were considered as part of the programme. Moreover, nurses have an understanding of mental health problems and therefore significant concerns can be identified and addressed.
		Coping Cat is an American programme, which is called *Coping Bear* in Canada, and is more targeted than the *FRIENDS* programme. It is designed for 8- to 13-year-olds experiencing problems with anxiety. The findings from evaluations indicate that the programme shows promise in reducing anxieties and fears and enables children to cope more effectively with most-dreaded situations, and that the children fared better than control group participants (Tarlton and Porter, 2012). However, the evaluations were completed by teams that included the programme developer, and follow-up was short term.

| The Pyramid Club | This club is designed for use in any primary school to build confidence, improve self-esteem and a sense of belonging, and develop social skills in children who present as withdrawn, socially isolated and are therefore emotionally and psycho-logically vulnerable. Although it uses similar cognitive-behavioural approaches to *FRIENDS*, it is a more targeted provision. The first stage of the process is for the whole year group within a school to be screened, usually using the Goodman *Strengths and Difficulties Questionnaire* to assess their socio-emotional needs. This is followed by profes-sionals involved with the children, such as teachers, social workers and educational psychologists, meeting to identify the most appropriate children for the club. *The Pyramid Club* itself is run as an after-school club by trained volunteers. It consists of weekly one-and-a-half hour group sessions for ten weeks. A cognitive-behavioural approach is taken, with the children given opportunities to rehearse social skills in a safe and supportive setting. A similar routine is followed each week: circle time, an art activity, physical activity, shared snack and closing circle time. Intervention fidelity is main-tained through ongoing supervision from a Pyramid coordinator. | The scheme was established in the late 1970s and has been subject to a number of evaluations which show promise, although most of the studies are small scale (Turnell, 2012). |

Box 12.1 cont.

Title of programme	Summary of programme content	Studies of effectiveness
PATHS Promoting Alternative THinking Strategies	The curriculum of systematic and developmentally based lessons, materials and instructions is designed for children of primary school age and can be used by teachers or counsellors. The *PATHS* curriculum is delivered in one-hour lessons per week and covers: • emotional literacy • self-control • social competence • positive peer relations • interpersonal problem-solving skills.	This American programme, whilst also focusing on emotional awareness, is also designed to address self-control and aggressive tendencies. Allen (2011) has included *PATHS* in his list of early interventions that show the most promise, and the charity Barnardo's has also evaluated it positively (Scottish Government, 2010). It is also being tried in Northern Ireland, Birmingham and Norfolk. *PATHS* is based on what is referred to as the Affective-Behavioural-Cognitive-Dynamic (ABCD) Model of Development. In other words, to fully appreciate the impact of one's behaviour on others it is necessary to assess the influence of emotions, thoughts and communications. Delivery of the programme has been shown to improve protective factors and reduce behavioural risk factors. Evaluations taking place in general and special needs settings and with hearing impaired children have demonstrated significant improvements for those who participated (Greenbaum *et al.*, 2008).

parenting practices and parents' perceptions of their child's behaviour (DHSSPS, 2005). Hutchings *et al.* (2011) completed a study in England of the *Incredible Years Parenting Programme* delivered to 280 parents of 8- to 13-year-olds attending in total 54 groups, all facilitated by practitioners. The children were at high risk of developing conduct disorders, they were demonstrating significant behavioural problems and were deemed to be at risk of adolescent antisocial behaviour. The programme was found to be effective in increasing parenting skills and improving the behaviour of the children. Moreover, the programme was found to improve parents' wellbeing amongst a sample that already had high baseline levels of depression. This could possibly be linked to their improved skills and a reduction in the problematic behaviour of their child. Despite these positive findings, the researchers add a note of caution: not all children's behaviour improved, and some problematic parenting skills and parental depression persisted. This was particularly the case with older children, where the problems are more established and influences such as peers, school and the community are competing with those of the parents.

Whilst the study above focused just on a parents' group for primary school age children with behavioural problems, Webster-Stratton recommends that this programme runs alongside a *Dinosaur School*. The *Dinosaur School* is designed to teach children how to manage their feelings, make friends and learn social and problem-solving skills using life-size puppets. Bell (2007b) provides an account of six programmes, consisting of the combined parents' programme and the *Dinosaur School* delivered by an interdisciplinary team in a local community centre to 29 families in total living in one community. The scheme was run in the evenings and was open to parents and children between the ages of 4 and 11, with different levels of need, and included families with complex needs. The children had a range of problems, including anger and defiance, soiling, poor peer relationships, bullying and lack of concentration. Bell, reflecting on the experience, makes the following points: first, these programmes require considerable preparation, careful presentation and time to bed down; second, a community venue, the evening timing, the provision of food and a crèche facilitated participation; and third, voluntary attendance by families with diverse levels of need reduced stigmatization. Moreover, the project (funded by a charitable trust) was perceived as belonging to the community rather than a particular agency.

Aldgate *et al.* (2008) evaluated the application of this intervention for primary school age children and their parents in Scotland. Their evaluation highlights the importance of maintaining programme fidelity whilst adapting materials and activities to the needs and circumstances of the children. For example, some of the children in their study found the video clips included in the *Dinosaur School* difficult to understand and became distracted. They also found that children needed to be assessed as ready for *Dinosaur School*, as some children, because of their family situation, might find the materials too emotional to manage. They also noted that the puppets and materials did not lend themselves to engaging and working with older children; some found the content boring and the puppets babyish. This is not surprising since the materials were originally designed for children under eight years of age, although additional materials have now been developed. The staff running the programmes, in the Aldgate study, found older children responded better to role play and discussions, cartoons with characters similar to those portrayed by the puppets, and discussing real and possible situations in their lives suggested by the cartoons.

The *Dinosaur School* is more likely to take place in school rather than in the community and to be run by teachers who have completed the *Incredible Years Teacher Classroom Management Programme*. Webster-Stratton and Reid (2010), in a study of 153 teachers and 1,768 students, representing low-income and multiethnic populations, where both programmes were in operation, found the pupils were more socially competent, had developed emotional regulation skills and had fewer conduct problems than students in the control groups (the sample were randomly assigned to the intervention or control conditions). In addition, the teachers using the programme reported more parent involvement than teachers in control conditions.

Baker-Henningham *et al.* (2012) wished to establish whether the *Incredible Years Teacher's Programme* would cross cultures. They concluded, based on focus group discussions with parents and teachers in the Caribbean, that the strategies and principles for managing conduct problems was largely compatible with the values and beliefs of the teachers and parents. Aldgate *et al.* (2008) also looked at ways in which this programme crosses cultures, using it in Scotland. They make some salutary points about the use of the *Incredible Years Programme*, which is applicable to the other social and emotional learning programmes. First, many of the problems encountered by the children and their parents are entrenched and will not be resolved through a short intervention. These programmes may help the children and families begin to change but more longer-term support is required to consolidate these changes. Second, with many of these programmes the focus is on group work, and for the most vulnerable children this is not enough; the group work needs to be augmented by individual work. Third, if the children and families are not able to actively engage in group work programmes, it is important that they are not made to feel they have failed and that positive attempts are made to engage them in more appropriate services. Finally, these are not programmes that can be delivered without skill and sensitivity. Motivated staff who appreciate, and are able to work with, complexity are crucial to the successful implementation of these programmes.

Interventions to improve cognitive functioning

For maltreated children the ability to think has often been damaged or distorted by the time they reach school age (Stafford *et al.*, 2011). This is clearly demonstrated in the findings from the Minnesota Longitudinal Study. By the time physically neglected children reach five, for example, the Minnesota study found their intellectual functioning and academic achievement are lower than other maltreated groups, including those who have been emotionally neglected. By school age they often have considerable problems, they struggle with school and rapidly require special educational services. The situation is exacerbated by an inability to concentrate and a lack of engagement in learning. They also appear to have problems using expressive and receptive language (Hildyard and Wolfe, 2002).

The day-to-day impact of neglect will also affect the child's ability to learn. Children who are hungry, cold, have not slept and are inappropriately dressed are not in a position to maximize the learning opportunities available to them. In a systematic review of interventions to assist teachers to increase attainment, Higgins *et al.* (2011) identified a number of activities including one-to-one tutoring, peer tutoring and after-school clubs. Moving beyond activities that focus on improving attainment, breakfast clubs, after-school activities and homework clubs can prove invaluable to neglected children.

Language delay and neglect

Neglect impacts on language development, affecting articulation, and verbal and grammatical development (Sedlak *et al.*, 2010). These neglected children are more prone to suffering language delay, in terms of both expression and comprehension, than children of similar age and ability, often because the parents have not facilitated the development of those skills. This in turn affects their academic attainment – for example, they have been found to be at greater risk of reading difficulties at school (Catts *et al.*, 2002). Moreover, it can cause difficulties for broader learning and socialization lasting into adolescence and beyond (Spencer and Baldwin, 2005). For example, Flouri *et al.* (2011), in a UK community sample of 207 children with a mean age of 13.4 years, found non-verbal cognitive ability was more likely to be associated with emotional arousal and problem behaviour. They argue that children are likely to be frustrated at not being able to articulate their feelings and therefore tend to demonstrate them in the only ways they know.

Central to early language development is the language stimulation style used by the mother: a supportive style focuses on what the child is trying to achieve through communication and follows the verbal and non-verbal cues from the child. A mother using a directive style, however, will pick up on the cues but follow up on them remaining focused on what they want to achieve. So for example, a mother is watching TV. A child asks her mother for a biscuit, the mother gets a biscuit and gives it to the child so she can watch her programme without further delay – a directive style. Using the supportive style, the mother would engage with the child, find out what type of biscuit she wants and why she wants it, and may let the child choose one, asking her why she selected that biscuit and so forth. Thus, the target for interventions in the early years should be the interactions between the child and their primary caregiver. This is borne out by Biemiller (2003), who concludes that parents' interactions with their children are important as children's vocabulary by seven years of age is significantly influenced by parents, the way they talk to children and the vocabulary they use.

A rigorous Cochrane review of studies into effective interventions for language delay was undertaken by Law *et al.* (2003). They examined the effectiveness of speech and language therapy interventions for children with primary speech and language delay/disorder. They concluded that there may be some research support to demonstrate the effectiveness of speech and language therapy for children who have difficulties with verbal and written expression, such as producing sentences or recalling words. However, the evidence concerning the effectiveness of interventions for expressive syntax is mixed, and no evidence is available to indicate the effectiveness of interventions for children with receptive language difficulties – that is, children who have difficulty understanding what is being said to them.

Whilst the findings of the Cochrane review are not as positive as one might wish, there are interventions that show promise. Most of those are designed for preschool-age children, such as the English *Stoke Speaks Out* (*SSO*). The purpose of *SSO* is to ensure that professionals know about the importance of speech and language development and are able to assist parents with early communication development whilst emphasizing the importance of early attachment and ensuring that children enter school with well-developed emotional and communication skills. A multidisciplinary approach has been taken involving midwives, health visitors, speech and language therapists, clinical psychologists, teachers, a bilingual co-worker and play workers. A staged pathway was developed between early intervention, such as the use of *Early Talk* programmes designed to promote communication between parents and infants, and specialist support facilitating referrals as and when necessary and ensuring that referrals for specialist help are only made if advice and support by professionals offering population-based and early help services have been provided. Over a five-year period, an improvement from 64 per cent of children having a language delay to 48 per cent was noted (Walker *et al.*, 2008). A follow-on programme, *One Step a Time*, is a structured programme used in schools for the systematic teaching of spoken language skills for children up to seven years of age. It concentrates on age-appropriate spoken language skills, conversation, listening, narrative and discussion, ensuring that all skills are taught to all children, taking their needs into account. At each stage children are screened to identify level of need.

An important way for children to develop speech and language – and indeed essential for educational attainment in school – is through shared book reading between parent and child, particularly when it includes open-ended questions and encourages interactions and response from the child. Moreover, the development of reading skills is crucial as it underpins nearly all school activities (Daniel, Taylor and Scott, 2010). *REAL (Raising Early Achievement in Literacy)* is aimed at three- to four-year-olds in an attempt to engage them in the four aspects considered key to early literacy: books, early writing and mark making, singing songs and rhymes, and reading and engaging with environmental print. It has been evaluated, with demonstrable increases in early language and literacy attainment in comparison to a control group, with the effects extending to children at seven years of age. The programme is based on what is referred to as 'ORIM', which involves a family-based approach to providing opportunities to learn, recognizing and valuing children's achievements, interacting with adults in learning situations, and using models of literacy and numeracy behaviours, learning strategies and dispositions (Siraj-Blatford and Siraj-Blatford, 2009).

The neglected child and physical development

Despite the lack of consistent evidence that neglect and weight issues are linked, factors associated with obesity exist amongst families from lower socio-economic groups, who we know are over-represented amongst families where neglect is an issue (Sabin *et al.*, 2004). These are families that are also likely to live in 'food deserts' where healthy, affordable food is difficult to obtain and, as I have argued elsewhere, the families often do not have the knowledge and skills to prepare and cook nutritious meals (Horwath, 2007). Obesity can have a considerable detrimental effect on children, including a poor self-image, isolation in school and bullying, not to mention medical problems such as high blood pressure and type 2 diabetes (Wright *et al.*, 2006).

Safron *et al.* (2011) completed a systematic umbrella review of 18 systematic reviews, which between them included 375 qualitative studies analysing the relationship between family variables and body weight, diet and physical activity amongst children and young people, looking specifically at ways of changing behaviours. They identified a number of key messages that should be taken into account when developing interventions to address obesity:

- Parental involvement can increase the effectiveness of obesity prevention programmes.
- Obesity may be reduced if interventions include cognitive and behavioural treatment strategies that parents can use, such as positive reinforcement techniques.
- Addressing behaviour-specific family behaviours, such as attitudes towards eating, can increase the effectiveness of interventions.
- Family variables, such as attitudes towards physical activity, should be considered when planning interventions that include physical activities for young people.

Part 3: Meeting the needs of the neglected adolescent

Up to now I have considered ways in which neglect affects a child's cognitive, behavioural and emotional development and have identified ways in which population-based, early help and more specialist interventions can be used to meet the primary school age child's needs. The focus shifts in this part of the chapter to consider interventions for young people from 12 to 18 years of age. As has been discussed earlier, children who have been neglected are likely to have poor attachments with their primary carer. As these children grow up, and if interventions fail to meet their needs, they may demonstrate poor self-organization, impaired mental health and problem behaviour (Howe, 2005). This is particularly so if they continue to live within a neglectful environment without support and interventions enabling them to manage the situation (Hildyard and Wolfe, 2002). They may deal with their pain and distress as they go through middle childhood and adolescence by internalizing behaviours, such as becoming depressed and isolated, engaging in self-destructive acts, for example self-harming and misuse of alcohol and drugs, or externalized, destructive acts, such as aggression towards others and to property (Howe, 2005). It is not possible in this book to consider all of these different types of behaviours and appropriate interventions. I have therefore focused on three, which, according to practitioners in the Anytown study, are particularly challenging: antisocial behaviour including offending, running away from home and homelessness, and sexual exploitation.

Offending

Chapple *et al.* (2005), using prospective longitudinal data from a community study in the USA, found that child neglect is associated with increased levels of violence in later adolescence. These findings are supported by Yun *et al.* (2011) who, in another American longitudinal study using a national representative study of adolescents, found that sexual abuse and neglect were significant predictors of violent delinquency. Bender (2010) argues, however, that it is not inevitable that maltreated children become violent and engage in delinquent activities, and concludes that there is a range of risk factors, including substance misuse, mental health problems, school difficulties, negative peer networks and running away from home, which form a pathway to crime. Many of these factors, sadly, are also associated with neglect.

Allen (2006) argues that in order to address these antisocial and criminal behaviours it is important to recognize the problems these young people have encountered and the pathways that have led them to crime. He suggests that system change is required, with services addressing the educational and mental health issues that often trigger offending behaviour; limits applied to the criminalization of children; and a wider range of community-based and residential provision for the more challenged young offenders. Ross *et al.* (2011), in their more recent review of early intervention programmes to reduce youth crime, support this view. They are clear what does *not* work: military-type boot camps, unstructured life skills training, community service activities, individual counselling that is not based on cognitive-behavioural techniques, and any intervention that is focused primarily on coercion and control, such as surveillance. They argue that the problems these young people encounter and the complex lives they lead require looking beyond simple solutions, such as allocating a key worker who cannot physically provide constant guidance and supervision or a mentor who is unable to change the complex family circumstances surrounding the young person.

Ross *et al.* (2011) provide examples of English projects that seek to take a holistic approach towards the young person and their needs. For example, the *Persistent Young Offender Project (PYOP)* in Portsmouth includes a designated key worker who coordinates a programme involving skills training, mentoring, cognitive behavioural therapy and non-academic activities designed to boost the young person's sense of self-worth and competence. A common multifaceted intervention used in the UK is *Youth Inclusion and Support Panels*. They too focus on the young offender with a key worker, but also engage with the family through family group conferencing, parenting support and mentoring. Ross *et al.* conclude that what is crucial to all these interventions is that the programmes have a clear social, emotional and cognitive focus, and that support and direction is provided to the young person.

Multisystemic therapy (MST) has already been described in Chapter 9, with questions raised by Littell (2005) as to the nature of the evidence and whether it can be demonstrated conclusively that *MST* has benefits over and above other interventions. Despite these reservations, the reviews into effective interventions in relation to offending behaviour, including engagement in gangs and violent behaviour, are positive about the benefits of *MST* (HM Government, 2011; Ross *et al.*, 2011). To remind ourselves, *MST* is an intensive intervention with a trained therapist working for between three and five months within the young offender's home. Ross *et al.* emphasize the importance of adhering to the original programme design in order to maximize effectiveness.

Detached children and young people: runaways and homelessness

'Detached' children is a term used here to describe those who have literally run away from their homes; young people who are away from their homes for periods of time, often 'sofa surfing'; those who have been forced to leave; and those who are estranged from their parents. Studies of this diverse group of young people indicate that many of them have been neglected and have been living in the complex family situations frequently associated with neglect. Rees (2011) for example, found, in his study of 7,000 young runaways between the ages of 14 and 16 years, that children living in low-warmth and high-conflict family environments are particularly likely to run away, as are children who are living out-of-home. He found, as have others (Smeaton, 2009; Mayock, 2011) that poor, single-parent households, parents who have misused drugs and alcohol or have mental health issues, fraught and stressful relationships, a history of state care, negative peer relationships and the young person's own challenging behaviour were common amongst detached youth.

Smeaton (2009), in a powerful UK study involving interviews with 103 young people under the age of 16 years who had run away, found that young people ended up on the streets for a variety of reasons. These included conflict at home, finding caring responsibilities and the behaviour of parents intolerable, and unhappiness in a care placement. The following example, taken from her study (p. 24), highlights the desperate lives these young people have led prior to running away:

> I had to wash all the clothes, cook my brother's and my sister's tea...I had to keep all that hush...My mum said 'if you tell them, they'll do this and they'll do that'. Sometimes she said [if the young person told social services] that she'd beat me or that she'd kick me out.

To survive on the streets they engaged in shoplifting, selling drugs and sex, begging and blagging. She found that these young people showed resilience, managing to find strategies to survive and, in some cases, felt supported and protected by the homeless community. Nevertheless, substance misuse, bullying, depression and other mental health issues, sexual activity and sexual exploitation were rife.

Stein *et al.* (2009), based on 38 interviews with professionals and 22 with young people who had experience of running away, as well as consultation exercises with a further 100 professionals and 18 young people, identified the barriers to accessing services or finding help to prevent running away. They found that the young people were often unaware of the available services, and if they were, they felt they would not be taken seriously, listened to or cared about. Moreover, they were worried about the consequences of seeking help from agencies, such as being returned home without any consideration given as to why they ran away in the first place. A continuum of services is required to address the needs of young runaways. The UK charity the Railway Children outlines the services that are beneficial in their *Reach* model (included as an appendix in Stein *et al.*, 2009). Universal provision is important, ensuring that young people are aware of the risks of running away and know what options are open to them if they do leave. Services should also be available to address issues to prevent the young person leaving. For example, in Warrington, England, there is a project called *Talk Don't Walk* that seeks to do this. Detached street workers, one-to-one outreach and helplines can also play a part. If the young person does decide to leave home then it is important that there are accessible and appropriate crisis response services enabling the young person to access emergency accommodation. The *Night Stop* scheme, for example, operating throughout the UK, provides such accommodation for one to three nights from approved volunteers within the community. Effective services are those that are accessible 24 hours a day and are perceived to be trustworthy and helpful to the young person. The *Safe@Last* project operating in South Yorkshire is such a scheme.

Once the young person is safe then reintegration needs to be considered for those young people where returning home is the preferred outcome. Mayock *et al.* (2011) completed a biographical, longitudinal study of youth homelessness in Dublin, Ireland, with 37 young people being interviewed twice, with a year's gap, about their experiences, life and homeless histories. They studied the pathways of the young people who had exited homelessness and found, first, that more stable living situations, albeit in state care, home or other accommodation, was significant. Second, access to and engagement in treatment for drug and alcohol misuse and participation in education or training was common. Third, support from families was significant, with improved relationships as well as increased contact with parents and other family members commonly reported. However, the researchers found that despite the reported improvement in relationships, there were differences in the quality and nature of these family relationships, with many remaining strained and stressful.

It is therefore important to work not only with the young person but also with their parent or carer, through mediation or relationship building and assisting them in developing skills required to parent adolescents. Mayock *et al.* (2011) argue that whilst this may be the case, little is known about how to re-establish and renegotiate these relationships following a period of limited or no contact. Moreover, it can be a complex process for young people whose problems at home led to their running way, particularly when the problems are so entrenched, as is the case with chronic neglect. Improved communication and trust, and a willingness to resolve past tensions and issues, is key but this can be a long, incremental process and, in some cases, being realistic about what is likely to change is important.

Sexual exploitation

Sexual exploitation occurs when children and young people are forced or manipulated into sexual activity. The exploitation can involve engaging in sexual activity in exchange for money, presents, accommodation, affection and attention or status (Barnardo's, 2012). Children who are missing from home or living on the streets are particularly vulnerable to sexual exploitation. The Child Exploitation and Online Protection Centre (CEOP, 2011), for example, completed an analysis of 2,083 victims of sexual exploitation and found the majority were female, most commonly aged between 14 and 15 years and from a range of ethnic groups, although the majority were white. Of these young people, 842 were reported missing (Stein *et al.*, 2009, found that many children who went missing were not reported, so this is likely to be an under-estimation), and 311 were in care. Many of the victims were found to have vulnerabilities associated with neglect. For example, they were not engaged in school because of truanting, bullying, lack of interest or poor behaviour, and they demonstrated chaotic and at times aggressive behaviour. These findings are supported by another study completed by Jago *et al.* (2011). The perpetrators were found to create or exacerbate vulnerabilities, such as family difficulties, and challenging or criminal behaviour, to retain control over the young person.

As with running away, CEOP recommends that a continuum of services is required to address sexual exploitation: from prevention through to addressing the consequences of exploitation for the victims. They argue that frontline agencies, such as sexual health clinics, Child and Adolescent Mental Health Services (CAMHS), GPs, youth workers, teachers, school nurses, members of youth offending teams, specialist services for the homeless and drug misusing young people, all need to be aware of the signs of sexual exploitation, which include:

- going missing for periods of time

- regularly returning home late
- missing school or not taking part in education
- appearing with unexplained gifts or new possessions
- associating with other young people involved in exploitation
- having older boyfriends or girlfriends
- suffering from sexually transmitted infections
- mood swings or changes in emotional wellbeing
- drug and alcohol misuse
- displaying inappropriate sexualized behaviour. (CEOP, 2011; Barnardo's, 2012)

Practitioners also need to identify and address concerns with the young people and ensure that their needs are met. This engagement needs to be a proactive process that takes into account the barriers that the perpetrators are likely to have in place to prevent young people disclosing the exploitation. According to the young people in the study, engagement was effective if workers invested time into building a rapport and gaining the trust of the young person. CEOP also point out the importance of a multi-agency approach that centres on an ongoing process of intensive outreach work. Unfortunately, Jago *et al.* (2011) found that the responses across the UK vary considerably, services often only being put into place if there is a local champion or there has been a high-profile case that has brought the issue to public and professionals' attention. Moreover, they expressed concern about the lack of awareness and training for staff working in residential units, who appeared to fail to recognize the indicators of sexual exploitation.

Barnardo's, a UK charity, is the largest provider of child sexual support exploitation services in the UK and works with more than 1,200 victims through 21 specialist services. Seeking to provide a safe and confidential environment where young people can go for help, advice and support, their outreach services seek to identify vulnerable young people at risk in the community and work with these young people, building trust and expressing concern to enable the young person to break free of the exploitative relationship. Children are offered a range of therapeutic interventions including one-to-one counselling, group-work sessions and drop-in support.

Part 4: The case for a coordinated approach

As described in Chapter 3, neglect can affect every aspect of a child or young person's life. Whilst specific interventions may be useful, in terms of addressing the particular needs of the child, a multidisciplinary, coordinated response, involving a diverse range of professionals, such as educational psychologists, learning support staff, school nurses and social workers, may also be necessary. Dyson *et al.* (2010), in a review of 52 studies on interventions for children with additional needs, which clearly include many neglected children, conclude that in order to identify and meet these needs schools should take the following into account:

- Children and young people have a diverse range of additional needs and therefore varied and flexible strategies are required in order to meet those needs.
- Schools need to be equipped to identify and respond to needs that may fall outside of their traditional areas of expertise. Therefore, multidisciplinary working is essential.
- Clear, shared aims, clearly identified roles and responsibilities, commitment from all staff, strong leadership, effective communication and information sharing systems, and structures for joint planning between the different services are important for effective partnership working.

There are a number of multidisciplinary projects that are designed to enable school staff to assist children with additional needs. Dyson *et al.* (2010) identify two that showed promise. The first, the *Full-Service Extended Schools (FSES)* initiative, provided additional funding to selected schools in socio-economically disadvantaged parts of England in order to develop additional services to children, families and local communities, including health services, adult learning and community activities, as well as study support and 8 am to 6 pm childcare. Services offered reflect local need, some services being universal, others targeted. The second, *Behaviour and Extended Support Teams (BESTs)*, are multiagency teams of practitioners from health, children's social services and education. The members of the team work with a cluster of schools to address the needs of children and young people with emotional and behavioural problems. Activities include one-to-one and family casework, and group work with guidance and support provided to teachers within the schools.

This multidisciplinary approach is similar to the cluster family support services that Barnardo's has piloted in parts of England. One of their projects, the *Moulsham Schools Cluster*, has been operating for over five years with a single worker covering four closely located primary and secondary schools. The worker has a caseload of approximately 20 cases – the result of referrals from school, parents or children – and also runs groups to address such issues as anger management and peer relationship problems. According to Evans (2011), there has been an improvement of 71 per cent in the attendance of children where this was an issue, an 86 per cent improvement in mental health and a 75 per cent improvement in parenting. However, it is not clear how these improvements were measured. The New Zealand *Social Workers in Schools* project takes a similar approach. Drawing on a strengths-based model, a social worker is available to respond flexibly to the needs of individual children and their families who use the service on a voluntary basis. An evaluation of this project indicated that the children's circumstances improved. For example, there were clearer family routines and better communication between the parents and their children, and improved engagement within the school (Belgrave *et al.*, 2002, cited in Daniel *et al.*, 2011).

Despite the effectiveness of a coordinated, multidisciplinary approach, Ward *et al.* (2012) found that primary school head teachers in England were particularly concerned by the lack of response by children's statutory social work services to serious neglect. As a result, they developed their own strategies for supporting these children. These included promoting relationships between school staff and parents; providing a nurture room where neglected children could work in small groups or on an individual basis with staff; free breakfast clubs; and employment of specialist staff to work with children and families. In their study, Ward *et al.* found that some children suffering gross neglect were also receiving intensive support from individual teachers. They expressed concerns that this response was, in the main, delivered outside a strategic plan and was at risk of being discontinued when children moved to different classes or schools. Moreover, they raise a question as to whether this type of individualized response masks the true extent of the neglect the child is experiencing and is therefore less likely to lead to decisive action by social work services.

Specialist services

The interventions above are most likely to be effective in addressing emerging concerns. If the needs of these neglected children cannot be met through the provision of such services, then these children are likely to need more specialist services from providers such as Child and Adolescent Mental Health Services (CAMHS). Mental health interventions for children and adolescents can improve behaviour, personal functioning, educational attainment and other needs (Hawkins and Shohet, 2000). However, those neglected children who internalize problems and feel depressed and suicidal may not necessarily be the ones who receive services. Zwaanswijk *et al.* (2003) completed a review of 47 empirical studies from various countries exploring problem recognition and seeking help from mental health services. They identified five themes that affected who received services. First, pre- and early adolescent boys were more likely to be referred to services. This appeared to be due to the externalizing behaviour exhibited by the boys causing disturbance. This changed, however, in adolescence, with girls being more likely to seek help. Second, parents tended to seek help when the problems with the child caused them distress or became a burden. They were also more likely to seek help if they themselves or family members had experience of mental health services. Third, active types of maltreatment, such as sexual and physical abuse, were more likely to lead to service use than the more passive forms of maltreatment, such as neglect. Fourth, school-related problems detected by the teacher played an important role in increasing parents' acceptance of the need for help and problem recognition. Finally, GPs and paediatricians varied in their ability to recognize problems. These problems may not be brought to the attention of the GP by the parent. However, they are more likely to be identified if the child is seen routinely by, for example, the school nurse.

It seems, therefore, that the children most likely to receive services are those who externalize their behaviour and make sure they cannot be ignored, leaving another group of neglected children:

> Empty, deadened, inhibited, passive, apparently self-contained and who have little ability to reflect on their own and others' emotions. Often their narrative is limited, they evince little pleasure, and do not easily inspire hope, affection or enjoyment in those around them. (Music, 2009, pp. 142–3)

In a very full and frank personal account, based on working with neglected children in a mental health setting, Music (2009) considers why this group of neglected children not only have difficulty accessing and using help but are also neglected by professionals who find difficulty in 'warming' to them. The children often present as self-sufficient and they are more likely to be ignored in schools as they are quiet and withdrawn. If they are referred to services, such as CAMHS, they can be difficult to engage with. Music describes how his whole persona changes when he knows he is seeing one of these children: he finds himself in 'a cotton-wool like deadness' (2009, p. 148) and has to guard against being bored, irritated, wanting to shake the child up or just walk away. The children often present as managing, do not appear to want to engage with services and often have parents who do not seem particularly concerned. Music argues that this leads to these cases getting closed more quickly than other cases, if indeed they are even referred. If the therapist does, however, continue to work with these children and manages to engage with them, what follows may be a display of more externalized behaviour, such as aggression and possibly sadism, which can also be difficult to manage. He argues that it is important to bear in mind why these children present in this way. This means recognizing their lack of awareness of mental states: a deficit of both language and ability to express emotions, a lack of agency and ability to use imagination and tell stories, and an inability to find enjoyment in daily life. It is therefore important to keep working with them rather than give up and leaving them with a 'dampened-down system' (p. 148). This can be achieved by helping them to engage in a relationship, as well as affording them opportunities to foster a sense of agency and enjoyment. This is more likely to occur if work is also undertaken with parents so that they can encourage and support the child to engage in the world.

Whilst therapists may find it challenging to engage with withdrawn, neglected children, such children and their families may find it as hard, if not harder, engaging with mental health services. In an Australian study, Watt *et al.* (2007) completed a review of the literature to identify the barriers to effective engagement by families with children with conduct problems, which included some neglected children. They found that the following appeared to promote engagement: making the service accessible; maintaining regular contact with families; extended opening, and telephone reminders of appointments; offering incentives, such as transport; creating a comfortable atmosphere, such as having drinks available; addressing family expectations and modifying treatments with these in mind; recognizing and addressing broader family needs; working towards achievable gains; and using behavioural change strategies. Drawing on these features they then provided clinicians with training as to how to incorporate these into practice. The clinicians who completed the training and made changes found that attendance improved and the families became more involved in the treatments.

Conclusion

Neglect can impact on every aspect of a child's life. It affects their ability to form relationships within and beyond the family, leaving them ill equipped to cope within a school setting or to establish meaningful friendships. This, together with poor hygiene and inadequate clothing, leaves them vulnerable to being bullied and in turn becoming bullies. Obesity may also be a cause of bullying, and consideration needs to be given to addressing the needs of the obese child; failure of a parent to address morbid obesity can be considered a form of neglect. The neglected child's cognitive development may also be affected; language delay can have significant effects on literacy and numeracy skills and academic attainment. Children and young people cope with neglect in different ways. Many externalize their behavioural response to neglect through aggression, disruption and conduct disorders, and they tend to be the children who receive services. There are, however, a group of children who internalize their response to neglect; because they present as quiet and withdrawn they may not be identified as in need of help and support.

In terms of interventions available for these children, the message is clear – early intervention is essential. Building the child's resilience through the development of a 'web of supportive relationships', which draws on the extended family and community resources, is crucial. Schools have a particularly important role to play. A caring school ethos with very clear boundaries and expectations about behaviour can be important to a neglected child. Interventions such as *SEAL* and *Dinosaur School* have a part to play in promoting social and emotional skills. For children with additional needs, programmes such as the *Pyramid Club* can assist the emotionally and psychologically vulnerable. However, these children are likely to require a more multidisciplinary and coordinated approach that takes into account their diverse range of needs and responds with a flexible and tailor-made package. This package may include mental health services, such as those provided by CAMHS.

What is of concern is an implicit view amongst parents, and indeed some professionals, that by the time the child has reached secondary school age they are old enough and sufficiently resilient to take care of themselves. In these situations it is all too easy to downplay ongoing neglect and separate out the externalized and internalized behaviours exhibited by the adolescent from the root cause: child neglect.

Chapter 13

Meeting the Needs of the Neglected Child through Out-of-Home Care

Thus far in this book I have focused on interventions that are designed to keep the neglected child within the family home. But what happens if these interventions fail to improve the quality of the child's daily lived experience? The short answer to the question is that out-of-home care has to be considered. However, what is essential is that the child receives the type of care placement that will meet their needs. The term 'out-of-home care' is used to describe a range of different interventions and approaches. The placement may result from parents making a request to have their child taken into the care of the state through to the state making the decision that the child needs to be removed from the home; the arrangements can be temporary or permanent. Moreover, the care may be provided by extended family, foster carers, care workers in a residential setting or adoptive parents.

The neglected child's experience of the out-of-home care system, and the extent to which any placement is likely to meet their needs, is influenced by a range of factors. In this chapter I consider four key factors: the way in which decisions are made to place the child in out-of-home care; being mindful of what works when providing care to neglected children; understanding and addressing the challenges of family reunification and, finally, recognizing and meeting the needs of neglected young people when they leave care. The Department for Education in England has published the findings of three studies which give considerable insight into out-of-home interventions for these neglected children. A summary of the studies is provided in Box 13.1, and the findings from the studies, as they relate to out-of-home care and reunification, will be considered, together with those from studies completed in other nation states.

Box 13.1: Summary of studies of out-of-home care

Case Management and Outcomes for Neglected Children Returning to Their Parents: A Five-Year Follow-up Study

In this longitudinal study Farmer and Lutman (2010) examined the interventions and outcomes for 138 neglected children from seven different

---

local authorities, from point of referral until five years after they were returned home from out-of-home placements. All the children had been looked after by the local authority and returned to their parents within a one-year period.

Maltreated Children in the Looked-after System: A Comparison of Outcomes for Those Who Go Home and Those Who Do Not

Wade *et al.* (2011) used a survey and census study which involved seven local authorities. The researchers considered 3,872 looked-after children, comparing the pathways and destinations of 2,291 of this sample who had entered care because of maltreatment with those who had not. They focused on a purposive sub-sample of 149 of these maltreated children to explore the experiences of those who had returned home at some point with those who had remained in care, and considered their outcomes four years after reunification or the decision not to reunify.

Infants Suffering or Likely to Suffer Significant Harm: A Prospective Longitudinal Study

The mixed methods study was completed by Ward and colleagues (Davies and Ward, 2012) and explored the early life pathways of very young children and infants who had been identified as suffering or likely to suffer significant harm. Forty-three children were followed in this study until they were three years of age.

Making the decision to remove children from parental care

Compulsory state intervention, in the UK and in other nations such as the USA, Australia and New Zealand, is reserved for cases where there is evidence that the child is suffering or is likely to suffer significant harm and professionals have been unable to work in partnership with the family to meet the needs of the child (Gilbert, 2012; Kojan and Loanne, 2012). Underpinning these interventions is a belief in limited state involvement in family life, with coercive state action used as a last resort only where there is compelling evidence to warrant it (Fox-Harding, 1997; Dickens, 2007). A forensic approach is usually taken to information gathering to ensure sufficient evidence of neglect is available to warrant removal of the child from the care of their parents. As a consequence, considerable emphasis is placed on medical professionals, in particular, demonstrating that any maltreatment is causing significant harm to the health and wellbeing of the child. In England, Wales and Northern Ireland, care proceedings are brought by the statutory child protection agency – the local authority – when concerns are such that compulsory action is considered necessary (Stafford *et al.*, 2011). Care proceedings are a legal procedure with the court having powers to curtail parental responsibility, which can lead, in some cases, to the child being freed for adoption (Masson, 2012). In Scotland, decisions about compulsory out-of-home care are made within the Children's Hearing System. The Children's Reporter makes the initial decision as to whether a hearing is necessary. The decisions at the hearing are, however, made by a panel of lay members from the community rather than by legal experts. Irrespective of jurisdiction, in the words of Masson (2012, p. 203), care proceedings should 'deliver the best welfare solution for the child whilst upholding both parents' and children's rights to family life'.

I now consider some of the factors that influence practitioners' ability to achieve this.

Making a case for compulsory state intervention in cases of child neglect: the challenges

Cases where parents are highly resistant to change and fail to cooperate with child protection agencies to ensure their child is safe from harm are the cases that are most likely to result in care proceedings (Fauth *et al.*, 2010). Wade *et al.* (2011) in their study, which is summarized in Box 13.1, found that neglected children who were subject to care proceedings in England come from highly troubled families, with the children experiencing chronic or severe neglect, often with other forms of maltreatment. Moreover, parenting issues, such as alcohol and substance misuse, offending and mental health issues were common, as was a history of both maltreatment and attempts by professionals to work with the parents to improve parenting. These findings are commensurate with those of earlier studies (Brophy, 2006). Thus, unsurprisingly, the cases that are likely to reach care proceedings are the most challenging, hard-to-reach families who do not engage with child protection services in a meaningful manner.

Prior to initiating care proceedings, as mentioned above, child protection agencies must demonstrate that they have attempted to work in partnership with families to meet the needs of the child. Thus, the child protection plans (discussed in Chapter 6) that were put in place to work in partnership with parents to keep the child safe will be subject to scrutiny. The courts will pay particular attention to the attempts that have been made to work with families. Practitioners will need to demonstrate that every effort has been made to engage with resistant families. What will be of particular concern to the courts is that appropriate services have been provided to meet the needs of the child and their family. This can be challenging for practitioners. For example, Fauth *et al.* (2010) completed an international knowledge review about highly resistant families and found, as discussed in Chapter 10, that the key to effective engagement is the provision of timely, focused, long-term interventions rather than episodic services. Moreover, as has already been emphasized in this book, interventions need to be multifaceted, recognizing the complex needs of family members. If this level of intervention has not been made available to the family it can be difficult for both professionals and the court to ascertain whether families are actively resisting engagement with services or whether part of the problem is that they have not received the services and support that they need. It is not surprising, therefore, that practitioners who participated in Wade *et al.*'s study (2010, described in Box 13.1) found it difficult to provide evidence for the court about attempted interventions and their lack of impact on the lived experience of the child. What was also of note was that applications for care orders were rejected in court if it was felt that the family had been given insufficient support to assist them make the necessary changes to safeguard and promote the welfare of their child.

This raises questions as to what constitutes sufficient support. Nine parents were interviewed as part of the Wade *et al.* (2011) study, and they indicated that they were initially provided with support from children's services to avoid their child going into care. However, as the concerns abated they felt the support had decreased, leaving them, in some cases, having to manage, for example, difficult and challenging behavioural problems exhibited by their children. These experiences seem to indicate, in terms of the Prochaska and DiClementi (1982) model of change, discussed in Chapter 4, that sufficient support can be described as the provision of focused, long-term interventions of adequate intensity and duration to ensure that parents have opportunities not only to take actions to change their concerning behaviours but also to ensure these changes have become routinized and can be maintained in times of stress and difficulty. By providing adequate support, practitioners are better placed to gather evidence as to whether the parents are unable to make the changes required of them through lack of ability or superficial compliance ('walking the walk', discussed in Chapter 6), or genuine engagement ('walking the walk and talking the talk') but needing longer to make those changes.

One of the problems, however, of providing parents with opportunities to make changes and demonstrate that they are able to sustain change is that, as Prochaska and DiClementi (1982) note, lapse and relapse to old behaviours are a common feature of the change process. Whilst accepting that neglectful parents need time to make changes to their often complex lives, it is essential that practitioners remain child-focused and recognize that children, if they are suffering or likely to suffer significant harm, cannot wait for the years it might take parents to make some substantial changes to their lifestyle and behaviours. All too often, in cases of neglect, cases are allowed to drift whilst parents who have lapsed or relapsed into old ways of behaving are given further opportunities to change, with little regard to the impact on the children in the family. This is brought home in the Wade *et al.* (2010) study, with some children indicating it was a relief when they were finally removed from the home. The situation can be further exacerbated by judges who, according to Speight and Wyne (2000), may err towards promoting the rights of a neglectful parent rather than promoting the welfare of the child. If decisions are delayed then there is a danger that opportunities for providing a permanent placement, where appropriate, are reduced.

Whilst there is promising evidence that in England local authorities are making more appropriate and timely care applications with regard to neglect than they did three years earlier, it is all too easy to see how drift can occur in cases of chronic neglect (Cafcass, 2012). As discussed in Chapter 3, the harm resulting from neglect is cumulative. Therefore, making decisions about exactly when to decide that enough is enough and argue for the removal of children from their parents' care is challenging. That slow creep and erosion of the health and wellbeing of the child are far more difficult to evidence than an immediate, visible, dramatic event or specific incident of physical injury or sexual abuse. It is not surprising, therefore, that it is all too easy to argue for giving the parents one more chance. When this occurs actions may be delayed until there is a decisive event, which according to Dickens (2007, p. 78) 'catapults' the child towards care proceedings, with professionals believing this event provides the strong evidence necessary to justify the removal of the child from their parents. Barber and Delfabbro (2009), in a study of the profile of abused and neglected children in long-term foster care in South Australia, also found this to be the case. With this in mind, it is not surprising that Masson *et al.* (2008) found, in many cases that went to care proceedings in England, that there was evidence of long-term involvement of children's services alongside unplanned initiation of care proceedings as a consequence of a crisis or incident.

In order to present a strong case to court it can be helpful if practitioners draw on what has been discussed in the earlier chapters on planning to address the following:

- What do we know about the daily lived experience of the child?
- What does this tell us about the harm the child is suffering or likely to suffer if we fail to remove the child from the care of their parent/s?

In answering these questions, practitioners should consider how the parent's neglectful behaviours and lifestyle are affecting the child's daily life. In addition, it should be possible to demonstrate how this experience – day in, day out – is causing cumulative and significant harm. For example, in

Dylan's description of a day in his life (Case study 3.1), he describes his sleeping arrangements, which leave him tired during the day and result in him falling asleep in class. Moreover, he is hungry and being bullied, and his mother is failing to ensure he attends school regularly and to assist him with reading. These factors combined are likely to have a significant effect on his ability to learn and on his cognitive development.

- What attempts have been made by agencies to work with the child and their family to improve the child's daily lived experience and reduce the risk of harm?
- What evidence do we have about the parent's or parents' acceptance of the need to change their behaviours and their engagement with interventions designed to assist them in making these changes?

In answering these questions practitioners should specify the interventions that have been tried, both in the past and more recently, paying attention to the breadth of services provided as well as the intensity and duration of service provision. They should also explain both the rationale informing the intervention and the desired outcomes in terms of improving the quality of the child's lived experience.

Consideration should also be given to analysing parental engagement in the change process, drawing on the model of change in Chapter 4, with specific attention paid to:

- parental recognition of both their failure to meet the needs of the child and the part they play in addressing this failure
- parental ability, motivation to change and the opportunities provided to address the concerning behaviours
- parental engagement in taking action to change behaviours and, where necessary, lifestyles: are they both committed to, and putting sustained effort into, changing, or is there evidence of superficial compliance, surface static or disengagement?
- how practitioners have supported parents not only to make the necessary changes but maintain them in times of crisis and stress
- whether patterns are emerging regarding past and present engagement with service providers.

Children in out-of-home care

Despite the commonly held belief that children do not do well within the care system, there are an increasing number of studies that raise questions as to whether this is the case. Davidson-Arad (2005), for example, studied

93 abused and neglected children in Israel for 15 months. He found that the quality of life for the children removed from home improved incrementally over the period of study, whilst that of the children who stayed at home remained the same. An American study by Mennen *et al.* (2010b) compared 302 maltreated children, including neglected children, between nine and 12 years of age to see if placements at home, and in kinship or foster care affected mental health functioning in terms of self-report and caregiver report. They found that the children who remained at home perceived themselves and were perceived as having less positive mental health functioning than those in either a kinship or foster placement. All three English studies in Box 13.1 provide information indicating 'incontrovertible evidence that many children benefit from being placed away from home' (Davies and Ward, 2012, p. 88). The most striking finding comes from the study by Wade *et al.* (2011, p. 201), who conclude that there was 'an almost unequivocal good' in removing children who had experienced chronic or severe neglect.

Jones *et al.* (2011) completed a correlates review (mapping factors that are related with each other) of features associated with outcomes for looked-after children and young people. They considered 92 studies, including four systematic reviews, five non-systematic reviews, eight randomized control trails, 66 cohort studies and nine cross-sectional studies. The majority of studies were American, and whilst recognizing that the findings may not be transferable, there are themes that emerge that fit with the findings from the studies described above commissioned by the English Department for Education. Drawing on these findings and those from other studies, there are a number of factors that practitioners should consider when planning quality out-of home placements (Doolan, 2006; MacMillan *et al.*, 2009; Darlington *et al.*, 2012). Three key factors: placement stability, meeting the specific needs of the child, and providing a support network are discussed below.

Placement stability

Placement stability was found to be significant in Jones *et al.*'s review. Wade *et al.* (2011) also found children in care fared well in stable placements, and Farmer and Lutman (2010) found that five years on from being removed from parents, 58 per cent of neglected children who were living away from home in stable conditions were likely to have good overall wellbeing.

Farmer and Lutman found that placement stability through permanency is more likely to be successful if the neglected child is under six years of age at the time of placement. Jones *et al.* (2011) also found age to be important.

Davies and Ward (2012) explore the reasons behind this and argue that early permanent placement avoids maladaptive attachments. Drawing on a meta-analysis of attachment in adopted children by van den Dries *et al.* (2012), they conclude that children adopted before 12 months were as securely attached to their carers as non-adopted peers, but those adopted over the age of a year showed a less secure attachment than non-adopted children. This finding supports the need for practitioners and the courts to take swift action. Placement breakdown and accompanying instability, according to Jones *et al.* (2011), is more likely amongst older children who have more entrenched behavioural and emotional problems, which are likely to become more evident and difficult to manage as the child grows up. Moreover, these children are likely to have contact with their birth families, and poor quality or problematic contact can destabilize placements (Sen and Broadhurst, 2011).

Whilst placement stability is important, placement changes may be advantageous. Wade *et al.* (2011) explored this and found that, in the main, moves for children in care had been for positive reasons: moving from a short-term to longer-term placement. The children who fared badly, however, were those who were moving in and out of the care system, living with family or kinship care and then returning to foster parents or residential units. For example, Farmer and Lutman (2010) found that neglected children who had experienced the most returns home had the poorest wellbeing, with 38 per cent of these children having experienced two or more failed returns. Wade *et al.* (2011) found 20 per cent of their sample appear never to have settled at home, moving between family, extended networks and care.

Stability can be enhanced if foster carers have ready access to services, such as mental health services, that can assist them in meeting the needs of the young person in their care. Peer support networks can also make foster carers feel supported, which in turn can prevent placement breakdown. Another way to support foster carers is by providing planned breaks for them. An example of this is *Dreamwall* in Southhampton, England. The scheme seeks to prevent foster carers reaching breaking point by ensuring they have planned breaks. It is attributed with reducing by 95 per cent the number of carers leaving fostering because of discontent or burnout (Mellor, 2009).

Children in foster homes are much more likely than children in children's homes to say that they feel they are in the right placement. Asylum-seeking young people are less likely to think they are in the right placement. The main reasons given by the young people for being satisfied with their placement were that they felt happy and settled, were well looked after and felt safe and were getting the help they needed (Ofsted, 2012).

Meeting the specific needs of the neglected child in substitute care

> I think there's a perception in pre-adoptive parents that neglect is one of the easier issues to deal with – love is all it takes to heal the child. But severe neglect can't be healed with a hug and a kiss. It's a long-term issue and requires enormous amounts of patience. (Pers. comm., adoptive mother of a child who had experienced eight years of chronic neglect)

Children do not achieve better outcomes in out-of-home care without considerable effort being put in to ensure that they receive good enough parenting as well as emotional and educational support. This means that their carers have to be equipped to meet their specific needs. Marquis *et al.* (2008), in a Canadian study of 79 neglected children placed in foster care, found that these children import their problems, particularly their attachment disorders, into the foster placement and are likely to exhibit issues of emotional regulation, social relatedness and behavioural problems. Foster carers and others providing long-term or permanent placements must, therefore, be equipped to address these issues, as is made clear in the quote above.

There are some specific interventions that show promise in terms of ensuring that substitute care meets the needs of the neglected children. One of these is considered below.

Multidimensional Treatment Foster Care (MTFC)

This programme, which originated in Oregon, USA, is a wrap-around intervention designed to meet the needs of children and young people in care who exhibit challenging behaviour, such as offending or mental health problems. It differs from foster care as it combines treatment and substitute care. Individual treatment plans are developed and may include individual and family therapy, social skills training and support with education. The young people are provided with a short-term foster placement for around nine months, followed by a short period of aftercare. Whilst behaviour management is a key element of the programme, there is also attention paid to developing interpersonal skills, emotional regulation and coping with relationships with family, peers and other adults. The programme centres on reinforcing positive behaviour and is delivered by specially trained foster carers. Whilst the original aim of the American programme was to return young people to their families, in England the programme has been used to meet the needs of young people who have been in out-of-home placements for a number of years with the aim of obtaining a family-based, stable placement and, if appropriate, improving the quality of contact with birth families once they have completed the programme. Once the programme is completed, therapists work with follow-on carers to ensure that there is consistency in approach and that desired behaviours are reinforced.

The programme has been piloted and evaluated in England by Biehal *et al.* (2010). They concluded that *MTFC* appears to work better with young people who are exhibiting antisocial behaviour and are prepared to both engage meaningfully with the programme and be enthusiastic about it. It is no surprise, bearing in mind what has been discussed earlier in this book, that a positive relationship between the *MTFC* foster carer and the young person was also important. The quality of placement provided once the programme was completed also had an impact, with foster carers needing to reinforce the messages of the programme and persist in supporting the young people.

Providing a support network

Children and young people appear to value and benefit from staying in contact with family and friends of their choice. This contact may be direct, through face-to-face meetings, which may or may not be supervised, or indirect through letters and emails. Placement stability, reunification, and the health and wellbeing of the child can be enhanced through appropriate contact (Schofield and Simmonds, 2009; Smith, 2009; Sen and Broadhurst, 2011). One of the challenges, when working with children in out-of-home care as a consequence of child neglect, is establishing the extent to which contact with particular family members can be beneficial to the child. Sen and Broadhurst have drawn on the research literature on contact and concluded that this needs to be well planned, supported and of high quality. In order to achieve this level of contact with family members, the research they reviewed indicated that:

- Contact should contribute to meeting the needs of the child. Therefore, when determining whether contact is appropriate, the needs of the child, the circumstances of family members, the previous history of professional involvement with the family, the quality of family relationships, and the capacity of carers to manage contact that meets the needs of the child should all be taken into account.
- The difficulties that parents and other family members may encounter in maintaining contact should be recognized and addressed.
- The aims and objectives of contact should be specified and included in the care plan.
- Social workers have a key role in ensuring that the aims and objectives of contact are achieved, the frequency and quality of contact is maintained and the child is safe.

- Assessments also need to be undertaken with regard to contact between siblings, most importantly whether it is in the interest of the siblings, taking into account their individual needs and, if it is appropriate, plans should be devised outlining the form of contact and frequency, as well as indicating how this will be achieved and maintained.
- The wishes and feelings of the child, family members and carers must be taken into consideration.
- The support required to make the contact successful should be provided to the child, the family and carers.
- If contact is considered to be detrimental to the health and wellbeing of the child then the child should be provided with explanations that take into account their age and ability.

Moving beyond the family, young people appear to value the quality of relationships with foster carers, childcare workers and other professionals. Minnis and Walker (2012), in a literature review of young people's experiences of the fostering and adoption processes, emphasize the importance of a positive relationship with their social worker. They conclude that children felt well looked after when the social worker supported them, offered reassurance at times of stress, and gave practical support and continuity. Mentoring has shown some promise in terms of educational and psychological outcomes, and focused education projects designed specifically to improve educational outcomes have also proved popular with looked-after children, as have schemes, particularly in schools, to tackle the bullying and stigma associated with being looked after. Interventions designed to improve the quality of the placement and the relationships between the child and professionals in their life are therefore important. Training for foster carers and case workers to address relationship-building and maintenance, as well as access to support services to help address relationship issues, can be useful.

One group of young people who appear to lack a supportive network are those who are in care but also in custody. There are currently 400 of those in England. A report by HM Inspectorate of Prisons (2011) found these young people are often not identified in young offender institutes (YOI), have a lack of involvement from social workers, and there can be confusion amongst professionals as to the assistance they receive and from what source. This means that some end up in unsuitable bed and breakfast accommodation with no support. The Youth Justice Board intends to fund social workers in YOIs and this should ensure a more coordinated approach to meeting the needs of this group.

It is not only contact with professionals and family that is important; children in out-of-home care need to develop friendships, informal social support and community networks, not only to improve their sense of self-worth but also to provide them with social support when they make the transition to independent living.

Kinship care

Jones *et al.* (2011) found that kinship care, whereby children are placed with members of the extended family network, can have benefits since it often means the child remains within their community, enabling them to maintain links with friends as well as staying at the same school. MacMillan *et al.* (2009), in their review, found studies indicated that these children are less likely to be maltreated and have fewer placement changes. Moreover, they found that there are few or no differences in terms of behavioural, cognitive, educational, emotional and interpersonal functioning from foster care, with a minority of studies indicating they fare better. MacMillan *et al.* (2009), however, signal some caution in interpreting these findings, noting that there is some suggestion that the children placed in kinship care are from less dysfunctional families and have fewer behavioural and emotional problems than those in foster care. Davies and Ward (2012), drawing on the findings from the English Department for Education commissioned studies, argue that there is a danger of these placements being made without taking into account the carers' history of caring, the quality of care they are able to provide and any current problems they are experiencing. It is also important to recognize that kinship carers, such as grandparents, may have provided poor-quality parenting to their own children. Moreover, as these children are likely to have a range of problems and needs associated with neglect by their parents, these carers need access to specialist help to enable them to meet the needs of the child and to manage the relationship with the birth parents.

Backhouse and Graham (2012), in an interesting Australian study of 34 grandparents raising their grandchildren, highlighted the additional challenges that grandparents in their own study – and in others completed in various nation states – encounter when caring for their grandchildren. These include financial problems, housing difficulties, damage to physical and emotional health, high levels of stress, anxiety and depression, and social isolation and lack of support. These grandparents also have to manage the demands of parenting a new generation of children whose values and norms, as well as the expectations placed on carers, will have changed since they parented their own children. Bearing in mind, particularly in cases of neglect, that many of these grandparents may have limited parenting skills themselves and will also be managing many of the behavioural problems associated with neglect exhibited by their grandchildren, this is a group of carers who are likely to need significant practical and emotional support in order to meet the needs of their grandchildren.

Reunification: does it work?

Cleaver (2000) found that children who enjoy regular contact with family are more likely to return home to parental care. However, she also noted that such factors as significant neglect militate against reunification. MacMillan *et al.* (2009), in their systematic review, found better outcomes for neglected children were recorded for children who were *not* reunified with their families of origin, in terms of greater overall wellbeing and criminal activity. Farmer and Lutman (2010) found that two years after returning home 59 per cent of the neglected children in their study had been maltreated. The children who were subjected to the most maltreatment, the severest neglect or had the poorest wellbeing were likely to be living with parents with alcohol problems. Wade *et al.* (2011) found that the children in their study who returned home were likely to be subject to further negative disruption, with 35 per cent re-entering the care system because of maltreatment, inadequate parenting or the parents' inability to manage the child's risky behaviours. Reunifications were most effective if the child returned to a different parent or the problems that led to the original admission had been addressed. This means that practitioners need evidence that change has taken place and will be maintained so that the child is safe not only in the short term but also in the longer term. Concerns about the child's safety often remain high for practitioners following reunification. Thus, reunification is not an easy option and is not always the best solution for neglected children.

Younger children appear to return home more successfully than older children. This may, in part, be the result of older children's behaviour and entrenched problems proving challenging for carers. However, what was also found was that there are diminishing levels of involvement from social work services to support parents as children get older (Davies and Ward, 2012). Moreover, according to Wade *et al.* (2011), when younger children return home they are more likely to remain on a care order as 'placement with parents', and because of this workers provide more support within an agreed plan. Children who return home with other looked-after siblings also fare better. Wade *et al.* (2011) found variations in approaches to reunification amongst local authorities, but a number of other factors make reunification of children *less* likely to be successful. These include the child:

- is considered to be at risk of harm and the problems that led to the admission into out-of-home care had not improved
- has been looked after for some time
- accepts the need to be in care
- has a learning disability
- comes from a family where substance misuse and domestic violence were issues. (Interestingly, mental health issues were not significantly associated with decisions as to whether a child should remain in care)

- has suffered neglect. These children 'were significantly less likely to have returned [home], were less likely to have wanted to return and were more likely than other maltreated children to be rated as having settled well in care' (Wade *et al.*, 2011, p. 193).

A key message from the studies is that neglected children achieved much better wellbeing if they remained in care. Amongst those who returned home, stability did not seem to impact on their wellbeing and they tended to fare worse than the other maltreated children who returned home but had not been neglected.

Most difficulties regarding reunification occur within the first few months. It is therefore important that practitioners continually assess whether the parent is meeting the needs of the child. The findings from the studies indicate that both children and families need intense and ongoing support after the child returns home from care, such as the multifaceted interventions described in Chapter 8. However, this is often not available, with services provided on return ceasing after a few months. The lack of services fails to recognize the deep-seated problems these families encounter and the support these parents require to meet the needs of their children. Wade *et al.* (2011) conclude that where children have suffered chronic or severe neglect, the potential for reunification should be viewed with considerable caution.

A group of neglected children who are particularly vulnerable regarding reunification are those who are accommodated by the local authority on a voluntary basis. Davies and Ward (2012) conclude, drawing on the three studies commissioned by the English Department for Education (see Box 13.1), that less rigorous practice takes place with regard to reunification for these children than those subject to care orders. This was particularly so when children were returned to their parents. Abrupt and unplanned reunification, as a result of placement disruption, was also more likely to occur amongst children accommodated on a voluntary basis.

Leaving care

There is a sub-population of young people, irrespective of nation state, who often leave placements abruptly and earlier than those living at home or those who have been adopted (Blakeslee, 2012). This group, which is likely to include young people who have experienced chronic neglect and display many of the challenging behaviours associated with this neglect, lack adequate resources and the longer-term support that they require to meet their needs as they make the transition from late adolescence to young adulthood (Stein *et al.*, 2009; Rees *et al.*, 2011). Attempts have been made to address this issue. For example, the Children (Leaving Care) Act 2000 places a duty on local authorities in England to assess and meet the needs of young people aged 16 and 17 who are in care or leaving care, and to keep in touch with care leavers until they are at least 21. Moreover, when they are 16 young people in care should receive a pathway plan that maps out a clear route to independence. They should also have an adviser who will coordinate the provision of support and assistance to meet the needs of the young person. Key to this plan is helping the young person into education, training or employment, ensuring they receive comprehensive financial support and ongoing assistance with education or training, even if it takes some past the age of 21. Whilst this sounds laudable it does not necessarily occur in a way that meets the needs of the young person.

Young people leaving care for independent living often feel not only that they entered the care system because of neglect but also that they have suffered further neglect at the hands of their corporate parents, the local authority who has failed to prepare them appropriately for life beyond care (Viner *et al.*, 2010). The kinds of skills the neglected young people in the Rees *et al.* (2011) study referred to were being able to cook, use a washing machine and know how to search for jobs. This lack of attention to vulnerable young carers, who already have significant needs, means their problems can be exacerbated by this further neglect by professionals. It is not surprising, therefore, that this group is vulnerable to homelessness, poor educational achievement, sexual exploitation, mental health issues and offending, and young women are much more likely to become young mothers. It is all too easy to see how this group can become the neglectful parents of the future.

Morgan and Lindsay (2006) explored leaving care with 117 young people. These young people provided a list of what they required from professionals as part of the leaving care process. This included:

- having everything in place, including secure, safe accommodation with sufficient time to prepare for the move
- a gradual move, timed for when the young person was ready, with options to return if necessary
- assistance and easier methods for dealing with housing benefits, and help in getting travel cards and driving lessons
- recognition of the cost of living independently and benefiting from money that the council has put aside for them
- being able to contact key people, with social workers understanding how difficult it is for them
- help in bringing up any children of their own.

Conclusion

Whilst the primary focus of this book has been on meeting the needs of neglected children in the community, there will be some children whose needs cannot be met in this way and for whom out-of-home placements are necessary. All too often, however, this difficult decision is delayed, to the detriment of the child. A major cause of delay is that in order for the state to intervene and remove a child from their family, professionals have to demonstrate that despite every effort having been made to work in partnership with parents and provide the family with the services and support they require to meet the needs of the child, the parents have not engaged in a manner that is preventing the child from suffering significant harm. Whilst it is important that decisions to remove children from the care of their parents are not taken lightly, it is also important, when making such decisions, that both professionals and the courts recognize that research is increasingly providing evidence that quality placements in care can be the salvation of neglected children, particularly if they are accessed before the child is six years old.

There are a number of factors that contribute to quality out-of-home placements. These include placement stability, meeting the specific needs of the child whilst they are in substitute care, and ensuring the child has a support network. A key question that professionals need to answer in cases of chronic neglect is whether the parents can be a source of support to the child and, in light of that response, whether it is advantageous for the child to remain in regular contact with their parents. Whilst the parents may not be able to provide the care and support a child needs, there may be other family members who can do so. With this in mind it is worth exploring the possibility of kinship care. This form of out-of-home placement has advantages because it frequently means the child can maintain links within their community. However, in cases of neglect workers have to consider that there may be some intergenerational concerns regarding parenting. Therefore, a thorough assessment of the parenting capacity of potential carers, such as grandparents, aunts and uncles, is essential.

Practitioners working with children in out-of-home care, unless the child is placed for adoption, have to consider whether reunification is both possible and appropriate. In cases of neglect, recent research (described in Box 13.1) seems to indicate that reunification is not always the best solution for neglected children. Often, children returning to their parents experience further neglect and maltreatment, and achieve poorer outcomes than those remaining in care. Parental issues, notably alcohol problems, exacerbate the situation.

Neglected children who spend their adolescence in out-of-home care may also experience additional neglect through the lack of services and support they receive from professionals when leaving care. If these young people are not equipped and supported to manage the transition to adulthood, they are vulnerable to becoming homeless, being sexually exploited, engaging in drug and alcohol misuse or offending. These are some of the issues that, taken together, make these young people vulnerable to becoming the neglectful carers of the future (Rees *et al.*, 2011).

Appendix: The Anytown Neglect Study

The overall aim of the study was to further understanding of multidisciplinary planning and intervention in cases of chronic neglect. The aim was achieved by:

- analysing the outline child protection plans made at initial child protection conferences in relation to the needs of children and their families in cases of chronic neglect
- exploring the ways in which these plans were developed by the core group[1] in partnership with family members
- identifying the ways in which members of core groups understood their roles and responsibilities in relation to planning and intervention in cases of chronic neglect
- establishing to what extent knowledge about family history, past patterns of behaviour, and motivation and capacity to change informed core group decision making and planning
- exploring the role of the social worker, acting as lead professional, in providing direction and support to members of the core group
- ascertaining the extent to which family members were actively engaged in the work of the core group
- identifying the personal, professional and organizational promoters and inhibitors to effective core group working in these cases
- identifying best core group practice in cases of chronic neglect.

For the purposes of this study chronic neglect was defined as either the child being registered[2] under the category of neglect and remaining on the register for over two years, or the child having their name placed on the register because of neglect, subsequently being de-registered and then being re-registered on at least one further occasion in a two-year period.

Research design and sample

The study was commissioned by a local safeguarding children board (LSCB)[3] in Wales. The first three stages of the study were completed in the area served by the board. This is a mixed urban and rural community of approximately 173,000, which centres around two main towns. The

250

area has experienced a decline in traditional industry with accompanying problems of high unemployment.

In order to achieve the aims and objectives, four different research methods were used:

- a review of case files
- interviews with social workers who act as lead professional and with conference chairs
- focus groups consisting of frontline practitioners who participate in core groups
- a survey of frontline staff working in three other regions of the UK.

Data collection, using the methods described above, enabled comparison of data from different sources and provided a reliability and validity check.

Stage 1: Review of case files: analysis of child protection plans and reports

The first stage of the study centred on an analysis of information contained in the case files, as these records provide the official record of decision making. The purpose of this review was, first, to ascertain from the case files and records the issues related to chronic neglect that were identified as of concern at initial child protection conferences; second, in light of these issues, to identify how members of the conference expected them to be addressed through the child protection plan; third, to ascertain how the core group translated the plan into a working, detailed, multidisciplinary child protection plan; fourth, to establish how the plan was implemented, monitored and evaluated.

A sample of 21 case files was interrogated. A purposive sampling method was used to ensure that the sample reflected the definition of chronic neglect used for this study but also included:

- adolescents
- children who are members of the same sibling group
- disabled children.

It was considered important to ensure these three groups were represented in the sample as there is limited research on these children in relation to child neglect. Moreover, the research that has been completed indicates that interventions into neglectful families can overlook the particular needs of these children and young people. (See Chapters 3 and 12 for more information.)

The brief was to analyse case conference minutes, chronologies, reports, child protection plans, core group minutes and reports contained in the case files of 21 children. The final sample included 12 boys and nine girls. However, this sample of 21 children and young people came from only seven families, as a significant number of parents declined to give permission for the research team to read the files on their children. This provided an opportunity to explore in some detail the ways in which different children in the same family are perceived and the efforts that are made to ensure that the needs of the different members of a sibling group are met. However, the information contained in the various files in relation to family background, past history and interventions was often duplicated. Therefore, the analysis on family background and so on can do little more than provide a commentary on what was recorded with regard to siblings in the seven families. Common themes did, however, emerge regarding practice in relation to these families, and the subsequent stages of the study provided an opportunity to explore these themes further to consider whether they are common in other cases of chronic neglect or unique to these families.

The ages of the selected sample of children ranged between 3 and 16. Of the 21 children, four had a physical disability or chronic health condition and three were considered to have special learning needs, such as autistic spectrum disorder. Figure A.1 shows the age spread of the sample.

To identify themes and sub-themes, the case files of all 21 children and young people were subject to content analysis, using a content analysis framework that drew on a review of the literature. Data was collated and analysed with the aim and objectives of the study in mind and included information on:

- referrals and re-referrals, nature and sources
- family and child background
- role of extended family
- specified concerns about the child or children
- case history: parents' past experiences, patterns emerging, past interventions
- parenting issues
- assessment of child's needs; parental potential to change; risk of significant harm
- engagement of other professionals in planning and their brief
- engagement with children and families in determining the content and operation of the plan
- interventions, rationale for interventions and decisions regarding effectiveness of interventions.

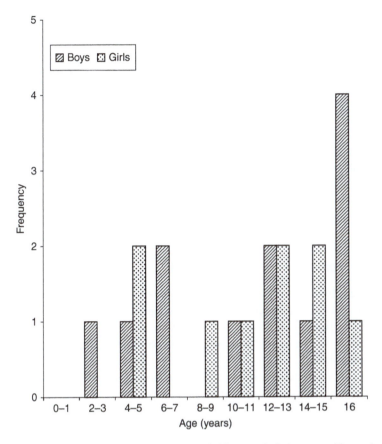

Figure A.1: Age distribution and gender of children included in case file analysis

Stage 2: Interviews with chairs of initial child protection conferences and social workers

All child and family social workers who were acting as lead professional for children on a child protection plan experiencing chronic neglect, as per the definition above, received an email providing information about the study and inviting them to participate in a semi-structured telephone interview. The first 15 social workers who responded to the invitation were contacted for interview. Twelve interviews were completed within the study timescales. In addition all six child protection conference chairs were interviewed. Each interview lasted between 40 and 60 minutes. The purpose of these interviews was to explore with the participants the themes from the case review. With this in mind, the participants were asked:

- what they considered important when preparing reports and assessments for the initial child protection conferences

- their views on analysis and decision making in the initial child protection conferences regarding the needs of children experiencing chronic neglect
- how plans were developed at the conference
- the issues encountered when implementing child protection plans in core groups
- factors that promoted and inhibited multidisciplinary working in core groups
- their views on the engagement of children and parents/carers in the planning process.

Discussions were recorded, transcribed and subject to content analysis using NVivo, a qualitative data analysis package.

Stage 3: Multidisciplinary focus groups

Having explored the themes from the analysis of case records with social workers and conference chairs, the next stage was to explore these emerging themes further with professionals who are members of core groups and work with the family and other professionals to implement the child protection plan.

With this in mind, the focus group questions centred on eliciting information from participants regarding their experiences of:

- interpretation of the function of the core group and processes associated with child protection planning
- participation in core groups in cases of chronic neglect
- engagement with children
- ways in which parental capacity and motivation to change are explored in the core group
- termination of child protection plans
- challenges and effective practice when working in a core group with chronic neglect.

Agencies represented on the local safeguarding children board, who commissioned the study, were invited to identify four frontline staff from their agency to attend. Out of a possible total of 40 participants, 34 took part in the focus groups. Membership of the focus groups was as follows:

- Focus group 1: representation from housing, school health, community midwifery, probation, children's social services, nursing (safeguarding) (total = 10).

- Focus group 2: representation from school health, housing, youth offending services, education welfare services, children's social services (total = 11).
- Focus group 3: representation from children's social services, probation, educational psychology, voluntary sector (total = 5).
- Focus group 4: representation from voluntary sector, probation, midwifery, educational psychology (total = 4).

Each focus group lasted between 60 and 80 minutes and was audio recorded.

Stage 4: The survey

Whilst the first three stages of this study yielded significant qualitative data, the researchers were mindful that the sample was small and the research had been completed in just one local authority area. Therefore, whilst the data collected and analysed thus far provided some insight into the ways in which planning in cases of chronic neglect occurs in that particular authority, it was difficult to ascertain whether the key practice issues identified by the respondents were unique to that authority. With this in mind, a survey was completed to establish whether practitioners working with similar cases in other parts of the UK encountered comparable issues. Three areas in England were identified as providing a contrasting context to Anytown: a large rural county which includes two large towns acting as service centres for the region, referred to below as County; a city with high rates of deprivation in the north of England, referred to as Metropolis; and a London borough, referred to as Borough. A series of 14 statements and questions was developed by the research team in order to identify the extent to which professionals working in a diverse range of practice settings felt some of the key findings that emerged consistently from the data analysis of the first three stages of the study reflected their practice experience. These statements and questions were:

- There is adequate time at conference for drawing up an outline child protection plan.
- I am confident that the parents leave the conference with a clear understanding as to why particular actions are included in the plan.
- I am confident that the professionals leave the conference with a clear understanding as to why particular actions are included in the plan.
- How often have you experienced:
  - children in the family being overlooked when initial child protection plans are developed

- 'start again syndrome' (ignoring what services had been provided previously and the family's responses to these interventions in the past)
- the outline child protection plan as a list of actions with no specified child-focused outcomes
- plans with too many actions
- the focus of the plan is on addressing one of a number of issues
- the plan is driven by resources?
- 'Core groups are no more than a chat in the family home.'
- All professional members attend core groups.
- Information sharing takes place outside the core group meeting.
- Decisions at core groups about progress are based on what has changed for the child or children in the family.
- The core group has 'teeth'.

A five-point Likert scale was included with each of the above, enabling the respondent to indicate the extent to which, in their experience, the practice described in the statement or question occurred.

Hard copies of the survey were distributed at training events, namely annual conferences and workshops organized by the local safeguarding child boards or local authority in the three different research sites described above. The participants were invited to complete the survey and return it to the event organizers at the end of the event. The survey was completed by 162 frontline staff. Table A.1 provides an overview of the different professional groups that responded.

Table A.1: Breakdown by profession of participants completing the survey

Profession	Frequency	To nearest %
Social work	51	32
Family health – health visitor/school nurse/ Family Nurse Partnership	14	9
Mental health – CAMHS/psychology/ psychiatry	11	7
Other health: hospital, general practitioners, speech and language therapists, physiotherapists	9	6
Voluntary sector	4	2
Children's centre/early years worker	6	4
Education	17	10
Family intervention/family support	10	6
Other	17	10
Not stated	23	14
Total	**162**	**100**

Key findings

These are considered in two sections: (a) from the first three stages of the study completed in Anytown, and (b) from the survey.

Findings from the Anytown case study

- Referrals from adult services regarding chronic neglect appear to be very limited. Moreover, referrals from members of the family, community and anonymous referrals are not always given as much weight as those from professionals.
- Assessments of risk of harm and the needs of the child are negatively affected by: limited time; emphasis on the presenting problem; lack of sufficient attention paid to both the past history of the family and past patterns of engagement with services; failure to engage meaningfully with children; and lack of attention to the identity of the child. The result is a lack of appreciation of the daily lived experience of the child.
- Participants recognized that attendance amongst professionals at conferences varies. General practitioners, paediatricians and representatives from adult services were considered the poorest attenders. The level of core group attendance with regard to the case analysis was found to reduce as concerns about a child abated; the participants agreed that this occurs. Core group meetings routinely consist of three or four professionals and the parent(s). The case review and the comments from practitioners indicate that when a professional has not seen the family between core group meetings they may absent themselves from the following core group meeting.
- Participants described how conference members struggle to get the balance right between sharing information and analysis. Some respondents in the study felt the analysis and plan should only focus on safeguarding the child from harm, whilst others felt it should go beyond this to promote the health and wellbeing of the child. Decisions could be overly influenced by the chair and/or social worker as other members look to them for guidance and advice.
- The majority of outline plans in the case review were vague and therefore open to different interpretations as to their purpose, expectations and measurement of success when developed further by the core group. Participants in the interviews and focus groups indicated this appears to be due, in part, to: lack of clarity regarding the detail that should be included; the very limited time spent on developing the plan (between 5 and 25 minutes); and planning taking place at the end of lengthy meetings.

- The evidence from the case review and some of the comments of practitioners indicated that often the outline plan was not developed further by the core group and plans therefore lacked specific indicators and timescales. Moreover, there was a perceived lack of shared understanding regarding the purpose of the plan and the responsibility of the core group to expand on the plan.
- A number of professionals noted a lack of clarity regarding what was negotiable and what was non-negotiable within a plan. A particular issue centred on giving families a 'last chance', with the indication that this was not negotiable. However, last chances seemed to be given on a number of occasions, leading both family members and professionals to question whether the core group has 'teeth'.
- There was a lack of consistency in terms of the content of plans. Furthermore, a number of different themes emerged in terms of the content of plans when discussed by the participants in the interviews and focus groups. These included: overlooking children in the family; the 'start again syndrome'; an overwhelming list of actions; no sense of priority regarding task completion; a focus on one issue; and resource-driven actions.
- An issue for those who participate in core groups was the frustration of not having a copy of the outline plan for the first core group meeting. The forms used for core groups also caused some confusion. Written agreements with families were not completed routinely and some study participants were not clear about their purpose and the weight that should be given to these agreements.
- Case drift was identified as a concern by those who were interviewed and also members of the focus groups. It was also evident in the cases reviewed. This was due, in part, to a lack of clarity regarding the purpose of the actions, the agreed outcomes of the plan and agreed indicators of progress. Drift was particularly evident in the case review with regard to making decisions about whether the children should be removed from the home.
- Participants acknowledged difficulties in identifying appropriate indicators that provide evidence of improvements to outcomes for children. Without clear indicators, cases can be allowed to drift with no specific ending to the plan. Moreover, a lack of clarity and vague actions and outcomes within the plan can lead to professionals using very different thresholds to measure success.
- Not all professionals appreciated their roles and responsibilities in relation to core group membership, and this led to different perceptions of the group and individuals' remit.
- Effective plans require an understanding of the way in which individuals manage change and the influence of the past on present engagement. All

too often there was little indication on the files of parents being taken through the change process. Only a minority of respondents appeared to routinely use models of change. There were also a number of factors that appeared to act as barriers to practitioners engaging parents meaningfully in the change process. These included:

- lack of time to establish working relationships
- limited information shared and analysed regarding change
- lack of consideration of what worked and did not work previously
- vague plans which were a list of actions with little explanation as to why these actions were necessary
- setting tasks and goals for the parents which they cannot, for whatever reason, achieve
- lack of indicators and outcome measures
- putting square pegs in round holes by failing to assess whether poor parenting is a result of lack of knowledge, motivation or parenting resources or a combination of these factors.

- The central role of the social worker is apparent in as much as some core groups do not appear to meet if the social worker is unable to attend. The social worker usually acts as chair and as minute taker, and organizes the venue and chases up core group participants. There was an acknowledgement by the participants in the study that it would be fairer to at least share minute taking and chairing of meetings between professionals.

- There was evidence in the case files of practitioners centring their assessment on gathering information from the primary caregiver, who is usually the mother, with transitory male caregivers often marginalized or ignored. What was also of note was the lack of assessment on the files of family members, particularly grandparents, who provided support to the family and on occasion had children in the family living with them. This focus on the primary caregiver was recognized by the participants in the study.

- There was evidence in the case files of practitioners going through reports with family members, but often the reports were lengthy, difficult to follow and full of technical terms and abbreviations, and it was not clear to what extent the parent(s) understood the content. Time constraints, according to the participants in the interviews and focus groups, appear to impact on a practitioner's ability to share assessments in a meaningful way prior to entering the conference. There was little evidence from the files included in the case review that reports were shared with children and young people, and this was also acknowledged by the participants in the focus groups and interviews.

- A striking feature of the case review was that workers in their reports frequently referred to 'seeing' the child, but in the majority of cases it appeared to be little more than registering the child's presence since there was rarely any evidence in files and reports that meaningful information had been gathered from the child. When workers did talk to children it tended to be generalized conversations regarding their wishes and feelings. There was very little evidence throughout the study of information being collected from children about their lived experience and the impact of plans on this experience.

- Respondents identified that, if managed well, children's levels of self-esteem and confidence can be boosted through attendance at conference and core group meetings. There were, however, some concerns expressed about attendance at conferences and core groups in terms of what children might hear, and professionals therefore feeling inhibited in their presence. Whilst attendance may not be appropriate, participants agreed that the child should have a voice.

A particular issue highlighted by this study is the way in which decisions are made regarding a sibling group, with a loss of focus on the individual children in a family. In this situation, the child who does not appear to have any significant problems is overlooked, whilst interventions may still be necessary to prevent problems occurring. The challenge of focusing on more than one child extended to the implementation of the plans. Two issues were identified at all three stages of the study: first, the size of core groups and, second, professionals may disengage when they have a particular interest in only one child and therefore feel they do not have a part to play in discussions that are not related to the particular child.

Findings from the survey

Whilst some common themes emerged in terms of practice in County, Metropolis and Borough, there were also some differences. What was of particular note was that, in the main, practitioners in Borough rated the quality of practice, with regard to the various statements, slightly higher than the practitioners in the two other areas. Practitioners in Metropolis and County tended to hold similar views. Any significant differences between the three areas are highlighted below.

- There was general agreement that there is inadequate time at the conference to draw up the outline plan, with 48 per cent of the respondents indicating that adequate time is available only some of the time. However, there were clear differences between the three survey site areas, with only 43 per cent of respondents from Borough indicating that adequate time is available only some of the time or rarely compared to 71 per cent from Metropolis and 73 per cent from County.

- There was a shared lack of confidence that parents left the conference understanding why particular actions were included in the plan, with only 12 per cent believing this occurs most of the time and 23 per cent half the time. However, there was slightly more confidence amongst the Borough respondents that this occurred most of the time (18 per cent) compared to 5 per cent in Metropolis and 10 per cent in County.
- Practitioners were more confident that their colleagues left the conference with a clear understanding of the reasons for actions in the plan, with 46 per cent believing this was the case most of the time. However, 47 per cent thought this happened only half or some of the time.
- Overall, the respondents did not think that children in sibling groups were overlooked when the outline child protection plan was developed, although 47 per cent did acknowledge that this can sometimes occur.
- The practitioners agreed that 'start again syndrome' can take place when preparing a plan, with only 10 per cent indicating this rarely occurs.
- The respondents did not agree as to whether the initial child protection plan was a list of actions with no specific child focus. For example, a fifth thought this happened most of the time; another fifth thought it rarely occurred. Comparing responses across the three survey sites, 67 per cent of respondents from Borough stated this happened some of the time or rarely, compared to 46 per cent from County and 50 per cent from Metropolis.
- There was agreement across all three survey sites that the plan included too many actions.
- There was a very mixed response across the three areas as to whether some plans only focused on one issue when a number of issues needed addressing.
- Opinion was divided as to whether the child protection plan was driven by resources, a split occurring depending on location, with only 37 per cent of respondents in Borough indicating this was an issue whilst 69 per cent in County thought this was the case.
- The respondents overwhelmingly disagreed (78 per cent) with the statement that core groups are no more than a chat in the family home.
- In terms of professional engagement and attendance at core groups there was general agreement that professionals did not attend all of the time but they did attend some (40 per cent), half (20 per cent) or most of the time (20 per cent).
- Information sharing outside of the core group was reported to happen some (42 per cent) or most of the time (32 per cent). Practitioners in Metropolis were most likely to think this took place (45 per cent) with those in County least likely (20 per cent) to think so.

- The respondents could not agree as to whether decisions in core groups about progress are based on what has changed for the child or children in the family: 39 per cent felt this only happened some of the time, 25 per cent half the time and 28 per cent most of the time.
- Regarding the question about whether the core group had 'teeth', 17 per cent (n = 28) did not answer. Of those who responded, 43 per cent felt the core group did. Respondents from Metropolis were most likely to say this was not usually the case, with 64 per cent of them saying this only happened some of the time or rarely, compared with 48 per cent from Borough and an overall figure of 56 per cent.

Notes

1. The study was completed in Wales, where multidisciplinary child protection plans are delivered and monitored by a 'core group' of professionals. The same system is used in other nation states such as England, Northern Ireland and Scotland. (For more information on core groups see Chapter 6.)
2. In Wales, as in Northern Ireland and Scotland, if there are concerns that a child is suffering and likely to continue to suffer significant harm and therefore be in need of a child protection plan, a decision is made at the initial child protection conference to place the name of the child on the child protection register. In England, instead of being registered, the name of the child is recorded as being the subject of a multidisciplinary child protection plan.
3. LSCBs consist of service directors and senior managers who have a statutory duty to coordinate and ensure the effectiveness of what is done by each person or body represented on the LSCB for the purposes of safeguarding and promoting the welfare of children.

References

4Children (2011) *Suffering in Silence: 70,000 reasons Why Help with Postnatal Depression Has to Be Better* (London: 4Children).

AC682 (1971) 'Re W (An Infant)' (Lexis Library).

ACT for Youth (2004) *Adolescent Brain Development*. Available: http://www.act-foryouth.net (accessed 26 June 2011).

Action for Children (2009) *Child Neglect: Experiences from the Frontline*. Available: http://www.actionforchildren.org.uk (accessed 12 June 2010).

Action for Children (2010) *Seen and Now Heard: Taking Action on Child Neglect* (London: Action for Children).

Action for Children (2011) *Intensive Family Support: The Evidence* (London: Action for Children).

Advisory Council on the Misuse of Drugs (2003) *Hidden Harm: Responding to the Needs of Children of Problem Drug Users* (London: Home Office).

Akister, J. (2009) 'Protecting Children through Supporting Parents', *Journal of Public Mental Health*, 8(4): 11–17.

Alcohol Concern and The Princess Royal Trust for Carers (2008) *Keeping It in the Family: Growing up with Parents Who Misuse Alcohol* (London: Alcohol Concern).

Aldgate, J. and W. Rose (2008) *Assessing and Managing Risk in Getting It Right for Every Child* (Edinburgh: Scottish Government).

Aldgate, J., W. Rose and M. McIntosh (2008) *Changing Directions for Children with Challenging Behaviour and Their Families: Evaluation of Children 1st Directions Projects* (Edinburgh: Children 1st). Available: http://www.children1st.org.uk/shop/files/SPR-PUB-007.pdf (accessed 3 August 2012.)

Allen, G. (2011) *Early Intervention: The Next Steps* (London: HM Government).

Allen, R. (2006) *From Punishment to Problem Solving: A New Approach to Children in Trouble* (London: Centre for Crime and Justice Studies).

Antle, B. F., A. P. Barbee, D. Sullivan *et al.* (2007) 'The Relationship Between Domestic Violence and Child Neglect', *Brief Treatment and Crisis Intervention*, 7(4): 364–82.

Asawa, L., D. Hansen and M. F. Flood (2008) 'Early Childhood Prevention Programs: Opportunites and Challenges for Preventing Child Maltreatment', *Education and Treatment of Children* 31(1): 73–110.

Aubrey, C. and S. Dahl (2006) 'Children's Voices: The Views of Vulnerable Children on Their Service Providers and the Relevance of Services They Receive', *British Journal of Social Work*, 36(1): 21–39.

Australian Institute of Health and Welfare (2011) *Child Protection Australia 2009–10* (Canberra: Australian Institute of Health and Welfare).

Backhouse, J. and A. Graham (2012) 'Grandparents Raising Grandchildren: Negotiating the Complexities of Role-Identity Conflict', *Child and Family Social Work*, 17(3): 306–15.

Baker-Henningham, H., S. Scott, K. Jones *et al.* (2012) 'Reducing Child Conduct Problems and Promoting Social Skills in a Middle-income Country: Cluster Randomised Controlled Trial', *The British Journal of Psychiatry*, 201(2): 101–8.

Banwell, C., B. Denton and G. Bammer (2002) 'Programmes for the Children of Illicit Drug-using Parents: Issues and Dilemmas', *Drug and Alcohol Review*, 21(4): 381–6.

Barber, J. G. and P. H. Delfabbro (2009) 'The Profile and Progress of Neglected and Abused Children in Long-term Foster Care', *Child Abuse and Neglect*, 33(7): 421–8.

Barlow, J. (2006) 'Home Visiting for Parents of Pre-school Children in the UK', in C. McAuley, P. J. Pecora and W. Rose (eds), *Enhancing the Well-being of Children and Families through Effective Interventions: International Evidence for Practice* (London: Jessica Kingsley Publishers).

Barlow, J. and R. Calam (2011) 'A Public Health Approach to Safeguarding in the 21st Century', *Child Abuse Review*, 20: 238–55.

Barlow, J. and A. Schrader McMillan (2010) *Safeguarding Children from Emotional Maltreatment: What Works* (London: Jessica Kingsley Publishers).

Barlow, J. and J. Scott (2010) *Safeguarding in the 21st Century: Where to Now?* (Dartington: Research in Practice).

Barlow, J., J. D. Fisher and D. Jones (2012) *Systematic Review of Models of Analysing Significant Harm*, DFE-RR 199 (London: Department for Education).

Barlow, J., D. Simkiss and S. Stewart-Brown (2006) 'Interventions to Prevent or Ameliorate Child Physical Abuse and Neglect: Findings from a Systematic Review of Reviews', *Journal of Children's Services*, 1(3): 6–28.

Barlow, K. M., S. Milne, K. Aitken *et al.* (1998) 'A Retrospective Epidemiological Analysis of Non-accidental Head Injury in Children in Scotland over the Last 15 Years', *Scottish Medical Journal*, 43: 112–14.

Barn, R., C. Ladino and B Rogers (2006) *Parenting in Multi-Racial Britain* (London: National Children's Bureau and Joseph Rowntree Foundation).

Barnard M. (2007) *Drug Addiction and Families* (London: Jessica Kingsley Publishers).

Barnardo's (2009) *Below the Breadline: A Year in the Life of Families in Poverty* (London: Barnardo's).

Barnardo's (2012) *Cutting Them Free. How Is the UK Progressing in Protecting Its Children from Sexual Exploitation?* (London: Barnardo's).

Barnes, J., M. Ball, P. Meadows *et al.* (2009) *Nurse-Family Partnership Programme: Second Year Pilot Sites Implementation in England: The Infancy Period*, DCSF-RR166 (London: Department for Children, Schools and Families).

Barnes, J., M. Ball, P. Meadows *et al.* (2011) *The Family-Nurse Partnership Programme in England: Wave 1 Implementation in Toddlerhood & a Comparison between Waves 1 and 2a of Implementation in Preganancy and Infancy* (London: Department of Health).

Barth, R. (2009) 'Preventing Child Abuse and Neglect with Parent Training: Evidence and Opportunities', *The Future of Children*, 19(2): 95–118.

Batchelor, J. A. (1999) *Failure to Thrive in Young Children. Research and Practice Evaluated* (London: The Children's Society).

Batchelor, J. (2008) '"Failure to Thrive" Revisited', *Child Abuse Review*, 17: 147–59.

Batmanghelidjh, C. (2006) *Shattered Lives: Children Who Live with Courage and Dignity* (London: Jessica Kingsley Publishers).

Baxter, E. and B. Print (1999) 'Groupwork Processes and the Impact on Working Together in Core Groups', in M. C. Calder and J. Horwath, *Working for Children on the Child Protection Register: An Inter-agency Practice Guide* (Aldershot: Ashgate), pp. 135–58.

Belgrave, M. M. Jakob-Hoff, S. Milne, L. Asiasiger, P. Mataira et al. (2002) *Social Workers in Schools, Expansion Evaluation, Final Report*. Wellington, New Zealand: Ministry of Social Development.

Bell, M. (1996) 'Why Some Conferences Are Difficult: A Study of the Professionals' Experience of Some Initial Child Protection Conferences', *Children & Society*, 10(1): 51–63.

Bell, M. (2007a) 'Safeguarding Children and Case Conferences', in K. Wilson and A. James, *The Child Protection Handbook*, 3rd edition (London: Baillière Tindall).

Bell, M. (2007b) 'Community-based Parenting Programmes: An Exploration of the Interplay between Environmental and Organizational Factors in a Webster Stratton Project', *British Journal of Social Work*, 37(1): 55–72.

Belsky, J. and T. Melhuish (2008) *National Evaluation: The Impact of Sure Start Local Programmes on Three Year Olds and Their families* (London: Department for Children, Schools and Families).

Bender, K. (2010) 'Why Do Some Maltreated Youth Become Juvenile Offenders? A Call for Further Investigation and Adaptation of Youth Services', *Children and Youth Services Review*, 32: 466–73.

Ben-Galim, D. (2011) *Parents at the Centre* (London: Institute for Public Policy Research).

Ben-Galim, T., P. T. Louis and A. P. Giardino (2010) 'Neglect and Failure to Thrive', in A. P. Giardino et al., *A Practical Guide to the Evaluation of Child Physical Abuse and Neglect*, 2nd edition (New York: Springer), pp. 261–90.

Bennett, D. S., M. Sullivan, S. M. Thompson et al. (2010) 'Early Child Neglect: Obesity or Underweight in Later Childhood?' *Child Maltreatment*, 15(3): 250–4.

Bentovim, A. (2010) 'Safeguarding and Promoting the Welfare of Children Who Have Been Sexually Abused: The Assessment Challenges', in J. Horwath (ed.), *The Child's World: The Comprehensive Guide to Assessing Children in Need* (London: Jessica Kingsley Publishers), pp. 260–81.

Bentovim, A., A. Cox, L. Bingley Miller et al. (2009) *Safeguarding Children Living with Trauma and Family Violence: Evidence-based Assessment, Analysis and Planning Interventions* (London: Jessica Kingsley Publishers), pp. 228–9.

Biehal, N., J. Dixon, E. Parry et al. (2010) *The Care Placements Evaluation (CaPE): Evaluation of Multidimensional Treatment Foster Care for Adolescents (MTFC-A)*, DFE-RR194 (London: Department for Education).

Biemiller, A. (2003) 'Vocabulary Needed if More Children Are to Read Well', *Reading Psychology*, 24: 323–35.

Blakeslee, J. (2012) 'Expanding the Scope of Research with Transition-age Foster Youth: Applications of the Social Network Perspective', *Child and Family Social Work*, 17: 326–36.

Boffey, D. and D. Wilkes (2008) 'Madeleine: one year on, Portuguese police "should not be ashamed" they have not found her, says Attorney General'. Available: http://www.dailymail.co.uk (accessed 19 July 2012).

Boiling, K., C. Grant, B. Hamlyn *et al.* (2005) *Infant Feeding Survey* (London: Department of Health).

Booth, T. and W. Booth (1994) *Parenting Under Pressure: Mothers and Fathers with Learning Difficulties* (Buckingham: Open University).

Booth, T. and W. Booth (1997) *Exceptional Childhoods, Unexceptional Children: Growing Up with Parents Who Have Learning Difficulties* (London: Family Policy Studies Centre in association with Joseph Rowntree Foundation).

Booth, T., W. Booth and D. McConnell (2004) 'Parents with Learning Difficulties, Care Proceedings and the Family Courts: Threshold Decisions and the Moral Matrix', *Child and Family Law Quarterly*, 16(4): 409–21.

Booth, W. and T. Booth (2004) 'A Family at Risk: Multiple Perspectives on Parenting and Child Protection', *British Journal of Learning Disabilities*, 32(1): 9–15.

Boseley, S. (2012) 'Put your baby down and walk away: new drive to cut toll of shaken babies'. Available: http://www.guardian.co.uk (accessed 19 July 2012).

Bowlby, J. (1979) *The Making and Breaking of Affectional Bonds* (London: Tavistock).

Brandon, M., S. Bailey, P. Belderson *et al.* (2009) *Understanding Serious Case Reviews and Their Impact.* (London: Department for Children, Schools and Families).

Brandon, M., S. Bailey and P. Belderson (2010) *Building on the Learning from Serious Case Reviews: A Two-Year Analysis of Child Protection Database Notifications 2007–2009* (London: Department of Health).

Brandon, M., P. Belderson, C. Warren *et al.* (2008) *Analysing Child Deaths and Serious Injury through Abuse and Neglect: What Can We Learn? A Biennial Analysis of Serious Case Reviews 2003–2005* (Nottingham: Department for Children, Schools and Families).

Brandon, M., P. Sidebotham, C. Ellis *et al.* (2011) *Child and Family Practitioners' Understanding of Child Development: Lessons Learnt from a Small Sample of Serious Case Reviews* (London: Department for Education).

Brayden, R., W. Atlemeier, D. Tucker *et al.* (1992) 'Antecedents of Child Neglect in the First Two Years of Life', *Journal of Pediatrics*, 120: 426–9.

Broadhurst, K., D. Wastell, S. White *et al.* (2009) 'Performing "Initial Assessments": Identifying the Latent Conditions for Error at the Front Door of Local Authority Children's Services', *British Journal of Social Work*, DOI: 10.1093/bjsw/ben162.

Bronfenbrenner, U. (1979) *The Ecology of Human Development* (Cambridge, MA: Harvard University Press).

Brophy, J. (2006) *Research Review: Child Care Proceedings under the Children Act 1989* (London: DCA Research Series).

Burgess, C. and B. Daniel (2010) *Neglecting the Issue: Impact, Causes and Responses to Child Neglect in the UK* (London: Action for Children).

Burgess, C., B. Daniel, J. Scott *et al.* (2012) *Child Neglect in 2011. An Annual Review by Action for Children in Partnership with the University of Stirling* (Watford: Action for Children).

Butchart, A., V. Poznyak and M. Bellis (2006) *Child Maltreatment and Alcohol* (Geneva: World Health Organization and John Moores University).

Butler-Sloss, E. (1988) *Report of the Inquiry into Child Abuse in Cleveland 1987* (London: HMSO).

Butt, J. and L. Box (1998) *Family Centres: A Study of the Use of Family Centres by Black Families* (London: Race Equality Unit).

C4EO (2010a) *Grasping the Nettle: Early Intervention for Children, Families and Communities* (London: C4EO).

C4EO (2010b) 'Stop That Shake – Babies Break! Staffordshire'. Available: http://www.c4eo.org.uk/themes/safeguarding/vlpdetails.aspx?lpeid=270 (accessed 9 January 2012).

Cafcass (2012) *Three Weeks in November... Three Years On... Cafcass Care Application Study 2012* (London: Cafcass).

Calam, R., M. R. Sanders, C. Miller *et al.* (2008) 'Can Technology and the Media Help Reduce Dysfunctional Parenting and Increase Engagement with Preventative Parenting Interventions?' *Child Maltreatment*, 13(4): 347–61.

Calder, M. C. and J. Horwath (eds) (1999) *Working for Children on the Child Protection Register: An Inter-agency Guide* (Aldershot: Arena).

Carter, B. (2012) 'Developing and Implementing an Appreciative "Quality of Care" Approach to Child Neglect Practice', *Child Abuse Review*, 21(2): 81–98.

Cash, S. J. and D. J. Wilke (2003) 'An Ecological Model of Maternal Substance Abuse and Child Neglect: Issues, Analyses, and Recommendations', *American Journal of Orthopsychiatry* 73(4): 392–404.

Catts, H., M. Fey, J. B. Tomblin *et al.* (2002) 'A Longitudinal Investigation of Reading Outcomes in Children with Language Impairments', *Journal of Speech and Hearing Research*, 32: 32–50.

CEOP (2011) *Out of Mind, Out of Sight* (London: CEOP).

Chambers, R. M. and C. C. Potter (2009) 'Family Needs in Child Neglect Cases: A Cluster Analysis', *Families in Society*, 90(1): 18–27.

Chand, A. and J. Thoburn (2005) 'Child and Family Support Services with Minority Ethnic Families: What Can We Learn from Research?' *Child and Family Social Work*, 10(2): 169–78.

Chapple, C. L., K. Tyler and B. E. Bersani (2005) 'Child Neglect and Adolescent Violence: Examining the Effects of Self Control and Peer Rejection', *Violence and Victims*, 20(1): 39–53.

Child Welfare Information Gateway (2009) 'Child Witnesses to Domestic Violence: Summary of State Laws'. Available: http://www.childwelfare.gov/systemwide/laws_policies/statutes/witnessdv.cfm (accessed 31 August 2012).

Children in Wales (2008) *All Wales Child Protection Procedures* (Cardiff: Local Safeguarding Children Boards in Wales).

The Children's Society (2011) *4 in Every 10: Disabled Children Living in Poverty* (London: The Children's Society).

Cleaver, H. (2000) *Fostering Family Contact: Studies in Evaluating the Children Act 1989* (London: Department of Health).

Cleaver, H. and D. Nicholson (2007) *Parental Learning Disability and Children's Needs* (London: Jessica Kingsley Publishers).

Cleaver, H., D. Nicholson, S. Tarr *et al.* (2007) *Child Protection, Domestic Violence and Parental Substance Misuse* (London: Jessica Kingsley Publishers).

Cleaver, H., I. Unell and J. Aldgate (2011) *Children's Needs – Parenting Capacity. Child Abuse: Parental Mental Illness, Learning Disability, Substance Misuse, and Domestic Violence* (London: The Stationery Office).

Cleaver, H., S. Walker with P. Meadows (2004) *Assessing Children's Needs and Circumstances* (London: Jessica Kingsley Publishers).

Cm 5730 (2003) *The Victoria Climbié Inquiry: Report of an Inquiry by Lord Laming* (London: The Stationery Office).

Coe, C., A. Gibson and N. Spencer (2008) 'Sure Start: Voices of the "Hard to Reach" ', *Child, Care, Health and Development*, 34(4): 447–53.

Condon, L. and J. Ingram (2011) 'Increasing Support for Breastfeeding: What Can Children's Centres Do?' *Health and Social Care*, 19(6): 617–25.

Connell-Carrick, K. (2003) 'A Critical Review of the Empirical Literature: Identifying Correlates of Child Neglect', *Child and Adolescent Social Work Journal*, 20(5): 389–425.

Coohey, C. (1995) 'Neglectful Mothers, Their Mothers, and Partners: The Significance of Mutual Aid', *Child Abuse and Neglect*, 19(8): 885–95.

Coohey, C. (1998) 'Home Alone and Other Inadequately Supervised Children', *Child Welfare*, LXXVII(3): 291–310.

Coohey, C. (2003) 'Making Judgements about Risk in Substantiated Cases of Supervisory Neglect', *Child Abuse and Neglect*, 27: 821–40.

Corby, B., M. Millar and L. Young (1996) 'Parental Participation in Child Protection Work: Rethinking the Rhetoric', *British Journal of Social Work*, 26(4): 475–92.

Cossar, J., M. Brandon and P. Jordan (2011) *'Don't Make Assumptions': Children and Young People's Views of the Child Protection System and Messages for Change* (London: Office of the Children's Commissioner).

Cox, A. and A. Bentovim (2000) *Framework for the Assessment of Children in Need and Their Families. The Family Pack of Questionnaires and Scales* (London: The Stationery Office).

Crittenden, P. (1996) 'Research on Maltreating Families: Implications for Intervention', in J. Briere, L. Berliner and J. Bulkley (eds), *The APSAC Handbook on Child Maltreatment* (Thousand Oaks, CA: Sage), pp. 158–74.

Crittenden, P. M. (1999) 'Child Neglect: Causes and Contributors', in H. Dubowitz (ed.), *Neglected Children: Research, Practice and Policy* (Thousand Oaks, CA: Sage), pp. 47–68.

Crittenden, P. M. and M. D. S. Ainsworth (1987) 'Child Maltreatment and Attachment Theory', in D. Cicchetta and V. Carton (eds), *Child Maltreatment: Theory and Research* (Cambridge: Cambridge University Press), pp. 432–62.

Cross, W. F. and J. C. West (2011) 'Examining Implementer Fidelity: Conceptualising and Measuring Adherence and Competence', *Journal of Children's Services* 6(1): 18–31.

Currie, J. and C. S. Widom (2010) 'Long-term Consequences of Child Abuse and Neglect on Adult Economic Well-being', *Child Maltreatment*, 15(2): 111–20.

Dahl, R. D. (2004) 'Adolescent Brain Development: A Period of Vulnerabilities and Opportunities', *Annals of the New York Academy of Sciences*, 1021: 1–22.

Dale, P., M. Davies and T. Morrison (1986) *Dangerous Families: Assessment and Treatment of Child Abuse* (London: Routledge).

Daly, M. (ed.) (2007) *Parenting in Contemporary Europe: A Positive Approach* (Strasbourg: Council for Europe).

Damashek, A., D. Doughty, L. Ware *et al.* (2011) 'Predictors of Client Engagement and Attrition in Home-based Child Maltreatment Prevention Services', *Child Maltreatment*, 16(1): 9–20.

Daniel, B. M. and N. Baldwin (2002) 'Assessment Practice in Cases of Child Neglect: A Developmental Project', *Practice* 13(4): 21–38.

Daniel, B. and J. Taylor (2001) *Engaging with Fathers. Practice Issues for Health and Social Care* (London: Jessica Kingsley Publishers).

Daniel, B., J. Taylor and J. Scott (2010) 'Recognition of Neglect and Early Response: Overview of a Systematic Review of the Literature', *Child & Family Social Work*, 15(2): 248–57.

Daniel, B., J. Taylor, J. Scott *et al.* (2011) *Recognizing and Helping the Neglected Child. Evidence-based Practice for Assessment and Intervention* (London: Jessica Kingsley Publishers).

Daniel, B., S. Wassell and R. Gilligan (1999) *Child Development for Child Care and Protection Workers* (London: Jessica Kingsley Publishers).

Daniel, B., S. Wassell and R. Gilligan (2010) *Child Development for Child Care and Protection Workers*, 2nd edition (London: Jessica Kingsley Publishers), p. 14.

Darlington, Y., J. A. Feeney and K. Rixon (2005) 'Interagency Collaboration between Child Protection and Mental Health Services: Practices, Attitudes and Barriers', *Child Abuse & Neglect*, 28(10): 1085–98.

Darlington, Y., K. Healy, J. Yellowlees *et al.* (2012) 'Parents' Perceptions of Their Participation in Mandated Family Group Meetings', *Children and Youth Services Review*, 34(2): 331–7.

Davidson-Arad, B. (2005). 'Fifteen-month Follow-up of Children at Risk: Comparison of the Quality of Life of Children Removed from Home and Children Remaining at Home', *Children and Youth Services Review*, 27: 1–20. DOI: 10.1016/j.childyouth.2004.07.002.

Davidson-Arad, B., R. Benishty, W. Chen *et al.* (2010) 'Distinguishing Neglect from Abuse and Accident: Analysis of the Case Files of a Hospital Child Protection Team in Israel', *Health and Social Care*, 18(6): 614–23.

Davidson, D., J. Devaney and T. Spratt (2010) 'The Impact of Adversity in Childhood on Outcomes in Adulthood', *Journal of Social Work*, 10(4): 369–90.

Davies, C. and H. Ward (2012) *Safeguarding Children across Services: Messages from Research on Identifying and Responding to Maltreatment* (London: Jessica Kingsley Publishers).

Davis, H. and C. Day (2007) *Current Family Partnership Model* (London: South London and Maudsley NHS Foundation Trust).

De Bellis, M. D. (2005) 'The Psychobiology of Neglect', *Child Maltreatment*, 10(2): 150–72.

DePanfilis, D. (2006a) *Child Neglect: A Guide for Prevention, Assessment, and Intervention* (Washington, DC: US Department of Health and Human Services).

DePanfilis, D. (2006b) 'Therapeutic Interventions with Children Who Have Experienced Neglect and Their Families in the US', in C. McCauley, P. J. Pecora and W. Rose (eds), *Enhancing the Well-being of Children and Families: International Evidence for Practice* (London: Jessica Kingsley Publishers).

DePanfilis, D., H. Dubowitz and J. Kunz (2008) 'Assessing the Cost-effectiveness of Family Connections', *Child Abuse & Neglect*, 32(3): 335–51.

DePaul, J. and M. Guibert (2008) 'Empathy and Child Neglect: A Theoretical Model', *Child Abuse and Neglect*, 32(11): 1063–71.

Devaney, J. (2009) 'Chronic Child Abuse: The Characteristics and Careers of Children Caught in the Child Protection System', *British Journal of Social Work*, 39(1): 24–45.

DfE (Department for Education) (2011) *Identifying Families with Multiple Problems and Management: Information Paper* (London: Department for Education).

DfE (Department for Education) (2012) *Working Together to Safeguard Children: Consultation* (London: Department for Education).

DH (Department of Health) (2000) *Assessing Children in Need and Their Families: Practice Guidance* (London: The Stationery Office).

DH (Department of Health) and DfES (Department for Education and Skills) (2007) *Good Practice Guidance with Parents with a Learning Disability* (London: DH and DfES).

DH (Department of Health), Department for Education and Employment and Home Office (2000) *Framework for the Assessment of Children in Need and Their Families* (London: The Stationery Office).

DHSSPS (Department of Health, Social Services and Public Safety) (2003) *Co-operating to Safeguard Children* (Belfast: DHSSPS).

DHSSPS (Department of Health, Social Services and Public Safety) (2004) *Equality and Inequalities in Health and Social Wellbeing: Young Mothers and Breastfeeding Rates* (Belfast: DHSSPS). Available: http://www.dhsspsni.gov.uk/breasfeedingratesyoungmothers.pdf (accessed 23 August 2012).

DHSSPS (Department of Health, Social Services and Public Safety) (2005) *Regional Safeguarding Policy and Procedures in Northern Ireland* (Belfast: DHSSPS).

Dias, M. S., K. Smith, K. DeGuehery et al. (2005) 'Preventing Abusive Head Trauma among Infants and Young Children: A Hospital Based Parent Education Programme', *Pediatrics*, 115(4): 470–7.

Dickens, J. (2007) 'Child Neglect and the Law: Catapults, Thresholds and Delay', *Child Abuse Review*, 16: 77–92.

Dillane, J., M. Hill, J. Bannister et al. (2001) *An Evaluation of the Dundee Families Project*, Development Department Research Programme Research Findings No. 121 (Edinburgh: Scottish Executive Central Research Unit).

Donohue, B. (2004) 'Coexisting Child Neglect and Drug Abuse in Young Mothers: Specific Recommendations for Treatment Based on a Review of the Outcome Literature', *Behavior Modification*, 28(2): 206–33.

Doolan, M. (2006) 'Statutory Social Work and Family Group Conferences: Exploring the Connections', *Protecting Children*, 21(1): 5–18.

Dorsey, S., S. A. Mustillo, E. M. Farmer *et al.* (2008) 'Caseworker Assessments of Risk for Recurrent Maltreatment: Association with Case-specific Risk Factors and Re-reports', *Child Abuse & Neglect*, 32(3): 377–91.

Dubowitz, H. (1999a) 'Neglect of Children's Health Care', in H. Dubowitz (ed.), *Neglected Children: Research, Practice and Policy* (Thousand Oaks, CA: Sage), pp. 109–31.

Dubowitz, H. (ed.) (1999b) *Neglected Children. Research, Practice and Policy* (London: Sage).

Dubowitz, H. (2007) 'Understanding and Addressing the "Neglect of Neglect": Digging in the Molehill', *Child Abuse & Neglect*, 31: 603–6.

Dubowitz, H., M. Black, M. Kerr *et al.* (2000) 'Fathers and Child Neglect', *Archives of Pediatric and Adolescent Medicine*, 154: 135–41.

Dubowitz, H., R. R. Newton, A. J. Litrownik *et al.* (2005) 'Examination of a Conceptual Model of Child Neglect', *Child Maltreatment*, 10(2): 173–89.

Dubowitz, H., S. C. Pitts and M. Black (2004) 'Measurement of Three Major Subtypes of Child Neglect', *Child Maltreatment*, 9(4): 344–56.

Dufour, S., C. Lavergne, M.-C. Larrivée *et al.* (2008) 'Who Are These Parents Involved in Child Neglect? A Differential Analysis by Parent Gender and Family Structure', *Children and Youth Services Review*, 30: 141–56.

Duke, N., S. Pettingell, B. McMorris *et al.* (2010) 'Adolescent Violence Perpetration: Associations with Multiple Types of Adverse Childhood Experiences', *Pediatrics*, 125(4): 778–86. DOI: 10.1542/peds.2009–0597.

Dumaret, A.-C., M. Constantin-Kuntz and M. Titran (2009) 'Early Intervention in Poor Families Confronted with Alcohol Abuse and Violence: Impact on Families' Social Integration and Parenting', *Families in Society: The Journal of Contemporary Social Services*, 90(1): 11–17.

Dunn, M. G., R. E. Tarter, A. C. Mezzich *et al.* (2002) 'Origins and Consequences of Child Neglect in Substance Abuse Families', *Clinical Psychology Review*, 22: 1063–90.

Durlak, J. A., R. P. Weissberg, A. B. Dymnicki *et al.* (2011) 'The Impact of Enhancing Students' Social and Emotional Learning: A Meta-analysis of School-based Universal Interventions', *Child Development*, 82(1): 405–32.

Dyson, A., F. Gallannaugh, N. Humphrey *et al.* (2010) *Narrowing the Gap in Educational Achievement and Improving Emotional Resilience for Children and Young People with Additional Needs* (London: Centre for Excellence and Outcomes in Children and Young People's Services). Available: http://www.c4eo.org.uk/themes/schools/educationalachievement/files/educational_achievement_research_review.pdf (accessed 20 August 2010).

Easton, C. and G. Gee (2012) *Early Intervention: Informing Local Practice*, Local Government Education and Children's Services Research Programme (London: NFER and LGA).

Eckenrode, J., B. Ganzel, D. Olds *et al.* (2000) 'Preventing Child Abuse and Neglect with a Program of Nurse Home Visitation: The Limiting Effects of Domestic Violence', *The Journal of the American Medical Association*, 284(11): 1385–91.

Edge, D. (2011) *Perinatal Mental Health of Black and Minority Ethnic Women: A Review of Current Provision in England, Scotland and Wales* (London: National Mental Health Development Unit, Department of Health).

Edwards, Y. (2011) *A Cupboard Full of Coats* (Oxford: Oneworld).

Egeland, B. and M. Bosquet (2002) 'Emotion Regulation in Early Childhood: The Role of Attachment-oriented Interventions', in E. Zuckerman, A. Lieberman and N. Fox (eds), *Socioemotional Regulations: Dimensions, Developmental Trends and Influences* (New Jersey: Johnson & Johnson Pediatric Institute), pp. 101–24.

Egeland, B., A. Sroufe and M. Erickson (1983) 'The Developmental Consequences of Different Patterns of Maltreatment', *Child Abuse and Neglect*, 7: 459–69.

Elkan, R., D. Kendrick, M. Hewitt *et al.* (2000) 'The Effectiveness of Domicillary Health Visiting: A Systematic Review of International Studies and a Selective Review of the British Literature', *Health Technology Assessment 2000*, 4(13).

English, D. J. (1999) 'Evaluation and Risk Assessment of Child Neglect in Public Child Protection Services', in H. Dubowitz (ed.), *Neglected Children: Research, Practice and Policy* (Thousand Oaks, CA: Sage), pp. 191–210.

English, D. J., D. Marshall and A. Stewart (2003) 'Effects of Family Violence on Child Behavior and Health during Early Childhood', *Journal of Violence*, 18: 43–57.

Epstein, J. and C. Jolly (2008) 'Credibility Gap? Parents' Beliefs about Reducing the Risk of Cot Death', *Community Practitioner*, 82(11): 21–4.

Erickson, M. F. and B. Egeland (2002) 'Child Neglect', in J. E. B. Myers, L. Berliner, J. Briere *et al.* (eds), *The APSAC Handbook on Child Maltreatment* (Thousand Oaks, CA: Sage), pp. 3–20.

Ernst, J., M. Meyer and D. DePanfilis (2004) 'Housing Characteristics and Adequacy of the Physical Care of Children: An Exploratory Analysis', *Child Welfare*, 83(5): 437–52.

Evans (2011) *Tough Love, Not Get Tough: Responsive Approaches to Improving Behaviour in Schools* (London: Barnardo's).

Farmer, E. and E. Lutman (2010) *Case Management and Outcomes for Neglected Children Returned to Their Parents: A Five Year Follow-up Study*, DCSF-RB214 (London: Department for Children, Schools and Families).

Farmer, E. and M. Owen (1995) *Child Protection Practice: Private Risks and Public Remedies* (London: HMSO).

Fatherhood Institute (2009) *Commissioning Father-Inclusive Parenting Programmes: A Guide* (London: The Fatherhood Institute).

Fauth, R., H. Jelicic, D. Hart *et al.* (2010). *Effective Practice to Protect Children Living in 'Highly Resistant' Families* (London: C4EO).

Feig, D. S. and V. A. Palda (2002) 'Type 2 Diabetes in Pregnancy: A Growing Concern', *The Lancet*, 359(9318): 1690–2.

Ferguson, H. (2011) *Child Protection Practice* (Basingstoke: Palgrave MacMillan).

Fergusson, D., J. Horwood, E. Ridder *et al.* (2005) *Early Start Evaluation Report* (Christchurch, NZ: University of Christchurch).

Ferrari, A. M. (2002) 'The Impact of Culture upon Child Rearing Practices and Definitions of Maltreatment', *Child Abuse and Neglect*, 26: 793–813.

Field, F. (2010) *The Foundation Years: Preventing Poor Children Becoming Poor Adults* (London: HM Government).

Firth, B. (1999) 'The Role of the Keyworker', in M. C. Calder and J. Horwath (eds), *Working for Children on the Child Protection Register* (Aldershot: Ashgate), pp. 119–34.

Fisher, D. and S. Gruescu (2011) *Children and the Big Society* (London: Action for Children).

Fletcher, R., G. Vimpani, G. Russell *et al.* (2008) 'The Evaluation of Tailored and Web-based Information for New Fathers', *Child: Care, Health and Development*, 34(4): 439–46.

Flouri, E., J. Hickey, S. Mavoreli *et al.* (2011) 'Adversity, Emotional Arousal, and Problem Behaviour in Adolescence: The Role of Non-verbal Cognitive Ability as a Resilience Promoting Factor', *Child and Adolescent Mental Health*, 16(1): 22–9.

Forrester, D. (2000) 'Parental Substance Misuse and Child Protection in a British Sample. A Survey of Children on the Child Protection Register in an Inner London District Office', *Child Abuse Review*, 9(4): 235–46.

Forrester, D. and J. Harwin (2011) *Parents Who Misuse Drugs and Alcohol* (Chichester: Wiley-Blackwell).

Forrester, D., S. Kershaw, H. Moss *et al.* (2008) 'Communication Skills in Child Protection: How Do Social Workers Talk to Parents?' *Child and Family Social Work*, 13(1): 41–51.

Forrester, D., S. Pokhrel, L. McDonald *et al.* (2008) 'How to Help Parents Who Misuse Drugs or Alcohol: Findings from the Evaluation of an Intensive Family Preservation Service', *Child Abuse Review*, 17(6): 410–26.

Forrester, D., D. Westlake and G. Glynn (2012) 'Parental Resistance and Social Worker Skills: Towards a Theory of Motivational Social Work', *Child & Family Social Work*, 17: 118–29.

Foundation for the Study of Infant Deaths (2007) *Factfile 2. Research Background to Reduce the Risk of Cot Death: Advice by the Foundation for the Study of Infant Deaths* (London: Foundation for the Study of Infant Deaths).

Fox-Harding, L. (1997) *Perspectives in Child Care Policy* (London: Longman).

Frederick, J. and C. Goddard (2010) '"School was just a nightmare": Childhood Abuse and Neglect and School Experiences', *Child and Family Social Work*, 15(1): 22–30.

Garbarino, J. and C. C. Collins (1999) 'Child Neglect: the Family with a Hole in the Middle', in H. Dubowitz (ed.), *Neglected Children: Research, Practice and Policy* (Thousand Oaks, CA: Sage), pp. 1–23.

Gardner, R. (2008) *Developing an Effective Response to Neglect and Emotional Harm to Children* (Norwich: University of East Anglia and NSPCC).

Gaudin, J. M. (1993) *Child Neglect: A Guide for Intervention* (Washington, DC: US Department of Health and Human Services Adminstration for Children and Families).

Gaudin, J. M. (1999) 'Child Neglect: Short-term and Long-term Outcomes', in H. Dubowitz (ed.), *Neglected Children: Research, Practice and Policy* (Thousand Oaks, CA: Sage), pp. 89–108.

Gaudin, J. M., N. A. Polansky, A. C. Kilpatrick *et al.* (1996) 'Family Functioning in Neglectful Families', *Child Abuse and Neglect*, 20(4): 363–77.

Ghate, D. and N. Hazel (2002) *Parenting in Poor Environments* (London: Jessica Kingsley Publishers).

Gilbert, N. (2012) 'A Comparative Study of Child Welfare Systems, Abstract Orientations and Concrete Results', *Children and Youth Services Review*, 34: 532–6.

Gilbert, N., N. Parton and M. Skivenes (eds) (2011) *Child Protection Systems: International Trends and Orientations* (Oxford: Oxford University Press).

Gilligan, R. (2010) 'Promoting Positive Outcomes for Children in Need – The Importance of Protective Capacity in the Child and Their Social Network', in J. Horwath (ed.), *The Child's World* (London: Jessica Kingsley Publishers), pp. 174–83.

Girvin, H. (2004) 'Beyond "Stages of Change": Using Readiness for Change and Caregiver-Reported Problems in Identifying Meaningful Subgroups in a Child Welfare Sample', *Children and Youth Services Review*, 26: 897–917.

Girvin, H., D. DePanfilis and C. Daining (2011) 'Predicting Program Completion among Families Enrolled in a Child Neglect Preventative Intervention', *Research on Social Work Practice*, 17(6): 674–85.

Gittens, D. (1998) *The Child in Question* (Basingstoke: Macmillan).

Glisson, C. and P. Green (2011) 'Organizational Climate, Services, and Outcomes in Child Welfare', *Child Abuse & Neglect*, 35: 582–91.

Glisson, C. and A. Hemmelgarten (1998) 'The Effects of Organizational Climate and Interorganizational Coordination on the Quality and Outcomes of Children's Service Systems', *Child Abuse and Neglect*, 22(5): 401–21.

Gorin, S. (2004) *Understanding What Children Say: Children's Experiences of Domestic Violence, Parental Substance Misuse and Parental Health Problems* (London: National Children's Bureau).

Govindshenoy, M. and N. Spencer (2006) 'Abuse of the Disabled Child: A Systematic Review of Population-based Studies', *Child: Care, Health and Development*, 33(5): 552–8.

Greenbaum, J., H. Dubowitz, J. Lutzker *et al.* (2008) *Practice Guidelines: Challenges in the Evaluation of Child Neglect* (Elmhurst, IL: Amercian Professional Society on the Abuse of Children).

Griffin, C., S. Guerin, J. Sharry *et al.* (2010) 'A Multicentre Controlled Study of an Early Intervention Programme for Young Children with Behavioural and Developmental Difficulties', *International Journal for Clinical and Health Psychology*, 10(2): 279–94.

Gudjonsson, G. H., J. F. Sigurdsson and H. B. Tryggvadóttir (2011) 'The Relationship of Compliance with a Background of Childhood Neglect and Physical and Sexual Abuse', *The Journal of Forensic Psychiatry and Psychology*, 22(1): 87–98.

Hamlyn, B., S. Brooker, K. Oleinikova *et al.* (2002) *Infant Feeding 2000: A Survey Conducted on Behalf of the Department of Health, the Scottish*

Executive, the National Assembly for Wales and the Department of Health, Social Services and Public Safety in Northern Ireland (London: Department of Health).

Hansen, D. J., G. M. Pallotta, A. C. Tishelman *et al.* (1989) 'Parental Problem-solving Skills and Child Behavior Problems: A Comparison of Physically Abusive, Neglectful, Clinic, and Community Families', *Journal of Family Violence*, 4(4): 353–68.

Hardiker, P., with B. Atkins, K. Exton, M. Perry and M. Pinnock (2002) 'A Framework for Conceptualising Need and Its Application to Planning and Providing Services', in H. Ward and W. Rose (eds), *Approaches to Needs Assessment in Children's Services* (London: Jessica Kingsley Publishers), pp. 49–70.

Hardiker, P., K. Exton and M. Barker (1996) 'The Prevention of Child Abuse: A Framework for Analysing Services', in National Commission of Inquiry into the Prevention of Child Abuse, *Childhood Matters: Report of the National Commission into the Prevention of Child Abuse*, Volume 2 (London: The Stationery Office).

Harlow, E. and S. Shardlow (2006) 'Safeguarding Children: Challenges to the Effective Operation of Core Groups', *Child and Family Social Work*, 11(1): 65–72.

Harnett, P. H. and S. Dawe (2008) 'Reducing Child Abuse Potential in Families Identified by Social Services: Implications for Assessment and Treatment', *Brief Treatment and Crisis Intervention*, 8(3): 226–35.

Harnett, P. and C. Day (2008) 'Developing Pathways to Assist Parents to Exit the Child Protection System in Australia', *Clinical Psychologist*, 12(2): 79–85.

Harris, N. (2012) 'Assessment: When Does It Help and When Does It Hinder? Parents' Experiences of the Assessment Process', *Child & Family Social Work*, 17: 180–91.

Harwin, J., M. Ryan, J. Tunnard *et al.* (2011) *The Family Drug and Alcohol Court (FDAC) Evaluation Project: Final report* (Uxbridge: Brunel University).

Hawkins, P. and R. Shohet (2000) *Supervision in the Helping Professions* (Buckingham: Open University).

HealthyStart (2009) 'Practice Point: Parent Education'. Available: http://www.healthystart.net.au/resources/practice-points (accessed 21 November 2011).

Healy, K., Y. Darlington and J. Yellowlees (2012) 'Family Participation in Child Protection Practice: An Observational Study of Family Group Meetings', *Child & Family Social Work*, 17(1): 1–12.

Hecht, D. B., J. F. Silovsky, M. Chaffin *et al.* (2008) 'Project SafeCare®: An Evidence-based Approach to Prevent Child Neglect', *APSAC Advisor*, 20(1): 14–17.

Heikkilä, K., A. Sacker, Y. Kelly *et al.* (2011) 'Breast Feeding and Child Behaviour in the Millennium Cohort Study', *Archives of Disease in Childhood*, 96(7): 635–42.

Heim, C., M. Shugart, W. E. Craighead *et al.* (2010) 'Neurobiological and Psychiatric Consequences of Child Abuse and Neglect', *Developmental Psychobiology*, 52(7): 671–90.

Helm, D. (2011) 'Judgements or Assumptions? The Role of Analysis in Assessing Children and Young People's Needs', *British Journal of Social Work*, 41: 894–911.

Hemmelgarn, A. L., C. Glisson and L. R. James (2006) 'Organizational Culture and Climate: Implications for Services and Interventions Research', *Clinical Psychology, Science and Practice*, 13(1): 73–89.

Hernández-Martinez, C., J. Canals Sans and J. Fernández-Ballart (2011) 'Parents' Perceptions of Their Neonates and Their Relation to Infant Development', *Child: Care, Health and Development*, 37(4): 484–92.

Hester, M. (2011) 'The Three Planet Model: Towards an Understanding of Contradictions in Approaches to Women and Children's Safety in Contexts of Domestic Violence', *British Journal of Social Work*, 41: 837–53.

Hester, M., C. Pearson and N. Harwin (2007) *Making an Impact: Children and Domestic Violence. A Reader* (London: Jessica Kingsley Publishers).

Higgins, S., D. Kokotsaki and R. Coe (2011) *Pupil Premium Toolkit: Summary for Schools. Spending the Pupil Premium* (London Education Endowment Foundation and the Sutton Trust).

Higgs, L. (2011) 'New Government Unit to Co-ordinate Help for Troubled Families'. Available: http://www.cypnow.co.uk (accessed 20 July 2012).

Hildyard, K. and D. Wolfe (2002) 'Child Neglect: Developmental Issues and Outcomes', *Child Abuse and Neglect*, 26: 679–95.

Hildyard, K. and D. Wolfe (2007) 'Cognitive Processes Associated with Child Neglect', *Child Abuse & Neglect*, 31(8): 895–907.

HM Government (2010) *Working Together to Safeguard Children: A Guide to Inter-agency Working to Safeguard and Promote the Welfare of Children* (London: The Stationery Office).

HM Government (2011) *Ending Gang and Youth Violence* (London: Home Office).

HM Inspectorate of Prisons (2011) *The Care of Looked After Children in Custody: A Short Thematic Review* (London: HM Inspectorate of Prisons). Available: http://www.justice.gov.uk/downloads/publications/inspectorate-reports/hmi-pris/thematic-reports-and-research-publications/looked-after-children-2011.pdf (accessed 12 September 2012).

Hoffman, K. T., R. S. Marvin, G. Cooper *et al.* (2006) 'Changing Toddlers' and Preschoolers' Attachment Classifications: the Circle of Security Intervention', *Journal of Consulting and Clinical Psychology*, 74(6): 1017–26.

Holland, S. (2011) *Child and Family Assessment in Social Work Practice* (London: Sage).

Holland, S. and S. O'Neill (2006) '"We had to be there to make sure it was what we wanted": Enabling Children's Participation in Family Decision-making through the Family Group Conference', *Childhood*, 13: 91–111.

Home Office, Department of Health, Department of Education and Science *et al.* (1991) *Working Together under the Children Act 1989: A Guide to Arrangements for Inter-agency Cooperation for the Protection of Children from Abuse* (London: HMSO).

Horwath, J. (2005) 'Is This Child Neglect? The Influences of Differences in Perceptions of Child Neglect on Social Work Practice', in J. Taylor and B. Daniel (eds), *Child Neglect: Practice Issues for Health and Social Care* (London: Jessica Kingsley Publishers).

Horwath, J. (2007) *Child Neglect: Identification and Assessment* (London: Palgrave Macmillan).

Horwath, J. and M. C. Calder (1998) 'Working Together to Protect Children on the Child Protection Register: Myth or Reality', *British Journal of Social Work*, 28(6): 879–95.

Horwath, J. and T. Morrison (2000) 'Identifying and Implementing Pathways for Organizational Change: Using the Framework for the Assessment of Children in Need and Their Families as a Case Example', *Child and Family Social Work*, 5(3): 245–54.

Horwath, J. and T. Morrison (2001) 'Assessment of Parental Motivation to Change', in J. Horwath (ed.), *The Child's World. Assessing Children in Need* (London: Jessica Kingsley Publishers), pp. 98–113.

Horwath, J. and T. Morrison (2001) 'Transtheoretical Therapy: Towards a More Integrative Model of Change', *Psychotherapy: Theory, Research and Practice*, 19(3): 276–88.

Hosking, G. and I. Walsh (2010) *International Experience of Early Intervention for Children, Young People and Their Families 2010* (London: Wave Trust).

Hoskins, M. L. and J. White (2010) 'Processes of Discernment When Considering Issues of Neglect in Child Protection Practice', *Child Youth Care Forum*, 39: 27–45.

Howe, D. (2005) *Child Abuse and Neglect: Attachment, Development and Intervention* (Basingstoke: Palgrave Macmillan).

Howe, D., M. Brandon, D. Hinings *et al.* (1999) *Attachment Theory, Child Maltreatment and Family Support* (Basingstoke: Palgrave Macmillan).

Humphrey, N., A. Kalambouka, J. Bolton *et al.* (2008) *Primary Social and Emotional Aspects of Learning (SEAL): Evaluation of Small Group Work* (Nottingham: Department for Children, Schools and Families).

Humphreys, C. and N. Stanley (2006) *Domestic Violence and Child Protection* (London: Jessica Kingsley Publishers).

Hutchings, J., T. Bywater, D. Daley, F. Gardner, C. Whitaker, K. Jones, C. Eames, and R. T. Edwards (2007) 'Parenting Intervention in Sure Start Services for Children at Risk of Developing Conduct Disorder: Pragmatic Randomised Controlled Trial', *British Medical Journal*, 334: 678–85. DOI:10.1136/bmj.39126.620799.55.

Hutchings, J., T. Bywater, M. E. Williams *et al.* (2011) 'The Extended School Age Incredible Years Parent Programme', *Child and Adolescent Mental Health*, 16(3): 136–43.

Ipsos MORI, Social Research Institute (2011) *Evaluation of Flying Start: Findings from the Baseline Survey of Families – Mapping Needs and Measuring Early Influence among Families with Babies Aged Seven to 20 Months* (Cardiff: Welsh Government Social Research).

Iwaniec, D. (2006) *The Emotionally Abused and Neglected Child* (Chichester: Wiley).

Jago, S. with L. Arocha, I. Brodie *et al.* (2011) *What's Going On to Safeguard Children and Young People from Sexual Exploitation? How Local Partnerships Respond to Child Sexual Exploitation* (Bedford: University of Bedfordshire).

James, A. and A. L. James (2000) *Constructing Childhood. Theory, Policy and Social Practice* (Basingstoke: Palgrave Macmillan).

Jeffreys, H., N. Rogers and C. Hirte (2011) *Keeping the Child in Mind. Child Protection Practice and Parental Mental Health* (Adelaide: Government of South Wales, Department for Families and Communities).

Johnson, W. (2010) *What Are the Barriers for Minority Ethnic Families Using Children's Centres in South West Devon?* (Leeds: Children's Workforce Development Council).

Johnson, Z., B. Molloy, E. Scallan *et al.* (2000) 'Community Mothers Programme: Seven Year Follow-up of a Randomized Control Trial of Non-professional Intervention in Parenting', *Journal of Public Health*, 22(3): 337–42.

Jones, D. (2010) 'Assessment of Parenting', in J. Horwath (ed.), *The Child's World: The Comprehensive Guide to Assessing Children in Need* (London: Jessica Kingsley Publishers), pp. 282–304.

Jones, J. and M. McNeely (1980) 'Mothers Who Neglect and Those Who Do Not: A Comparative Study', *Journal of Contemporary Social Work*, 424–31.

Jonson-Reid, M., B. Drake and P. L. Kohl (2009) 'Is the Overrepresenation of the Poor in Child Welfare Caseloads Due to Bias or Need?' *Children and Youth Services Review*, 31(3): 422–7.

Jonson-Reid, M., C. R. Emery, B. Drake *et al.* (2010) 'Understanding Chronically Reported Families', *Child Maltreatment*, 15(4): 271–81.

Joseph Rowntree Foundation (2010a) 'Child Poverty in the UK'. Available: http://www.jrf.org.uk/work/workarea/child-poverty (accessed 22 May 2012).

Joseph Rowntree Foundation (2010b) *Monitoring Poverty and Social Exclusion 2010* (York: The Joseph Rowntree Foundation).

Kendall-Tackett, K. A. and J. Eckenrode (1996) 'The Effects of Neglect on Academic Achievement and Disciplinary Problems: A Developmental Perspective', *Child Abuse and Neglect*, 20(3): 161–9.

Kerr, M., M. Black and A. Krishnakumar (2000) 'Failure-to-thrive, Maltreatment and the Behavior and Development of 6-year-old Children from Low-income, Urban Families: a Cumulative Risk Model', *Child Abuse and Neglect*, 24(5): 587–98.

Kilroy, S., J. Sharry, C. Flood *et al.* (2010) 'Parental Training in the Community: Linking Process to Outcome', *Clinical Child Psychology and Psychiatry*, 16(3): 459–73.

Koenig, A. L., D. Cicchetti and F. A. Rogosch (2004) 'Moral Development: the Association between Maltreatment and Young Children's Prosocial Behaviour and Moral Transgressions', *Review of Social Development*, 13(1): 87–106.

Kojan, B. and B. Loanne (2012) 'A Comparison of Systems and Outcomes for Safeguarding Children in Norway and Australia', *Child and Family Social Work*, 17: 96–107.

Kolb, D. (1988) *Experience as the Source of Learning and Development* (London: Prentice-Hall).

Korbin, J. E. and J. C. Spilsbury (1999) 'Cultural Competence and Child Neglect', in H. Dubowitz (ed.). *Neglected Children: Research, Practice and Policy* (Thousand Oaks, CA: Sage), pp. 69–88.

Kotch, J. B., T. Lewis, J. M. Hussey *et al.* (2008) 'The Importance of Early Neglect for Childhood Aggression', *Pediatrics*, 121(4): 725–31.

Kumpfer, K. L., R. Alvarardo, P. Smith *et al.* (2002) 'Cultural Sensitivity and Adaptation in Family-based Prevention Interventions', *Prevention Science*, 3(3): 241–6.

Lacharité, C., L. Ethier and G. Couture (1996) 'The Influence of Partners on Parental Stress of Neglectful Mothers', *Child Abuse Review*, 5(1): 18–33.

Lambert, M. J. and D. E. Barley (2001) 'Research Summary on the Therapeutic Relationship and Psychotherapy Outcome', *Psychotherapy: Theory, Research, Practice, Training*, 38(4): 357–61.

Lamont, A. and L. Bromfield (2009) *Parental Intellectual Disability and Child Protection: Key Issues* (Canberra: National Child Protection Clearing House).

Law, J., Z. Garrett and C. Nye (2003) 'Speech and Language Therapy Interventions for Children with Primary Speech and Language Delay or Disorder', Review, 3CD4110, The Cochrane Collaboration.

Law, J., C. Plunkett, J. Taylor *et al.* (2009) 'Developing Policy in the Provision of Parenting Programmes: Integrating a Review of Reviews with the Perspectives of Both Parents and Professionals', *Child: Care, Health and Development*, 35(3): 302–12.

Lawrence, R. and P. Irvine (2004) 'Redefining Fatal Child Neglect', *Child Prevention Issues*, 21 (Spring).

Lazenbatt, A. (2010) *The Impact of Abuse and Neglect on the Health and Mental Health of Children and Young People* (London: NSPCC).

Lee, S. J., J. L. Bellamy and N. B. Guterman (2009) 'Fathers, Physical Child Abuse, and Neglect: Advancing the Knowledge Base', *Child Maltreatment*, 14(3): 227–31.

Lefever, J. B., K. S. Howard, R. Gaines Lanzi *et al.* (2008) 'Cell Phones and the Measurement of Child Neglect: the Validity of the Parent–Child Activities Interview', *Child Maltreatment*, 13: 320–33.

Levy, A. and C. Scott-Clark (2010) 'Death of a child: what does the death of three-year-old Tiffany Wright reveal about the growing problem of child neglect? Available: http://www.guardian.co.uk/society/2010/feb/06/child-neglect-adrian-levy-cathy-scott-clark (accessed 20 July 2012).

Lewis, C. and M. E. Lamb (2007) *Understanding Fatherhood: A Review of Recent Research* (York: Joseph Rowntree Foundation).

LGA, ADSS, Women's Aid *et al.* (2006) *Vision for Services for Children and Young People Affected by Domestic Violence* (London: LGA).

Lindsey, M. A., R. A. Hayward and D. DePanfilis (2010) 'Gender Differences in Behavioral Outcomes among Children at Risk of Neglect: Findings from a Family-focused Prevention Intervention', *Research on Social Work Practice*, 20(6): 572–81.

Littell, J. H. (2005) 'Lessons from a Systematic Review of Effects of Multisystematic Therapy', *Children and Youth Services Review*, 27: 445–63.

Littlechild, B. (2000) 'Children's Rights to Be Heard in Child Protection Processes: Laws, Policy and Practice in England and Wales', *Child Abuse Review*, 9: 403–15.

Lloyd, C., I. Wollny, C. White *et al.* (2011) *Monitoring and Evaluation of Family Intervention Services and Projects between February 2007 and March 2011* (London: Department for Education).

Long, T., M. Murphy, D. Fallon *et al.* (2010) *Evaluation of the Action for Children UK Neglect Project* (Salford: University of Salford).

The Lord Laming (2009) *The Protection of Children in England: A Progress Report* (Norwich: The Stationery Office).

Luther, S. S., N. E. Suchman and M. Altomare (2007) 'Relational Psychotherapy Mothers' Group: A Randomized Clinical Trial for Substance Abusing Mothers', *Development and Psychopathology*, 19(1): 243–61.

McConnell, D., R. Breitkreuz and A. Savage (2011a) 'Independent Evaulation of the Triple P Postive Parenting Program in Family Support Service Settings', *Child & Family Social Work*, 17(1): 43–54.

McConnell, D., M. Feldman, M. Aunos *et al.* (2011b) 'Child Maltreatment Investigations Involving Parents with Cognitive Impairment in Canada', *Child Maltreatment*, 16(1): 21–32.

McCurdy, K. and D. Daro (2001) 'Parent Involvement in Family Support Programs: An Integrated Theory', *Family Relations*, 50: 113–21.

Macdonald, G. (2005) 'Intervening with Neglect', in J. Taylor and B. Daniel (eds), *Child Neglect: Practice Issues for Health and Social Care* (London: Jessica Kingsley Publishers), pp. 279–90.

McGaw, S., K. Ball and A. Clark (2002) 'The Effect of Group Intervention on the Relationships of Parents with Intellectual Disabilities', *Journal of Applied Research in Intellectual Disabilities*, 15(4): 354–66.

McGee, C. (2000) *Childhood Experiences of Domestic Violence* (London: Jessica Kingsley Publishers).

MacMillan, H. L., N. Wathen, J. Barlow *et al.* (2009) 'Interventions to Prevent Child Maltreatment and Associated Impairment', *Lancet*, 373 (January): 250–66.

McSherry, D. (2007) 'Understanding and Addressing the "Neglect of Neglect": Why Are We Making a Mole-hill out of a Mountain?' *Child Abuse & Neglect*, 31: 607–14.

Mackner, L. and R. Starr (1997) 'The Cumulative Effect of Neglect and Failure to Thrive on Cognitive Functioning', *Child Abuse and Neglect*, 21(7): 691–700.

Maiter and Stalker (2011) 'South Asian Immigrants' Experience of Child Protection Services: Are We Recognizing Strengths and Resilience?' *Child and Family Social Work*, 16(2): 138–48.

Mardani, J. (2010) *Preventing Child Neglect in New Zealand: A Public Health Assessment of the Evidence, Current Approach, and Best Practice Guidance* (Wellington, New Zealand: Office of the Children's Commissioner).

Marquis, R. A., A. W. Leschied, D. Chiodo *et al.* (2008) 'The Relationship of Child Neglect and Physical Maltreatment to Placement Outcomes and Behavioral Adjustment in Children in Foster Care: a Canadian Perspective', *Child Welfare*, 87(5): 5–25.

Mason, P. (2011) *Learning from the Early Implementation of the Families First Pioneers* (Birmingham: GHK and Arad Research).

Masson, J. (2012) '"I Think I Do Have Strategies": Lawyers' Approaches to Parent Engagement in Care Proceedings', *Child & Family Social Work*, 17: 202–11.

Masson, J., J. Pearce and K. Bader (2008) *Care Profiling Study* (London: Ministry of Justice).

Maxwell, N., J. Scourfield, B. Featherstone *et al.* (2012) 'Engaging Fathers in Child Welfare Services: A Narrative Review of Recent Research Evidence', *Child & Family Social Work*, 17: 160–9.

Mayock, P. (2011) 'Homeless Young People, Families and Change: Family Support as a Facilitator to Exiting Homelessness', *Child & Family Social Work*, 16: 391–401.

Mellor, G. (2009) *Dreamwall. Time Out Programme Monitoring and Evaluation Report 2008* (Southhampton: Dreamwall and Southhampton City Council).

Mennen, F. E., K. Kim, J. Sang *et al.* (2010a) 'Child Neglect: Definition and Identification of Youth's Experiences in Official Reports of Maltreatment', *Child Abuse & Neglect*, 34(9): 647–58.

Mennen, F.E., M. Brensilver and P.K. Trickett (2010b) 'Do Maltreated Children Who Remain at Home Function Better Than Those Who Are Placed?' *Children and Youth Services Review*, 32: 1675–82.

Mikton, C. and A. Butchart (2009) 'Child Maltreatment Prevention: a Systematic Review of Reviews', *Bulletin of the World Health Organization*, 87: 353–61. DOI: 10.2471/BLT.08.057075. Available: http://www.who.int/bulletin/volumes/87/5/08–057075/en/index.html (accessed 20 November 2012).

Millar, M. and B. Corby (2006) 'The Framework for the Assessment of Children in Need and Their Families: a Basis for a "Therapeutic" Encounter', *British Journal of Social Work*, 36: 887–8.

Miller, W. R. and S. Rollnick (2002) *Motivational Interviewing: Preparing People for Change* (New York: Guilford Press).

Milner, J. (1993) 'A Disappearing Act: the Differing Career Paths of Fathers and Mothers in Child Protection Investigations', *Critical Social Policy*, 38: 48–63.

Mind (2009) *Men and Mental Health: Get It Off Your Chest* (London: Mind).

Minnis, M. and F. Walker (2012) *The Experiences of Fostering and Adoption Processes – The Views of Children and Young People: Literature Review and Gap Analysis* (London: Local Government Association and National Foundation for Educational Research).

Mitchell, P. F. (2011) 'Evidence-based Practice in Real-world Services for Young People with Complex Needs: New Opportunites Suggested by Recent Implementation Science', *Children and Youth Services Review*, 33: 207–16.

Moraes, S., J. Durrant, D. Brownridge *et al.* (2005) 'Professionals' Decision-making in Cases of Physical Punishment Reported to Child Welfare Authorities. Does Family Poverty Matter?' *Child and Family Social Work*, 11(2): 157–69.

Moran, P. (2010) *Neglect: Research Evidence to Inform Practice* (London: Action for Children).

Moran, P., D. Ghate and A. van der Merwe (2004) *What Works in Parenting Support? A Review of the International Evidence*, RR574 (London: Department for Children, Schools and Families).

Morgan, R. (2011) *Younger Children's Views: A Report of Children's Views by the Children's Rights Director for England* (Manchester: Ofsted).

Morgan, R. and M. Lindsay (2006) *Young People's Views on Leaving Care. What Young People in and Formerly in Residential and Foster Care Think about Leaving Care.* London: Commission for Social Care Inspection.

Morris, K. and M. Connolly (2012) 'Family Decision Making in Child Welfare: Challenges in Developing a Knowledge Base for Practice', *Child Abuse Review*, 21: 41–52.

Morrison, T. (1998) 'Partnership, Collaboration and Change under the Children Act', in M. Adcock and R. White (eds), *Significant Harm: Its Management and Outcome*, 2nd edition (Croydon: Significant Publications).

Morrison, T. (2007) 'Emotional Intelligence, Emotion and Social Work: Context, Characteristics, Complications and Contribution', *British Journal of Social Work*, 37: 245–63.

Morrison, T. (2010) 'Assessing Parental Motivation for Change', in J. Horwath (ed.), *The Child's World: The Comprehensive Guide to Assessing Children in Need* (London: Jessica Kingsley Publishers), pp. 305–25.

Mullins, J. L., J. A. Cheung and C. A. Lietz (2011) 'Family Preservation Services: Incorporating the Voice of Families into Service Implementation', *Child & Family Social Work*, 17(3): 265–74.

Munro, E. (1999) 'Common Errors of Reasoning in Child Protection Work', *Child Abuse & Neglect*, 23(8): 745–58.

Munro, E. (2002) *Effective Child Protection* (London: Sage).

Munro, E. (2010) *The Munro Review of Child Protection Part One: A Systems Analysis* (London: Department for Education).

Munro, E. (2011a) *The Munro Review of Child Protection Interim Report: The Child's Journey* (London: Department for Education).

Munro, E. (2011b) *The Munro Review of Child Protection Final Report: A Child-centred System* (Norwich: The Stationery Office).

Munro, E. R. and E. Manful (2012) *Safeguarding Children: A Comparison of England's Data with That of Australia, Norway and the United States* (London: Department for Education).

Music, G. (2009) 'Neglecting Neglect: Some Thoughts about Children Who Have Lacked Good Input, and Are "Undrawn" and "Unenjoyed"', *Journal of Child Psychotherapy*, 35(2): 142–56.

Myors, K. A., V. Schmied, M. Johnson *et al.* (2011) 'Collaboration and Integrated Services for Perinatal Mental Health: an Integrative Review', *Child and Adolescent Mental Health*, DOI: 10.1111/j.1475–3588.2011.00639.x.

National Center for Injury Prevention and Control (2004) *Using Evidence-based Parenting Programs to Advance the Disease Control of Prevention Efforts in Child Maltreatment Prevention* (Atlanta, GA: Centers for Disease Control and Prevention).

National Child Protection Clearinghouse (2009) *Parental Intellectual Disability and Child Protection: Key Issues* (Canberra: Australian Institute of Family Studies).

National Clearing House on Child Abuse and Neglect (2001) 'Short and Long Term Consequences of Neglect'. Available: http://www.calib.com/nccanch/pubs/usermanuals/negelct/conseq.cfm (accessed 13 August 2001).

National Collaborating Centre for Mental Health (2007) *Antenatal and Postnatal Mental Health: The NICE Clinical Guideline Management and Service Guidance* (London: NICE).

National Institute for Health and Clinical Excellence (NICE) (2010) *Pregnancy and Complex Social Factors: A Model for Service Provision for Pregnant Women with Complex Social Factors* (London: NICE).

National Institute for Mental Health (2010) 'Teenage Brain: A Work in Progress', Fact Sheet. Available: www.nimh.nih.gov/health/publications/teenage-brain-a-work-in-progress-fact-sheet/index.shtml (accessed 4 July 2011).

National Scientific Council on the Developing Child (2004) 'Young Children Develop in an Environment of Relationships', Working Paper No. 1. Available: www.developingchild.harvard.edu (accessed 13 July 2012).

National Scientific Council on the Developing Child (2007) 'The Science of Early Childhood Development: Closing the Gap between What We Know and What We Do'. Available: http://www.developingchild.net (accessed 17 June 2010).

National Scientific Council on the Developing Child (2010) 'Early Experiences Can Alter Gene Expression and Affect Long-term Development', Working Paper No. 10. Available: www.developingchild.harvard.edu (accessed 27 November 2012).

Nelson, K., B. Walters, D. Schweitzer *et al.* (2009) *A Ten-Year Review of Family Preservation Research: Building the Evidence Base* (Seattle: Casey Family Programs).

Nolan, M. L. (1995) 'A Comparison of Attenders at Antenatal Classes in the Voluntary and Statutory Sectors: Education and Organisation Implications', *Midwifery*, 11(3): 138–45.

Nolin, P. and L. Ethier (2007) 'Using Neuropsychological Profiles to Classify Neglected Children with or without Physical Abuse', *Child Abuse and Neglect*, 31: 631–43.

NSPCC (2008) *Poverty and Child Maltreatment*, Child Protection Research Briefing (London: NSPCC).

NSPCC (2011) *Child Cruelty in the UK 2011* (London: NSPCC).

Office of the Children's Commissioner (2010) *Family Perspectives on Safeguarding and on Relationships with Children's Services* (London: Office of the Children's Commissioner).

Ofsted (2010) *Supporting Young People: An Evaluation of Recent Reforms to Youth Support Services in 11 Local Areas* (London: Ofsted).

Ofsted (2012) *Children's Care Monitor 2011: Children on the State of Social Care in England. Reported by the Children's Rights Director for England* (Manchester: Ofsted).

Olds, D. L. (2006) 'The Nurse–Family Partnership: an Evidence-based Preventive Intervention', *Infant Mental Health Journal*, 27: 5–25.

Owen, C. and J. Statham (2009) *Disproportionality in Child Welfare: Prevalence of Black and Ethnic Minority Children within 'Looked After' and 'Children in Need' Populations and on Child Protection Registers in England*, Research Report DCSF-RR-124 (London: Department for Children, Schools and Families).

Page, J., G. Whitting and C. McLean (2008) *A Review of How Fathers Can Be Better Recognised and Supported through DCSF Policy* (Nottingham: Department for Children, Schools and Families).

Parrott, L., G. Jacobs and D. Roberts (2008) *Stress and Resilience Factors in Parents with Mental Health Problems and Their Children*, SCIE Research Briefing 23 (London: Social Care Institute for Excellence).

Parton, N. (2006) *Safeguarding Childhood: Early Intervention and Surveillance in a Late Modern Society* (Basingstoke: Palgrave Macmillan).

Patel, A., R. Calam and A. Latham (2011) 'Intention to Attend Parenting Programmes: Does Ethnicity Make a Difference?' *Journal of Children's Services*, 6(1): 45–58.

Payton, J., R. P. Weissberg, J. A. Durlak, A. B. Dymnicki, R. D. Taylor, K. B. Schellinger and M. Pachan (2008) *The Positive Impact of Social and Emotional Learning for Kindergarten to Eight Grade Students: Findings from Three Scientific Reviews*. Chicago, IL: CASEL.

Pearson, A. (2008) 'Sorry, but I blame Scarlett Keeling's mother'. Available: http://www.dailymail.co.uk/debate/columnists/article-531289/Sorry-I-blame-Scarlett-Keelings-mother.html (accessed 20 July 2012).

Perry, B. D. (2002) 'Childhood Experience and the Expression of Genetic Potential: What Childhood Neglect Tells Us about Nature and Nurture', *Brain and Mind*, 3: 79–100.

Pianta, R., B. Egeland and M. Farrell Erickson (1989) 'The Antecededents of Maltreatment: Results of the Mother-Child Interaction Research Projects', in D. Cicchetti and V. Carlson (eds), *Child Maltreatment: Theory and Research on the Causes of Child Abuse and Neglect* (Cambridge: Cambridge University Press), pp. 203–53.

Platt, D. (2007) 'Congruence and Co-operation in Social Workers' Assessments of Children in Need', *Child and Family Social Work*, 12(4): 326–35.

Platt, D. (2012) 'Understanding Parental Engagement with Child Welfare Services: an Integrated Model', *Child & Family Social Work*, 17: 138–48.

Polansky, N. A., M. A. Chalmers, E. Werthan *et al.* (1981) *Damaged Parents* (Chicago: University of Chicago Press).

Polansky, N., C. DeSaix and S. Sharlin (1972) *Child Neglect: Understanding and Reaching the Parent* (New York: Child Welfare League of America).

Polonko, K. A. (2006) 'Exploring Assumptions about Child Neglect in Relation to the Broader Field of Maltreatment', *Journal of Health and Human Services*, 29(3): 260–84.

Portwood, S. (1998) 'The Impact of Individuals' Characteristics and Experiences on Their Definitions of Child Maltreatment', *Child Abuse & Neglect*, 22(5): 437–52.

Prince, J., A. Gear, C. Jones *et al.* (2005) 'The Child Protection Conference: a Study of Process and an Evaluation of the Potential for On-line Group Support', *Child Abuse Review*, 14(2): 113–31.

Prochaska, J. and C. DiClementi (1982) 'Transtheoretical Therapy: Towards a More Integrative Model of Change', *Psychotherapy: Theory, Research and Practice*, 19(3): 276–88.

Puckering, C., M. Mills, A. Cox, *et al.* (1999) *Improving the Quality of Family Support: An Intensive Intervention: Mellow Parenting. Final Report* (London: Department of Health).

Pugh, G., E. De'Ath, C. Smith *et al.* (1994) *Confident Parents, Confident Children. Policy and Practice in Parent Education and Support* (London: National Children's Bureau).

Reder, P. and S. Duncan (1999) *Lost Innocents? A Follow-up Study of Fatal Child Abuse* (London: Routledge).

Reder, P. and S. Duncan (2003) 'Understanding Communication in Child Protection Networks', *Child Abuse Review*, 12(2): 82–100.

Rees, G. (2011) *Still Running 3: Early Findings from Our Third National Survey of Young Runaways, 2011* (London: The Children's Society).

Rees, G., S. Gorin, A. Jobe *et al.* (2010) *Safeguarding Young People: Responding to Young People Aged 11 to 17 Who Are Maltreated* (London: The Children's Society).

Rees, G., M. Stein, L. Hicks *et al.* (2011) *Adolescent Neglect: Research, Policy and Practice* (London: Jessica Kingsley).

Reynolds, A. J., L. C. Mathieson and J. Topitzes (2009) 'Do Early Childhood Interventions Prevent Child Maltreatment? A Review of Research', *Child Maltreatment*, 14(2): 182–206.

Rigby, K. (2004) 'Addressing Bullying in Schools: Theoretical Perspectives and Their Implications', *School Psychology International*, 25(3): 287–300.

Ritchie, C. and A. Buchanan (2011) 'Self Report of Negative Parenting Styles, Psychological Functioning and Risk of Negative Parenting by One Parent Being Replicated by the Other in a Sample of Adolescents Aged 13–15', *Child Abuse Review*, 20(6): 421–38.

Rooney, B. L. and C. W. Schauberger (2002) 'Excess Pregnancy Weight Gain and Long-term Obesity: One Decade Later', *Obstetrics & Gynecology*, 100(2): 245–52.

Rose, S. and W. Meezan (1997) 'Defining Child Neglect: Evolution, Influences and Issues', in J. Duerr Berrick, R. Barth and N. Gilbert (eds), *Child Welfare Research Review*, Volume 2 (New York: Columbia University Press).

Rose, S. and J. Selwyn (2000) 'Child Neglect: an English Perspective', *International Social Work*, 32: 179–92.

Rose, W. (2010) 'The Assessment Framework', in J. Horwath (ed.), *The Child's World: The Comprehensive Guide to Assessing Children in Need* (London: Jessica Kingsley Publishers), pp. 34–55.

Rose, W. and J. Barnes (2007) *Improving Safeguarding Practice: Study of Serious Case Reviews 2001–2003* (Nottingham: Department for Children, Schools and Families).

Ross, A., K. Duckworth, D. J. Smith *et al.* (2011) *Prevention and Reduction: A Review of Strategies for Intervening Early to Prevent or Reduce Youth Crime and Anti-social Behaviour* (London: Department for Education and Centre for Analysis of Youth Transitions).

Sabin, M. A., E. C. Crowne and J. P. H. Shield (2004) 'The Prognosis in Childhood Obesity', *Current Paediatrics*, 14(2): 110–14.

Safron, M., A. Cislak, T. Gaspar *et al.* (2011) 'Effects of School-based Interventions Targeting Obesity-related Behaviors and Body Weight Change: a Systematic Umbrella Review', *Behavioral Medicine*, 37(1): 15–25.

Sanders, M., R. Calam, M. Durand *et al.* (2008) 'Does Self-directed and Web-based Support for Parents Enhance the Effects of Viewing a Reality Televison Series Based on the Triple P-Positive Parenting Programme?' *Journal of Child Psychology and Psychiatry*, 49(9): 924–32.

Sanders, M. R., C. Markie-Dadds and K. M. T. Turner (2000) *Practitioner's Manual for Standard Triple P* (Brisbane, QLD: Families International Publishing).

Sanders, M., A. Pidgeon, F. Gravestock *et al.* (2004) 'Does Parental Attribution Retraining and Anger Management Enhance the Effects of Triple-P Postive Parenting Program with Parents at Risk of Child Maltreatment?' *Behavior Therapy*, 35: 513–35.

Sanson, A. V., S. S. Havighurst and S. R. Zubrick (2011) 'The Science of Prevention for Children and Youth', *Australian Review of Public Affairs*, 10(1): 79–93.

Scannapieco, M. and K. Connell-Carrick (2005) 'Focus on the First Years: Correlates of Substantiation of Child Maltreatment for Families with Children 0 to 4', *Children and Youth Services Review*, 27(12): 1307–23.

Schaffer, H. R. (2004) *Introducing Child Psychology* (Oxford: Blackwell).

Schofield, G. and J. Simmonds (eds) (2009) *The Child Placement Handbook* (London: BAAF).

Schrader McMillan, A., J. Barlow and M. Redshaw (2009) *Birth and Beyond: A Review of the Evidence about Antenatal Education* (London: Department of Health).

Schumacher, J., A. Smith Slep and R. Heyman (2001) 'Risk Factors for Child Neglect', *Aggression and Violent Behaviour*, 6: 231–54.

Scott, D. (2010) 'Working Together to Support Families of Vulnerable Children', *Social Work Now*, 45(April): 20–5.

Scottish Government (2010) *National Guidance for Child Protection in Scotland* (Edinburgh: Scottish Government).

Scourfield, J. (2006) 'The Challenge of Engaging Fathers in the Child Protection Process', *Critical Social Policy*, 26(2): 440–9.

Seaman, P., K. Turner, M. Hill *et al.* (2006) *Parenting and Children's Resilience in Disadvantaged Communities* (York: Joseph Rowntree Foundation).

Sedlak, A. J., J. Mettenburg, M. Basena *et al.* (2010) *Fourth National Incidence Study of Child Abuse and Neglect*, NIS-4 (Washington: US Department of Health and Human Services).

Self-Brown, S., K. Fredrick, S. Binder *et al.* (2011) 'Examining the Need for Cultural Adaptations to an Evidence-based Parent Training Program Targeting the Prevention of Maltreatment', *Child and Youth Services Review*, 33: 1166–72.

Sen, R. and K. Broadhurst (2011) 'Contact between Children in Out-of-home Placements and Their Family and Friends Network: a Research Review', *Child & Family Social Work*, 16(3): 298–309.

Sen, R., P. Green-Lister, P. Rigby and A. Kendrick (2012) 'Grading the Graded Care Profile', *Child Abuse Review*. Online at: DOI: 10.1002/car.2257.

Senge, P., R. Ross, B. Smith *et al.* (1994) *The Fifth Discipline Fieldbook: Strategies for Building a Learning Organization* (New York: Currency).

Sharp, C. and C. Filmer-Sankey (2010) *Early Intervention and Prevention in the Context of Integrated Services: Evidence from C4EO and Narrowing the Gap Reviews* (London: C4EO).

Sharry, J., S. Guerin, C. Griffin *et al.* (2005) 'An Evaluation of the Parents Plus Early Years Programme: A Video-based Early Intervention for Parents of Preschool Children with Behavioural and Developmental Difficulties', *Clinical Child Psychology and Psychiatry*, 10(3): 319–36.

Shaw, R., L. M. Wallace and M. Bansal (2003) 'Is Breast Best? Perception of Infant Feeding', *Community Practitioner*, 76(8): 299–303.

Sheffield Area Child Protection Committee (2005) 'Executive Summary of the W Children Serious Case Review'. http://www.sheffield.gov.uk/safe--sound/protection-from-abuse/sscb/serious-case-review (accessed 16 January 2006).

Shipman, K., A. Edwards, A. Brown *et al.* (2005) 'Managing Emotion in a Maltreating Context: a Pilot Study Examining Child Neglect', *Child Abuse & Neglect*, 29: 1015–29.

Shortt, A. L., P. M. Barrett and T. L. Fox (2001) 'Evaluating the Friends Program. A Cognitive-behavioural Group Treatment for Anxious Children and Their Parents', *Journal of Clinical Child and Adolescent Psychology*, 30(4): 525–35.

Simmel, C. (2010) 'Why Do Adolescents Become Involved with the Child Welfare System? Exploring Risk Factors That Affect Young Adolescents', *Children and Youth Services Review*, 32(12): 1831–6.

Siraj-Blatford, I. and J. Siraj-Blatford (2009) *Improving Children's Attainment through a Better Quality of Family-based Support for Early Learning* (London: C4EO).

Skuse, D., S. Reilly and D. Wolke (1994) 'Psychosocial Adversity and Growth during Infancy', *European Journal of Clinical Nutrition* 48(Supplement 1): 113–30.

Slack, K. and M. Webber (2008) 'Do We Care? Adult Mental Health Professionals' Attitudes towards Supporting Service Users' Children', *Child and Family Social Work*, 13(1): 72–9.

Small, M. L. (2009) *Unanticipated Gains: Origins of Network Inequality in Everyday Life* (Oxford: Oxford University Press).

Smeaton, E. (2009) *Off the Radar: Children and Young People on the Streets of the UK* (Sandbach: Railway Children).

Smith, M. (2009) *Rethinking Residential Child Care* (Bristol: Policy Press).

Speight, N. and J. Wynne (2000) 'Controversy: Is the Children Act Failing Severely Abused and Neglected Children?' *Archives of Disease in Childhood*, 82: 192–6.

Spencer, N. and N. Baldwin (2005) 'Economic, Cultural and Social Contexts of Neglect', in J. Taylor and B. Daniel (eds), *Child Neglect: Practice Issues for Health and Social Care* (London: Jessica Kingsley Publishers), pp. 26–42.

Spratt, T. (2011) 'Families with Multiple Problems: Some Challenges to Identifying and Providing Services to Those Experiencing Adversities across the Life Course', *Journal of Social Work*, 11(4): 343–67.

Spratt, T. and J. Devaney (2009) 'Identifying Families with Multiple Problems: Perspectives of Practitioners and Managers in Three Nations', *British Journal of Social Work*, 39: 418–34.

Srivastava, P., R. Fountain, P. Ayre *et al.* (2003) 'The Graded Care Profile: A Measure of Care', in M. C. Calder and S. Hackett (eds), *Assessment in Child Care* (Lyme Regis: Russell House Publishing), pp. 227–46.

Srivastava, O. P., J. Stewart, R. Fountain *et al.* (2005) 'Common Operational Approach Using the "Graded Care Profile" in Cases of Neglect', in J. Taylor and B. Daniel (eds), *Child Neglect: Practice Issues for Health and Social Care* (London: Jessica Kingsley Publishers), pp. 131–46.

Stafford, A., N. Parton, S. Vincent *et al.* (2011) *Child Protection Systems in the United Kingdom: A Comparative Analysis* (London: Jessica Kingsley Publishers).

Stanley, J. and C. Goddard (2002) *In the Firing Line: Violence and Power in Child Protection Work* (Chichester: Wiley).

Stanley, N. (2011) *Children Experiencing Domestic Violence: A Research Review* (Dartington: Research in Practice).

Stanley, N., H. Cleaver and D. Hart (2010) 'The Impact of Domestic Violence, Parental Mental Health Problems, Substance Misuse and Learning Disability on Parenting Capacity', in J. Horwath (ed.), *The Child's World: The Comprehensive Guide to Assessing Children in Need*, 2nd edition (London: Jessica Kingsley Publishers), pp. 326–53.

Stein, M., G. Rees, L. Hicks *et al.* (2009) *Neglected Adolescents – Literature Review*, DCSF-RBX-09–04 (London: Department for Children, Schools and Families).

Stevenson, O. (2005) 'Working Together in Cases of Neglect: Key Issues', in J. Taylor and B. Daniel (eds), *Child Neglect: Practice Issues for Health and Social Care* (London: Jessica Kingsley Publishers), pp. 97–112.

Stevenson, O. (2007) *Neglected Children and Their Families* (Oxford: Blackwell Publishing).

Stewart, A., M. Livingston and S. Dennison (2008) 'Transitions and Turning Points: Examining the Links between Child Maltreatment and Juvenile Offending', *Child Abuse and Neglect*, 32: 51–66.

Stith, S. M., L. Ting Liu, C. Davies *et al.* (2009) 'Risk Factors in Child Maltreatment: a Meta-analytic Review of the Literature', *Aggression and Violent Behaviour*, 14(1): 13–29.

Stokes, J. and G. Schmidt (2011) 'Race, Poverty and Child Protection Decision Making', *British Journal of Social Work*, 41: 1105–21.

Suchman, N., C. DeCoste, N. Castiglione *et al.* (2008) 'The Mothers and Toddlers Program: Preliminary Findings from an Attachment-based Parenting Intervention for Substance Misusing Mothers', *Psychoanalytic Psychology*, 25(3): 499–517.

Sullivan, P. and J. F. Knutson (2000) 'Maltreatment and Disabilities: a Population-based Epidemiological Study', *Child Abuse and Neglect*, 24(10): 1257–73.

Swenson, C. C., C. M. Schaeffer, S. W. Henggeler *et al.* (2010) 'Multisysytemic Therapy for Child Abuse and Neglect: a Randomized Effectiveness Trial', *Journal of Family Psychology*, 24(4): 497–507.

Sykes, J. (2011) 'Negotiating Stigma: Understanding Mothers' Responses to Accusations of Child Neglect', *Children and Youth Review*, 33: 448–56.

Sylvestre, A. and C. Mérette (2010) 'Language Delay in Severely Neglected Children: a Cumulative or Specific Effect of Risk Factors?' *Child Abuse & Neglect*, 34(6): 414–28.

Tanner, K. and D. Turney (2006) 'Therapeutic Interventions with Children Who Have Experienced Neglect and Their Families in the UK', in C. McAuley, P. J. Pecora and W. Rose (eds), *Enhancing the Well-being of Children and Families through Effective Interventions: International Evidence for Practice* (London: Jessica Kingsley Publishers), pp. 118–30.

Tarlton, B. and S. Porter (2012) 'Crossing No Man's Land: a Specialist Support Service for Parents with Learning Disabilities', *Child & Family Social Work*, 17: 233–43.

Tarlton, B., L. Ward and J. Howarth (2006) *Finding the Right Support? A Review of Issues and Positive Practice in Supporting Parents with Learning Difficulties and Their Children* (London: Baring Foundation).

Taylor, J. and B. Daniel (eds) (2005) *Child Neglect: Practice Issues for Health and Social Care* (London: Jessica Kingsley Publishers).

Templeton, L., R. Velleman and C. Russell (2010) 'Psychological Interventions with Families of Alcohol Misusers: a Systematic Review', *Addiction Research & Theory*, 18(6): 616–48.

Thiara, R. K. and A. K. Gill (2012) *Domestic Violence, Child Contact, Post-Separation Violence: Issues for South Asian and African Caribbean Women and Children. A Report of Findings* (London: NSPCC).

Thoburn, J. and Members of the Making Research Count Consortium (2009) *Effective Interventions for Complex Families Where There Are Concerns about, or Evidence of, a Child Suffering Significant Harm*, Safeguarding: Briefing 1 (London: C4EO).

Thoburn, J., J. Wilding and J. Watson (2000) *Family Support in Cases of Emotional Maltreatment and Neglect* (London: The Stationery Office).

Traustadottir, R. and H. B. Sigurjonsdottir (2010) 'Parenting and Resistance Strategies', in G. Llewellyn, R. Trautstadottir, D. McConnell *et al.* (eds), *Parents with Intellectual Disabilities* (Chichester: Wiley), pp. 107–18.

Triple P (2011) 'American University Granted $2 Million to Study Triple P and Child Welfare'. Available: http://www.triplep.net/cicms/assets/pdfs/pg1as100-gr5so212.pdf (accessed 20 July 2012).

Trocmé, N., B. Fallon, B. MacLaurin *et al.* (2005) *Canadian Incident Study of Reported Child Abuse and Neglect – 2003* (Ottowa: National Clearing House on Family Violence).

Truman, P. (2004) 'Problems in Identifying Cases of Child Neglect', *Nursing Standard*, 18(29): 33–8.

Turnell, A. (2012) *The Signs of Safety*, Comprehensive Briefing Paper (Perth: Resolutions Consultancy).

Turney, D. (2012) 'A Relationship-based Approach to Engaging with Involuntary Clients: the Contribution of Recognition Theory', *Child & Family Social Work*, 17: 149–59.

Turning Point (2006) *Bottling It Up: The Effects of Alcohol Misuse on Children, Parents and Families* (London: Turning Point).

Twardosz, S. and J. R. Lutzker (2010) 'Child Maltreatment and the Developing Brain: a Review of Neuroscience Perspectives', *Aggression and Violent Behavior*, 15: 59–68.

Tyrer, P., E. Chase, I. Warwick *et al.* (2005) '"Dealing with It": Experiences of Young Fathers in and Leaving Care', *British Journal of Social Work*, 35: 1107–21.

Tyuse, S. W., P. P. Hong and J. J. Stretch (2010) 'Evaluation of an Intensive In-home Family Treatment Program to Prevent Out-of-home Placement', *Journal of Evidence-Based Social Work*, 7(3): 200–18.

US Department of Health and Human Services (2011) 'Definitions of Child Abuse and Neglect'. Available: http://www.childwelfare.gov/pubs/factsheets/whatis-can.cfm (accessed 15 May 2012).

van den Dries, L., F. Juffer, M. H. Van Ljzendoom *et al.* (2012) 'Infants' Responsiveness, Attachment and Indiscriminate Friendliness after International Adoption from Institutions or Foster Care in China: Application of Emotional Availability Scales to Adoptive Families', *Development and Psychopathology*, 24: 49–64.

Viner, R. M., E. Roche, S. A. Maguire *et al.* (2010) 'Childhood Protection and Obesity: Framework for Practice', *British Medical Journal*. DOI: 10.1136/bmj. c3074.

Wade, J., N. Biehal, N. Farrelly *et al.* (2010) *Maltreated Children in the Looked After System: A Comparison of Outcomes for Those Who Go Home and Those Who Do Not*, DFE-RBX-10–06 (London: Department for Education).

Wade, J., N. Biehal, N. Farrelly *et al.* (2011) *Caring for Abused and Neglected Children. Making the Right Decisons for Reunification or Long-term Care* (London: Jessica Kingsley Publishers).

Waldman, J. and A. Storey (2004) *There4me Evaluation Final Report* (Southhampton: University of Southhampton).

Walker, J., K. Crawford and F. Taylor (2008) 'Listening to Children: Gaining a Perspective of the Experiences of Poverty and Social Exclusion from Children and Young People of Single-parent families', *Health and Social Care in the Community*, 16(4): 429–36.

Ward, H., R. Brown and D. Maskell-Graham (2012) *Young Children Suffering, or Likely to Suffer, Significant Harm: Experiences on Entering Education*, DFE-RB209 (London: Department for Education).

Ward, T., A. Day, K. Howells *et al.* (2004) 'The Multifactor Offender Readiness Model', *Aggression and Violent Behavior*, 9: 645–73.

Watt, B. D., M. Hoyland, D. Best, *et al.* (2007) 'Treatment Participation among Children with Conduct Problems and the Role of Telephone Reminders', *Journal of Child and Family Studies*, 16: 522–30.

Webster-Stratton, C. and M. J. Reid (2006) 'Treatment and Prevention of Conduct Problems: Parenting Training Interventions for Young Children (Two to Seven Years old)', in K. McCartney and D. A. Phillips (eds), *Blackwell Handbook on Early Childhood Development* (Malden, MA: Blackwell), pp. 616–41.

Webster-Stratton, C. and M. J. Reid (2010) 'Adapting The Incredible Years, an Evidence-based Parenting Programme, for Families Involved in the Child Welfare System', *Journal of Children's Services*, 5(1): 25–42.

Welsh Assembly Government (2006) *Safeguarding Children: Working Together under the Children Act 2004* (Cardiff: Welsh Assembly Government).

Whittaker, J. K., J. Kinney, E. M. Tracy *et al.* (eds) (1990) *Reaching High-Risk Families: Intensive Family Preservation in Human Services* (New York: Aldine de Gruyter).

Whitaker, R. C., S. M. Phillipp, S. M. Orzol, *et al.* (2007) 'The Association between Maltreatment and Obesity among Pre-school Children', *Child Abuse & Neglect*, 31(11–12): 1187–99.

Wiehe, V. R. (1996) *Working with Child Abuse and Neglect: A Primer* (Thousand Oaks, CA: Sage).

Williams, R. (2008) 'Madeleine anniversary: McCanns tell of regrets in TV documentary'. Available: http://www.guardian.co.uk/uk/2008/apr/30/madeleinemccann.itv (accessed 20 July 2012).

Wilson, C., L. Thompson, A. McConnachie *et al.* (2011) 'Matching Parenting Support Needs to Service Provision in a Universal 13-month Child Health Surveillance Visit', *Child: Care, Health and Development*. DOI: 10.1111/j.1365–2214.2011.01315.x.

Wilson, D. and W. Horner (2005) 'Chronic Child Neglect: Needed Developments in Theory and Practice', *Families in Society: The Journal of Contemporary Social Services*, 86(4): 471–81.

Wilson, S. R., J. J. Rack and A. M. Norris (2008) 'Comparing Physically Abusive, Neglectful and Non-maltreating Parents during Interactions with Their Children: a Meta-analysis of Observational Studies', *Child Abuse & Neglect*, 32: 897–911.

Wonnacott, J. (2012) *Mastering Social Work Supervision* (London: Jessica Kingsley Publishers).

Wright, C. M. (1995) 'A Population Approach to Weight Monitoring and Failure to Thrive', in T. J. David (ed.), *Recent Advances in Paediatrics* (Edinburgh: Churchill Livingstone), pp. 73–8.

Wright, C. M., S. K. Jeffrey, M. K. Ross *et al.* (2009) 'Targeting Health Visitor Care: Lessons from Starting Well', *Archives of Disease in Childhood*, 94: 23–7.

Wright, C. M., K. N. Parkinson and R. F. Drewett (2006) 'How Does Maternal and Child Feeding Behavior Relate to Weight Gain and Failure to Thrive? Data from a Prospective Birth Cohort', *Pediatrics*, 117(4): 1262–9.

York Consulting (2011) *Turning Around the Lives of Families with Multiple Problems – an Evaluation of the Family and Young Carer Pathfinders Programme*, DFE-RR154 (London: Department for Education).

Yun, I., J. D. Ball and H. Lim (2011) 'Disentangling the Relationship between Child Maltreatment and Violent Delinquency: Using a Nationally Representative Sample', *Journal of Interpersonal Violence*, 26(1): 88–110.

Zielewski, E. H., K. Malm and R. Geen (2006) *Children Caring for Themselves and Child Neglect: When Do They overlap?* (Washington: The Urban Institute).

Zolotor, A. and D. R. Runyan (2006) 'Social Capital, Family Violence and Neglect', *Pediatrics*, 117: 1124–31.

Zwaanswijk, M., P. F. Verhaak, J. M. Bensing *et al.* (2003) 'Help Seeking for Emotional and Behavioural Problems in Children and Adolescents. A Review of the Recent Literature', *European Child and Adolescent Psychiatry*, 12(4): 153–61.

Index

Printed and bound in Great Britain by
CPI Antony Rowe, Chippenham and Eastbourne